Ian Lee

THE THIRD WOR*D WAR

*Apostrophe Theory

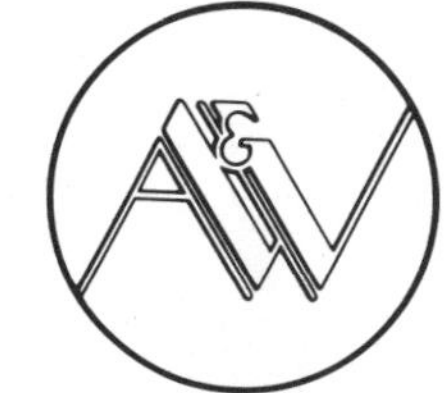

A & W Visual Library
New York

First published in the United States of America in 1978 by
A & W Publishers, Inc.
95 Madison Avenue
New York, New York 10016
By arrangement with Thames and Hudson Ltd., London

Library of Congress Catalog Card Number: 78-55111
ISBN 0-89104-115-X

Printed in the United States of America

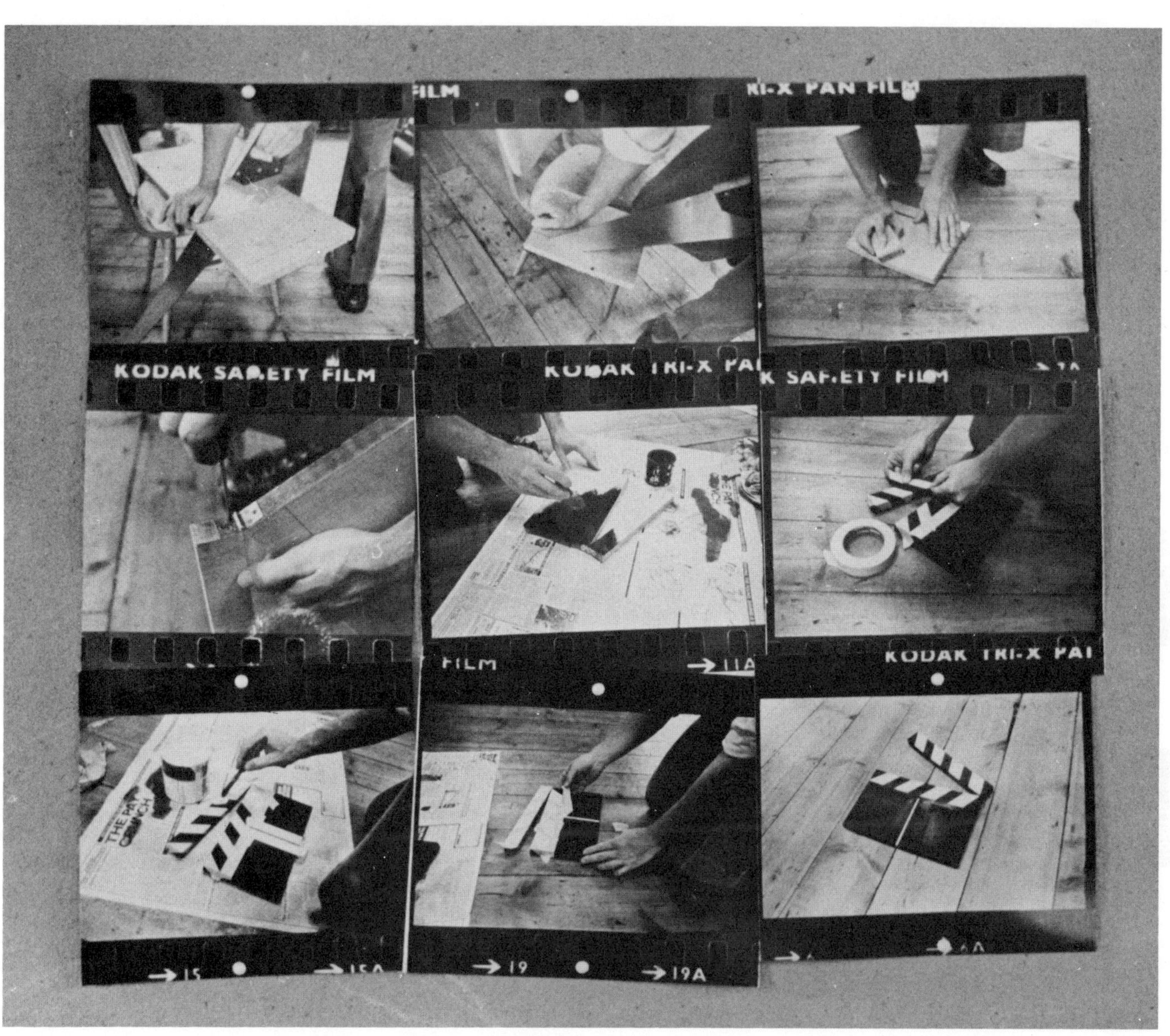

A documentary

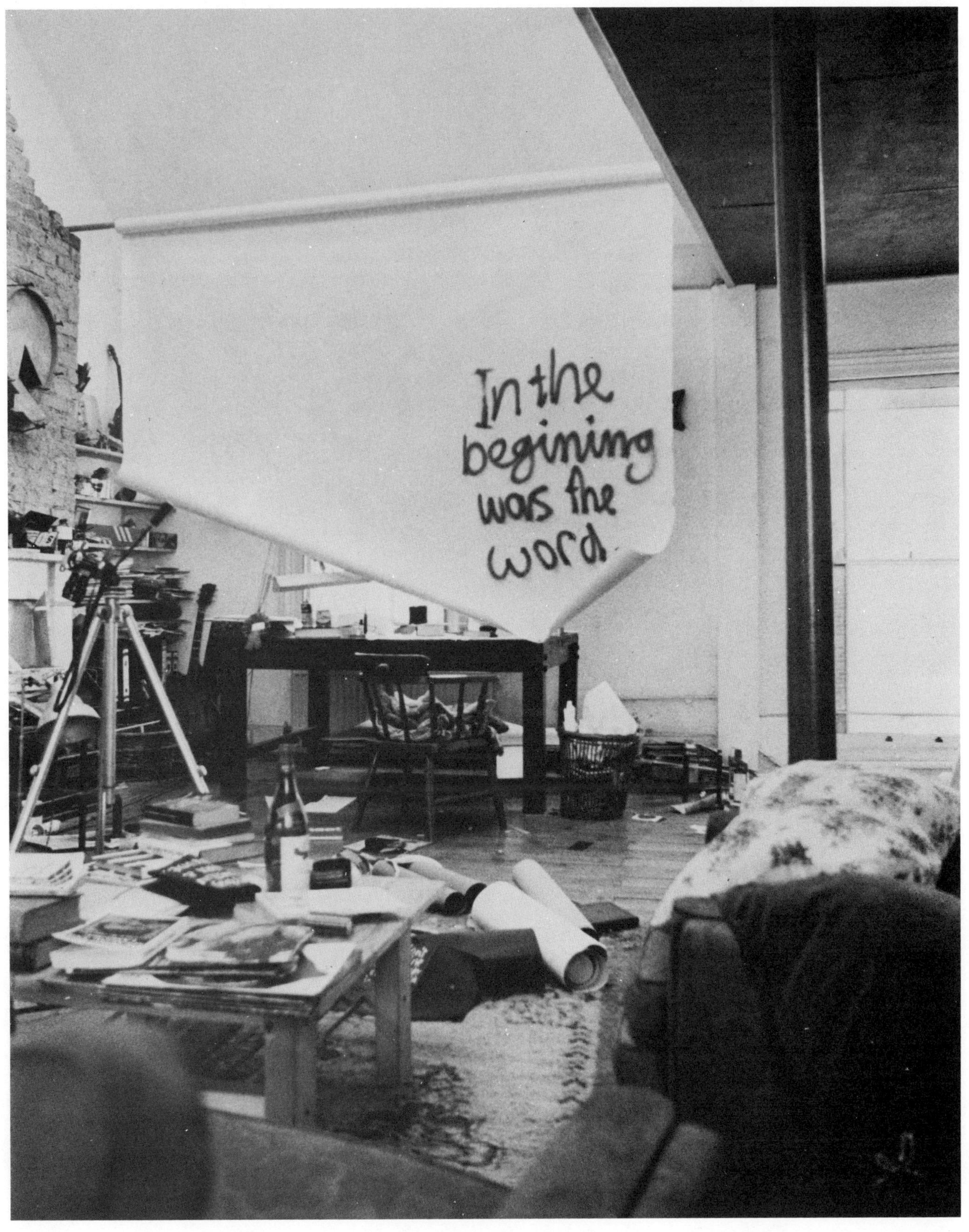

Stop me if you've heard it

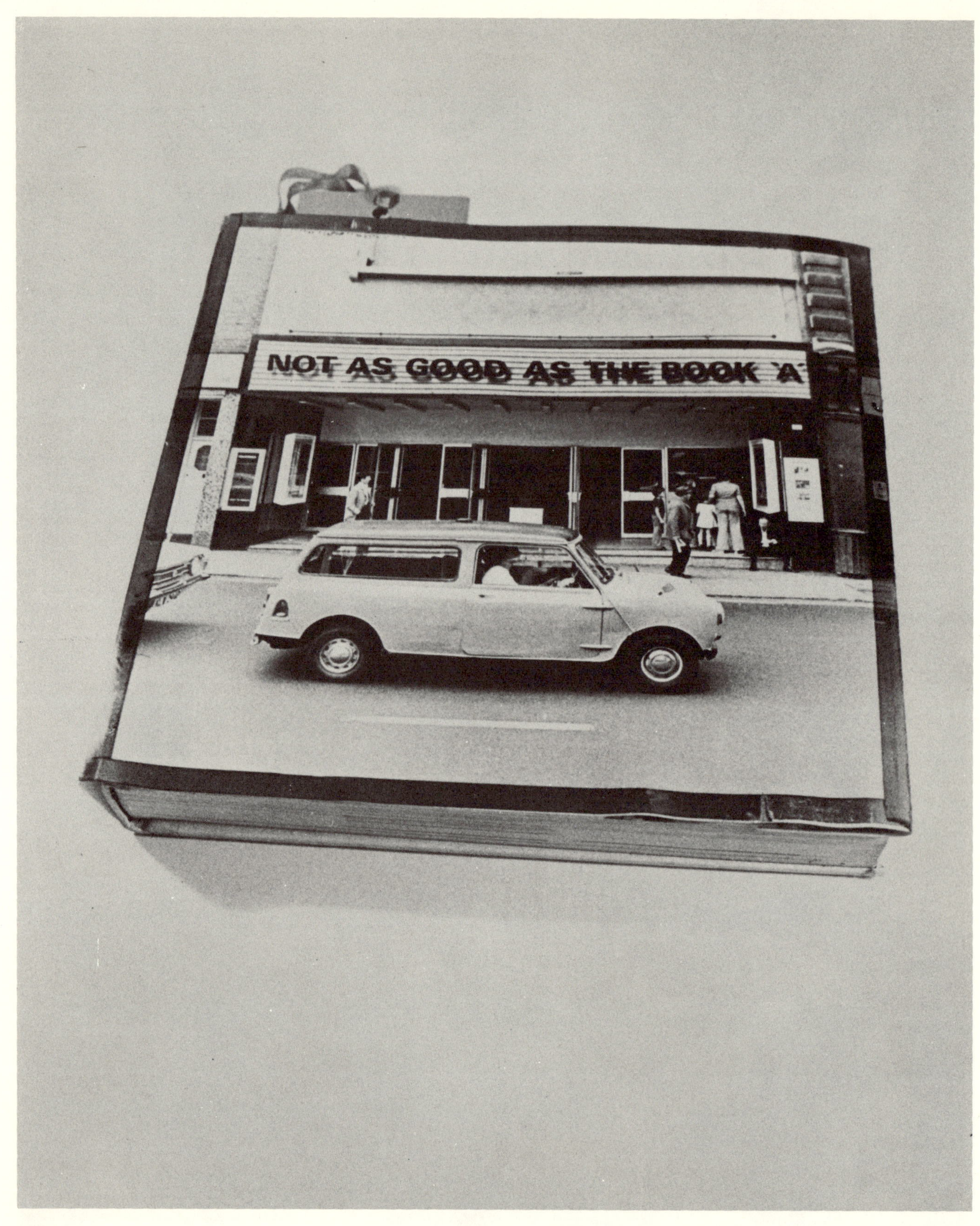

Stop me if you've seen it

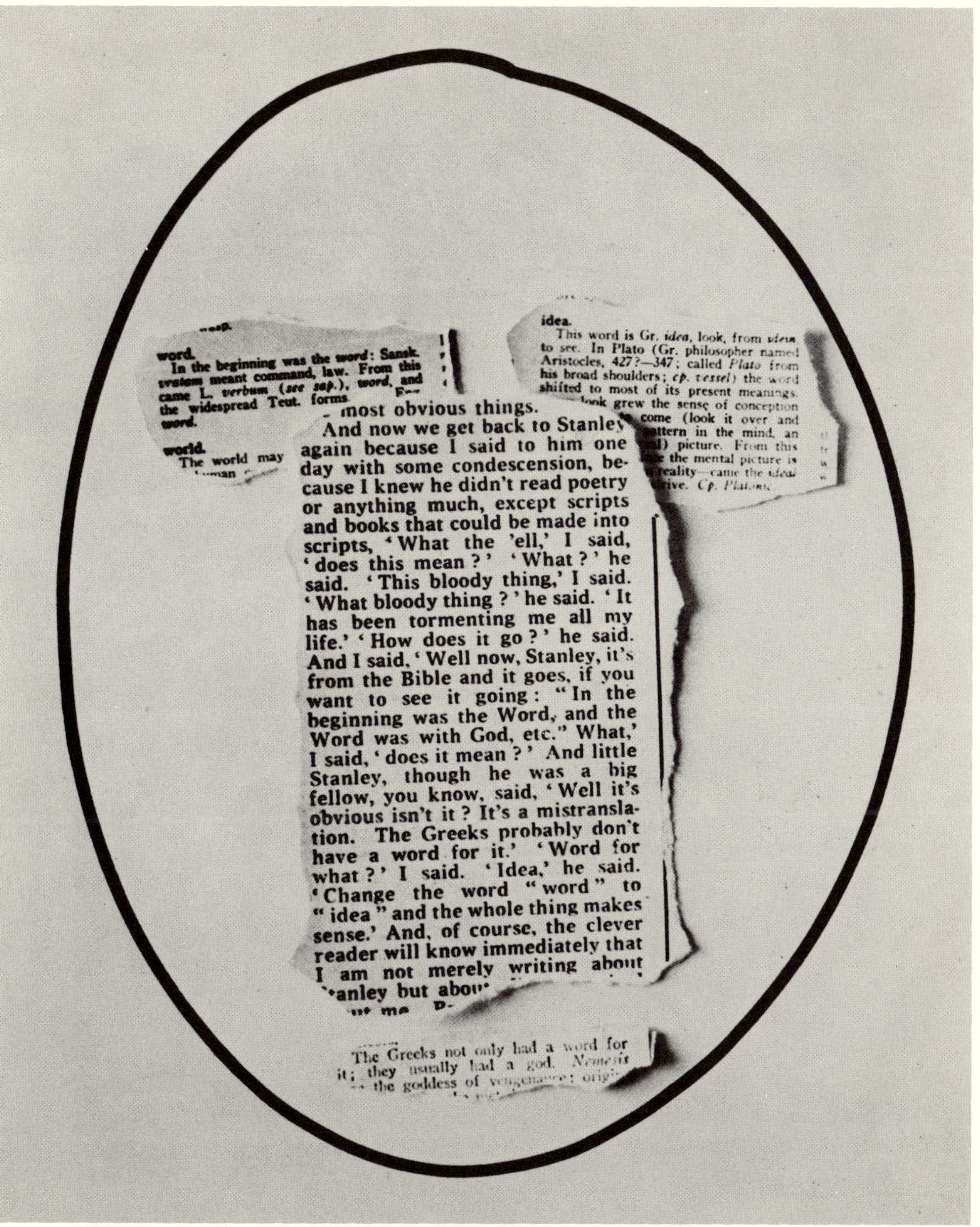

But first an idea from our sponsor

These little lines were a bright idea!

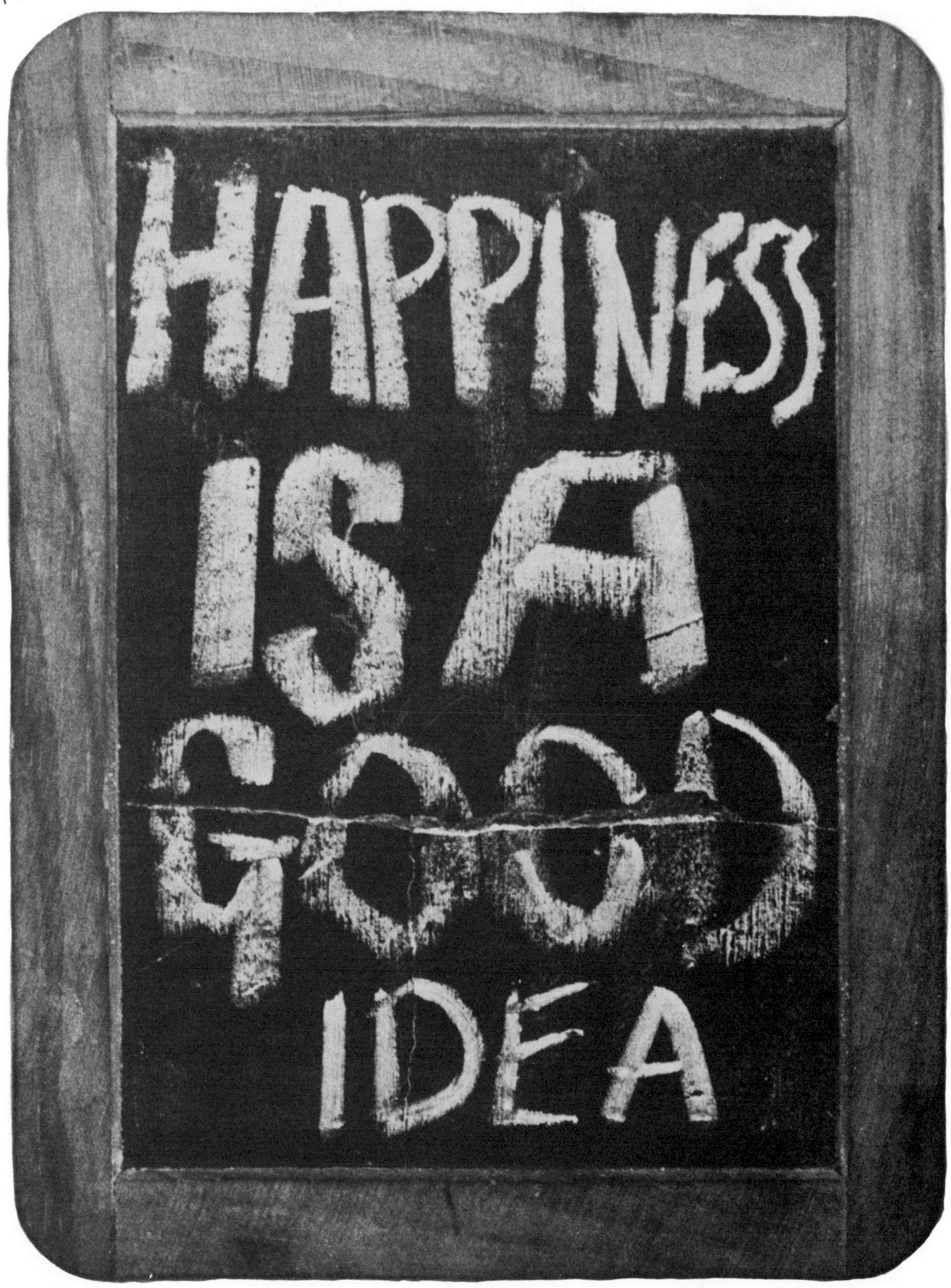

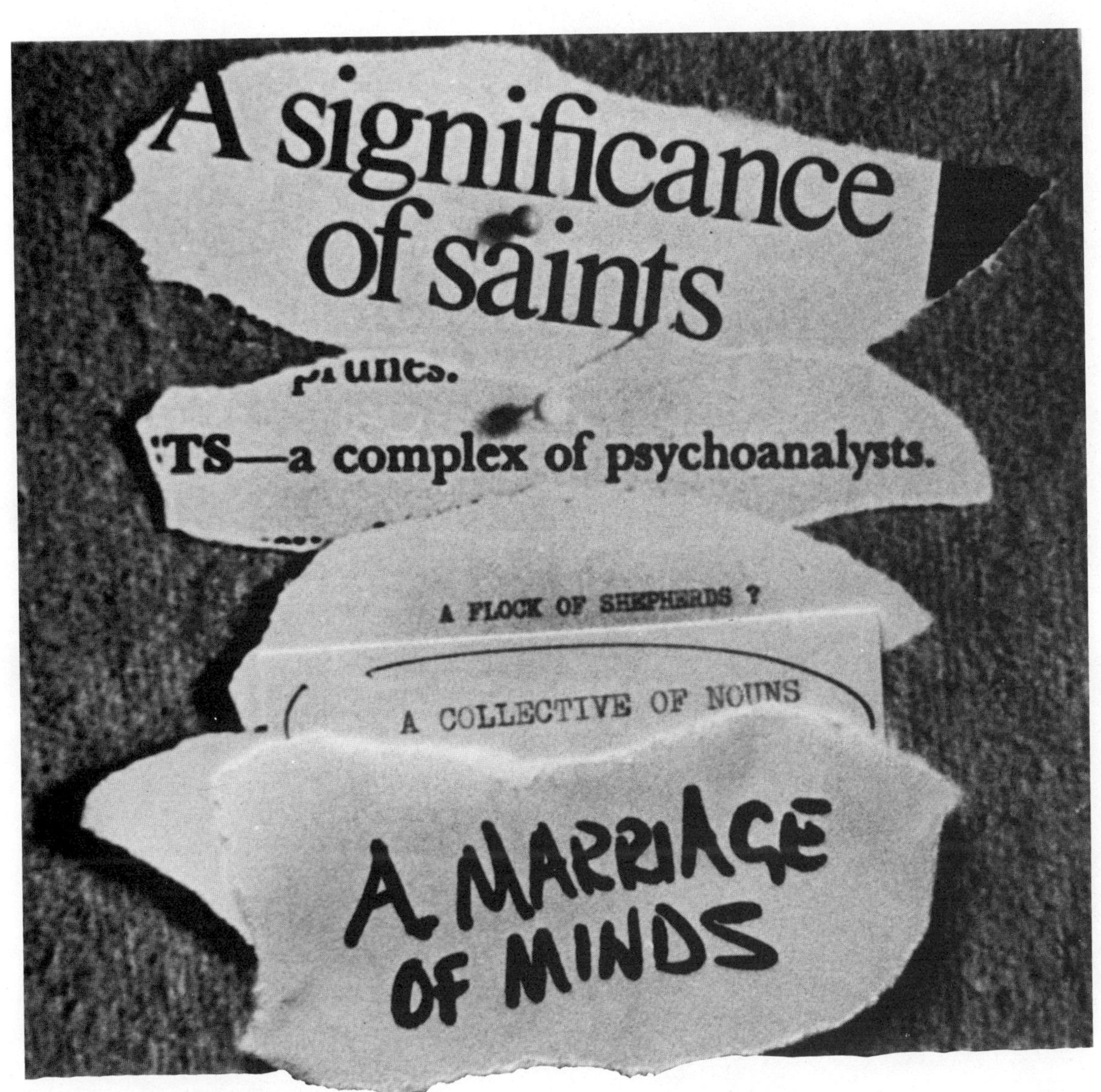

An association of ideas

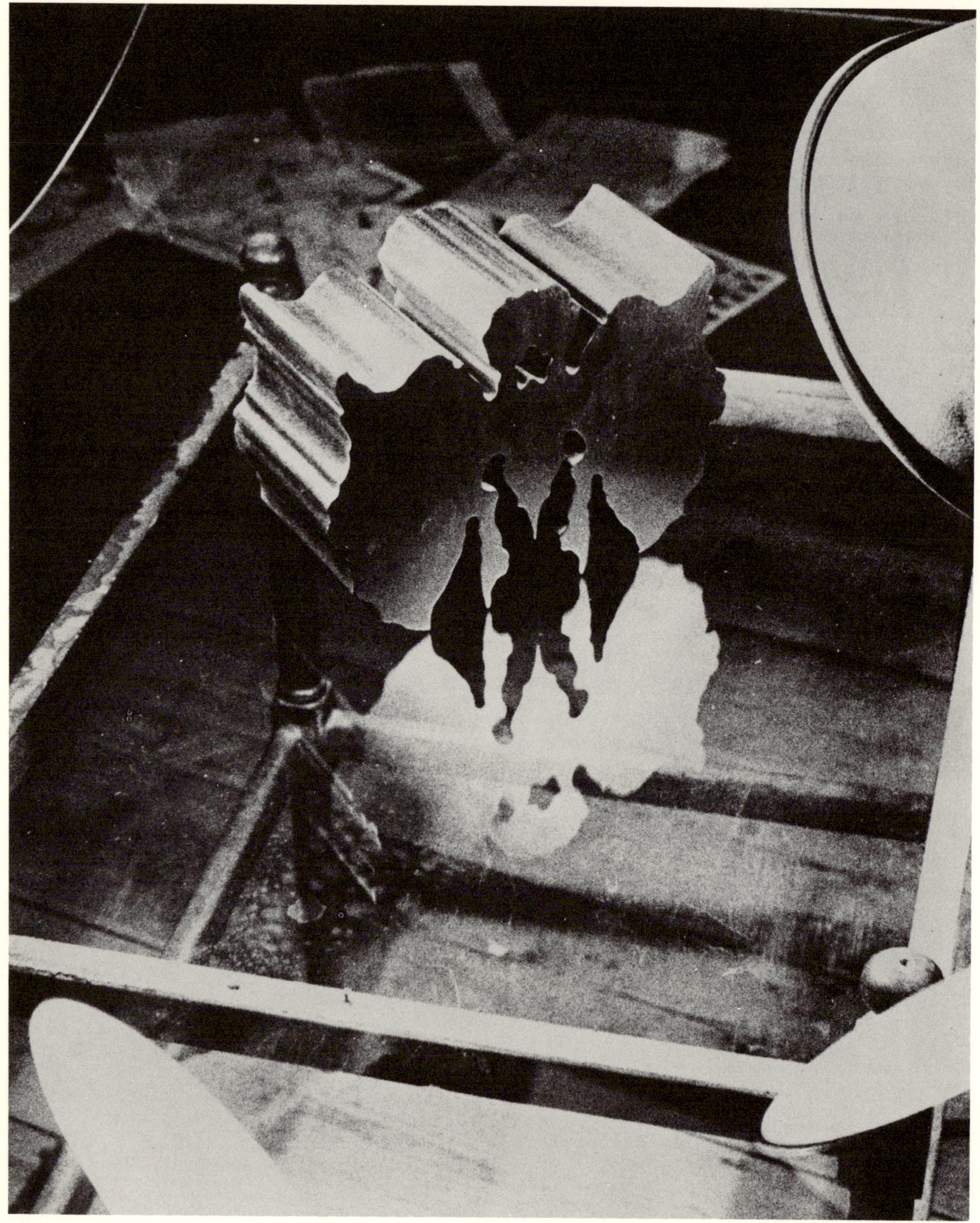

The blot

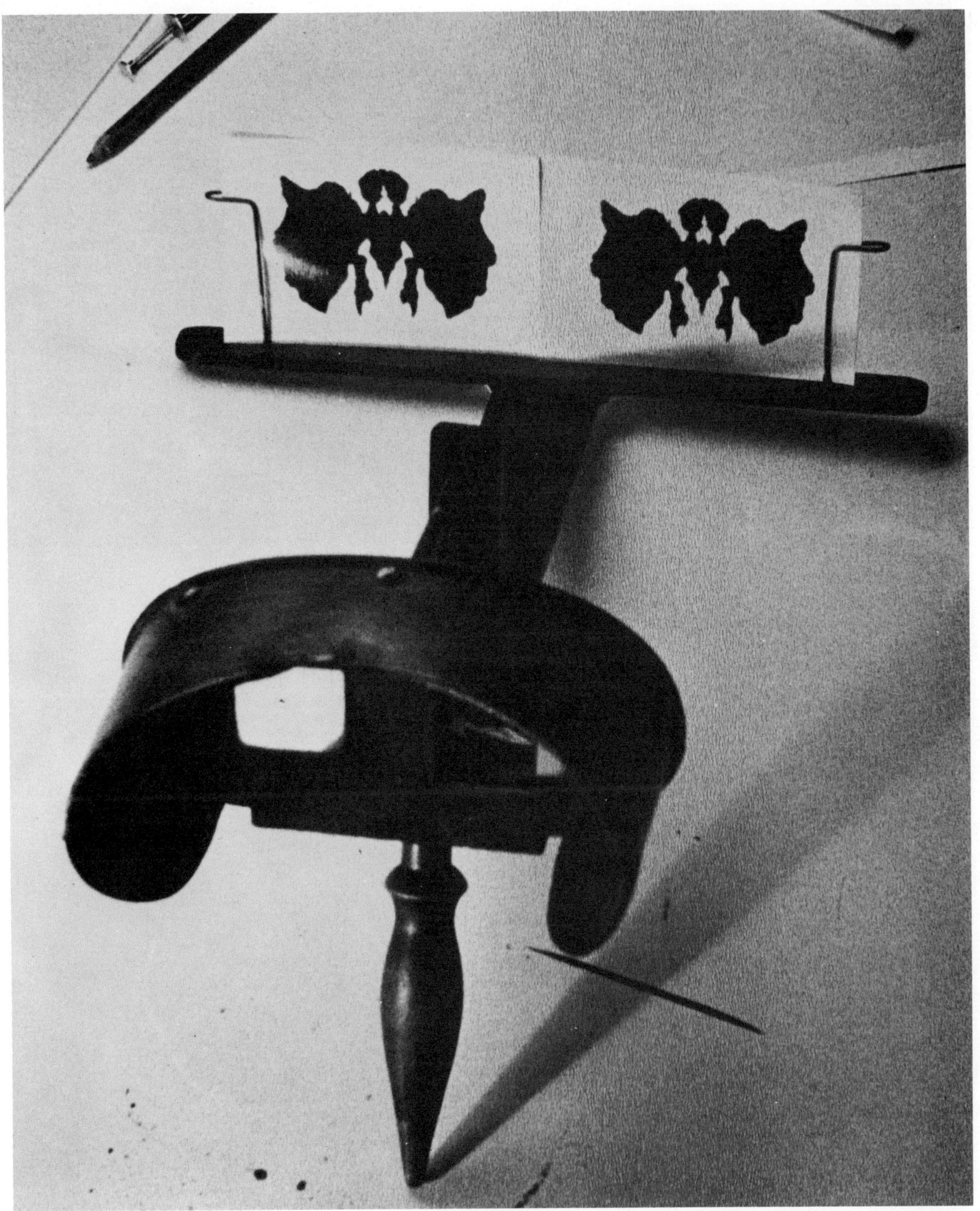

Thickens

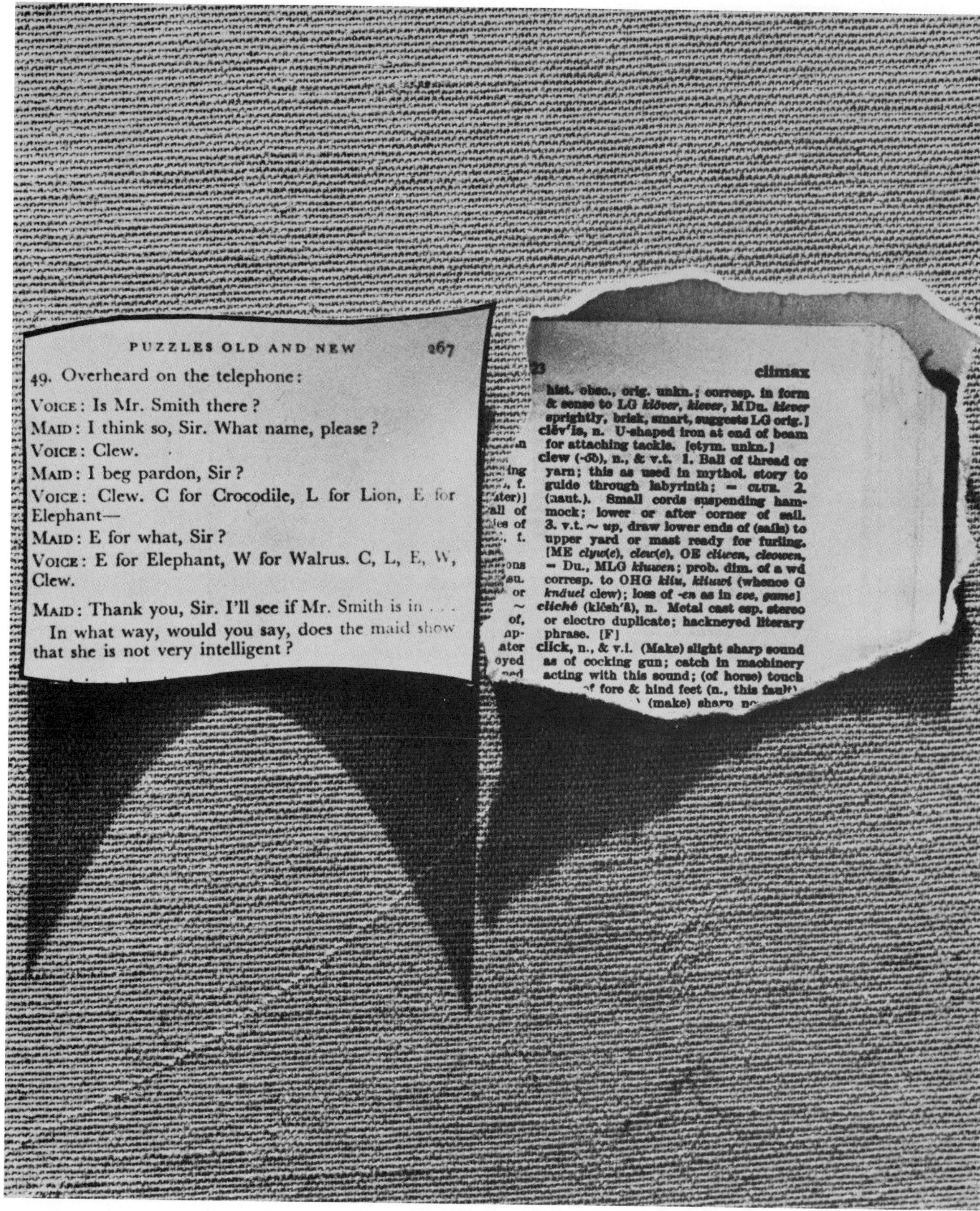

The cliché is the clue

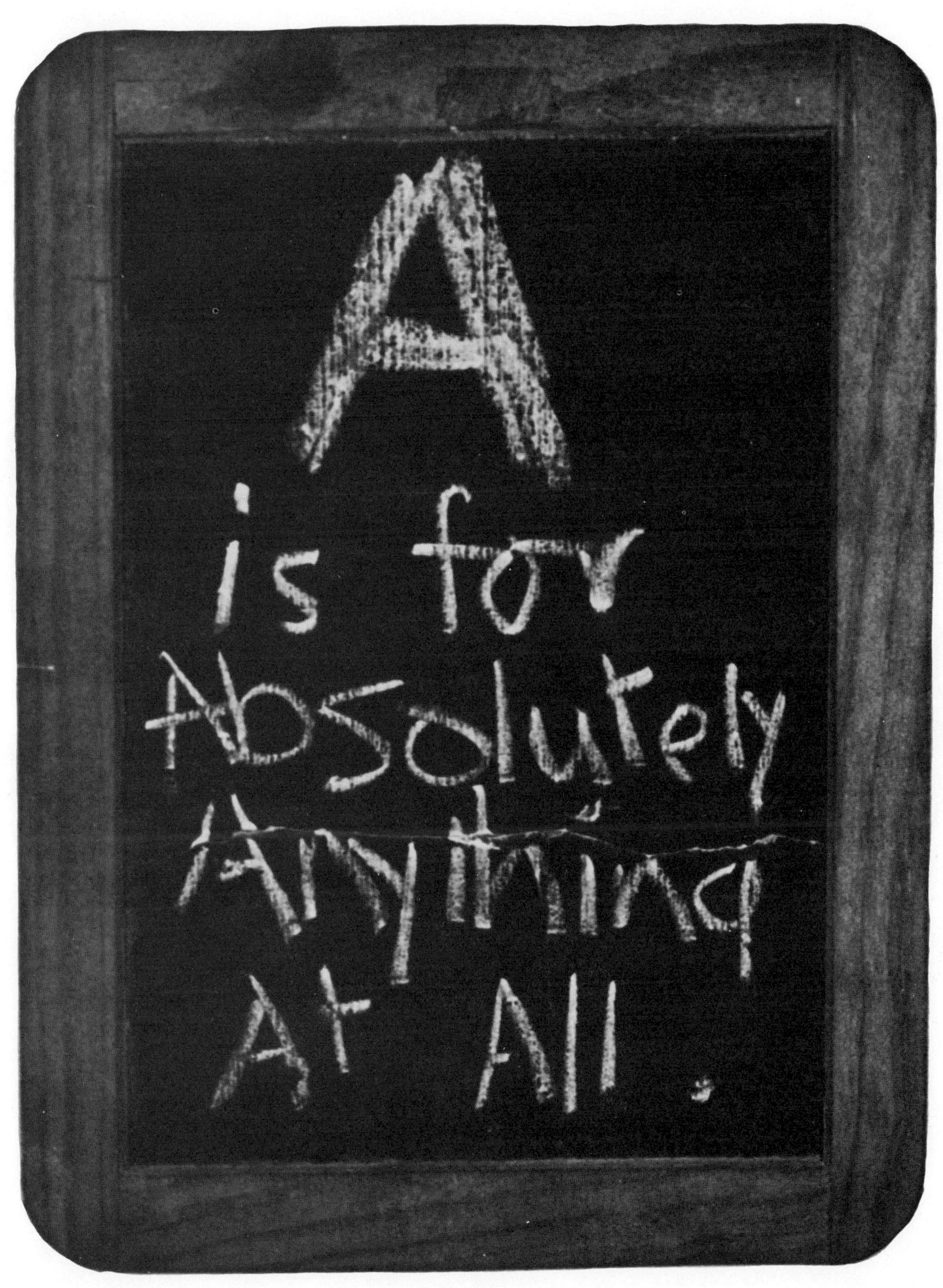

The Initial Premise

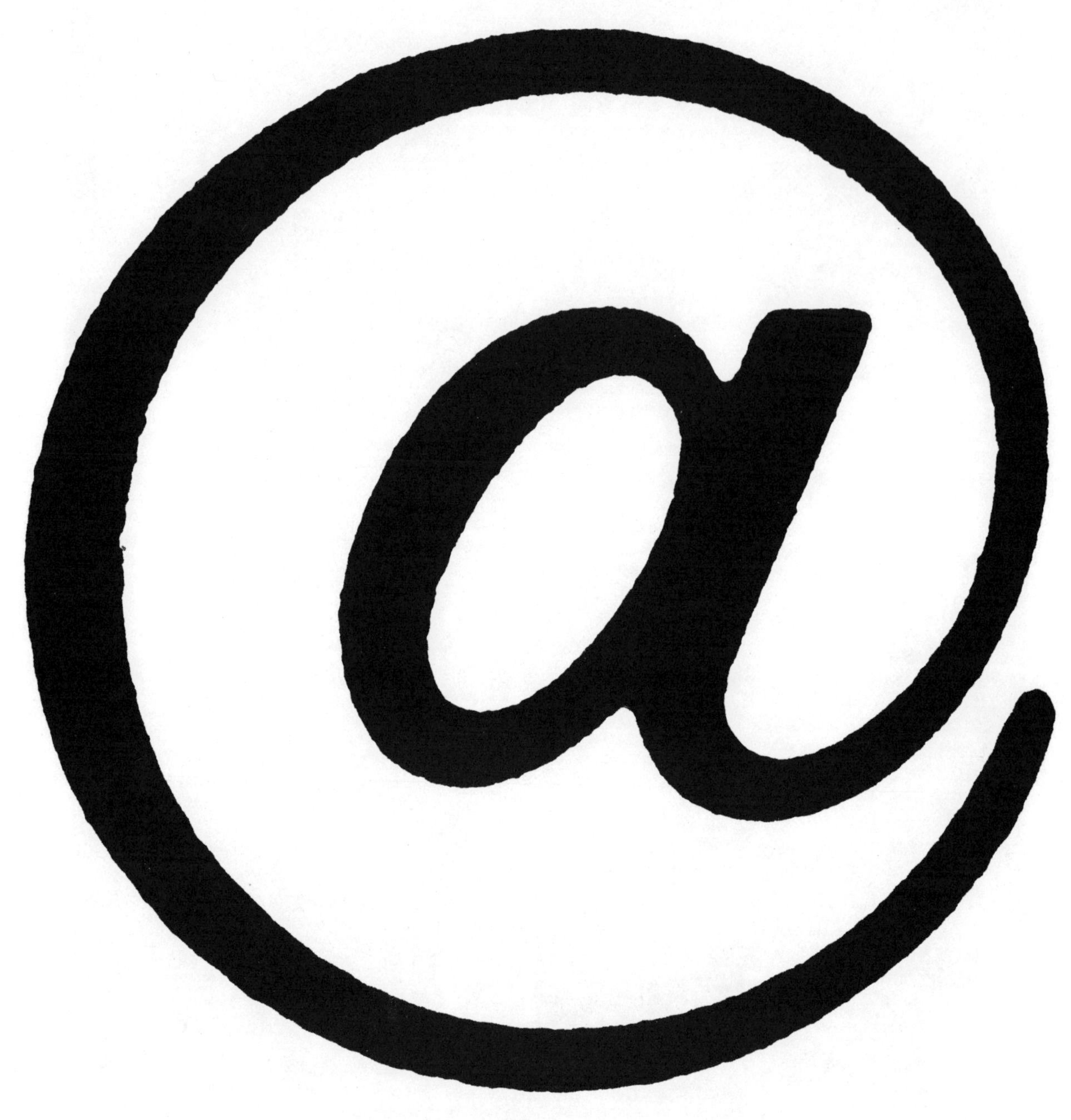

Convers'ion piece

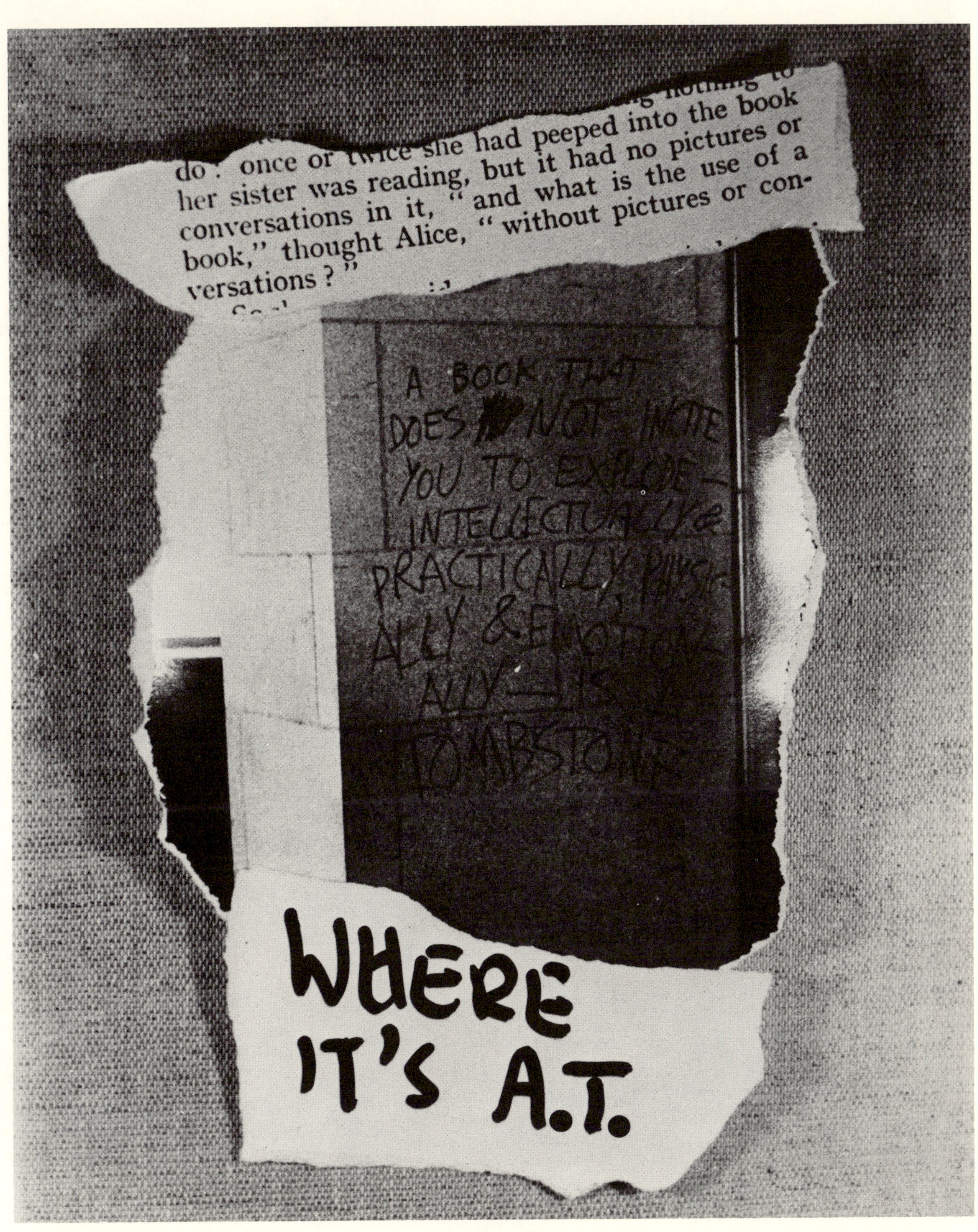

Apostrophe Theory

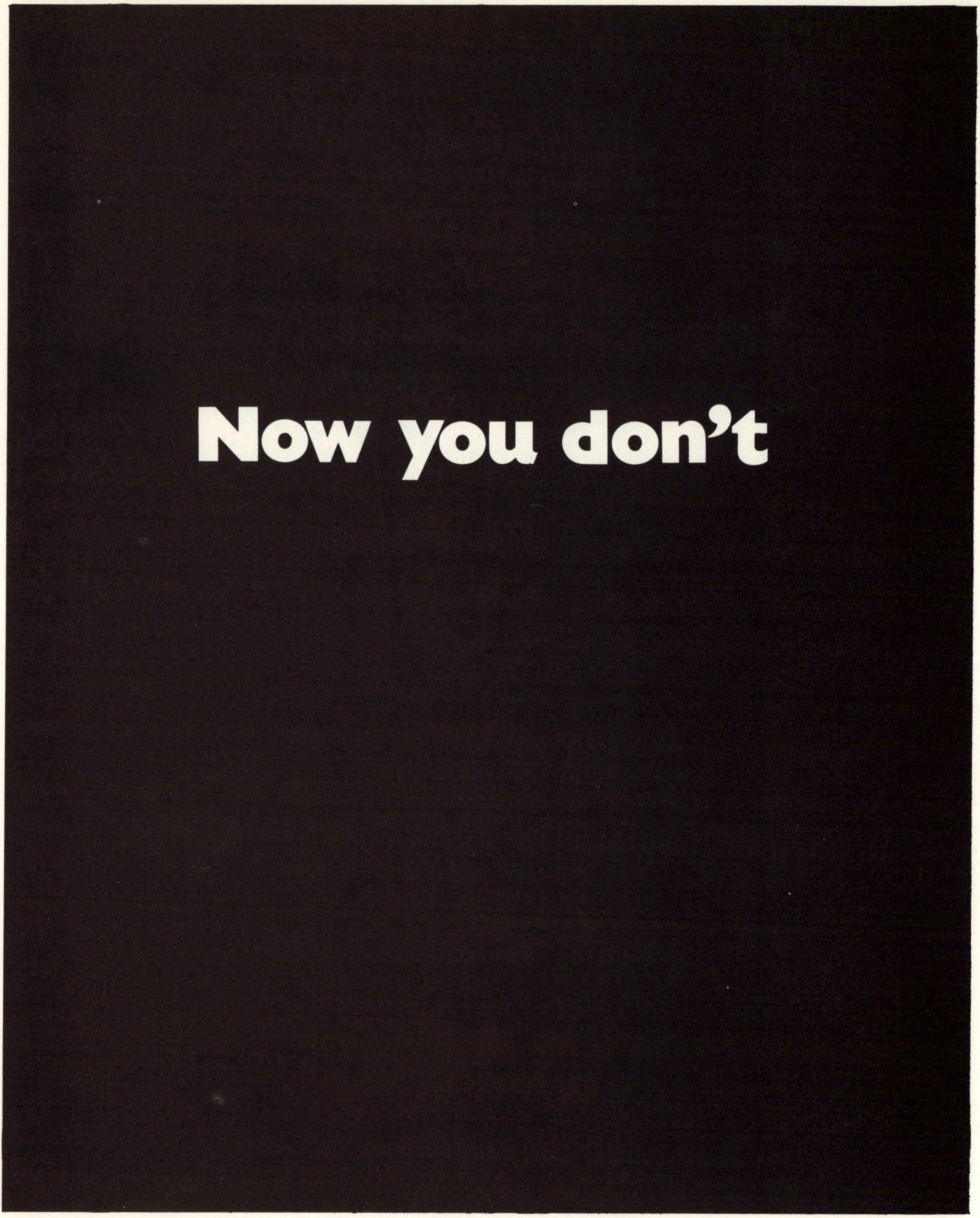

Now you don't

Fig 1 The Apostrophe

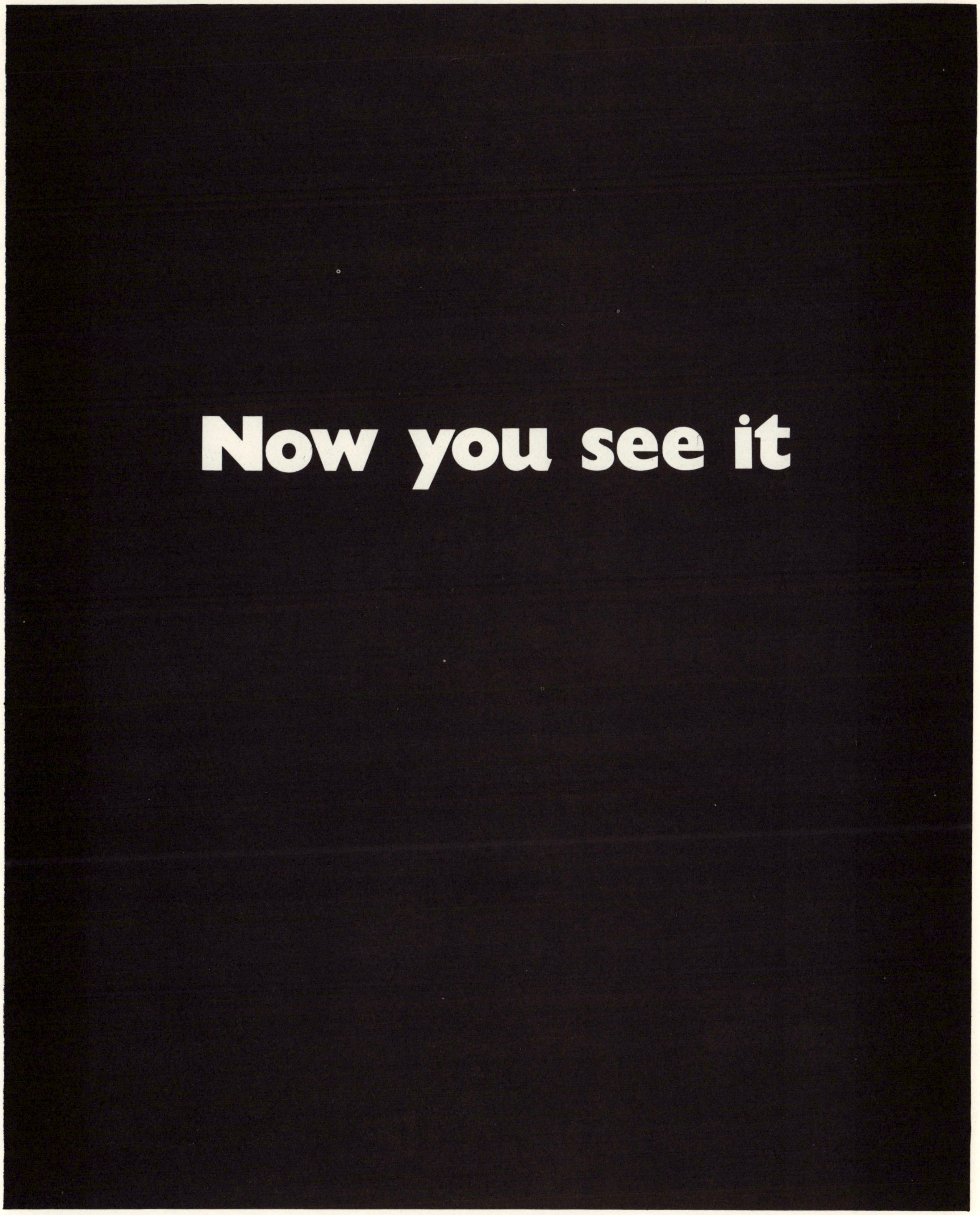

Now you see it

Fig 2 The Theory

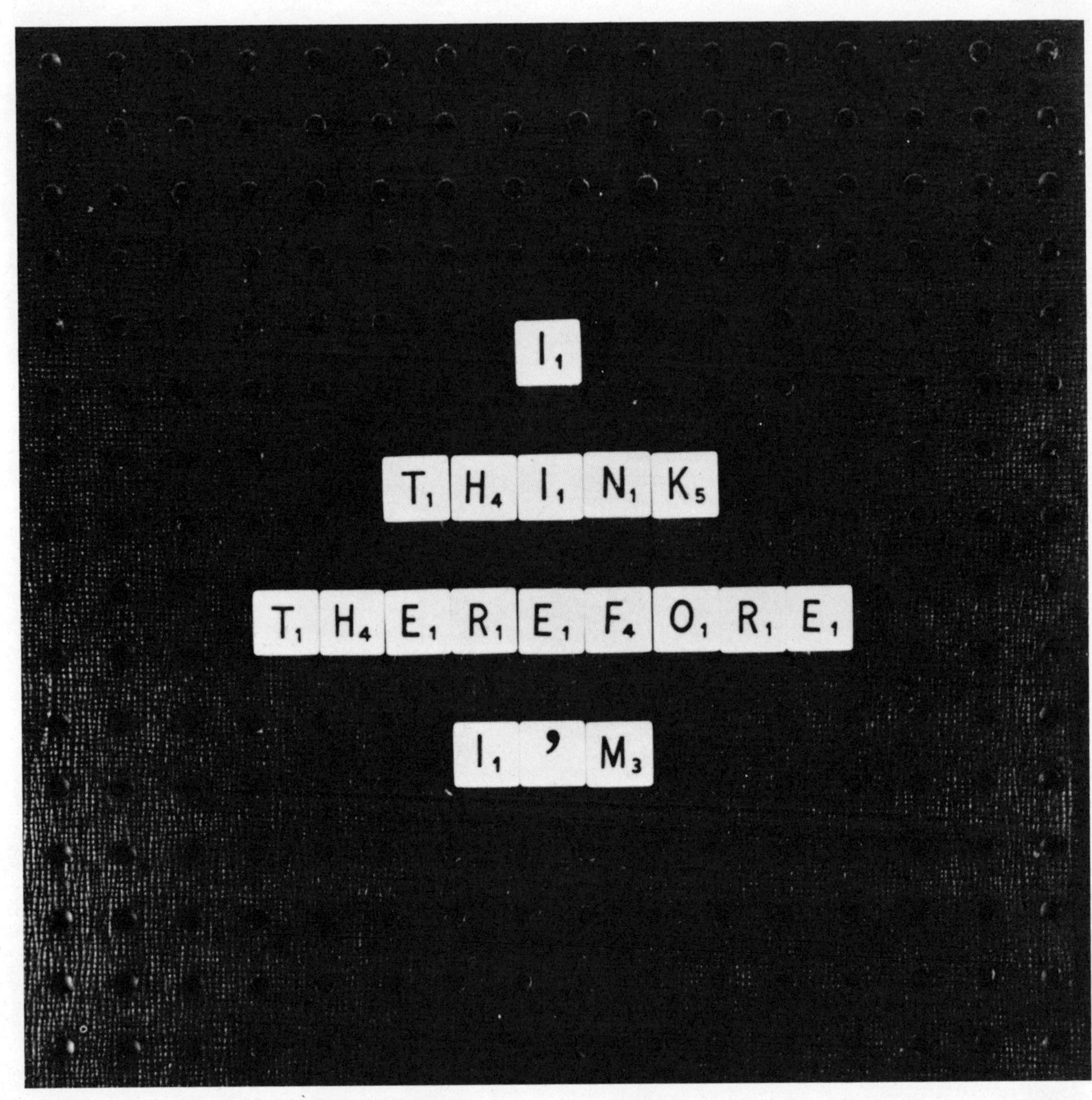

Fig 1 The Apostrophe

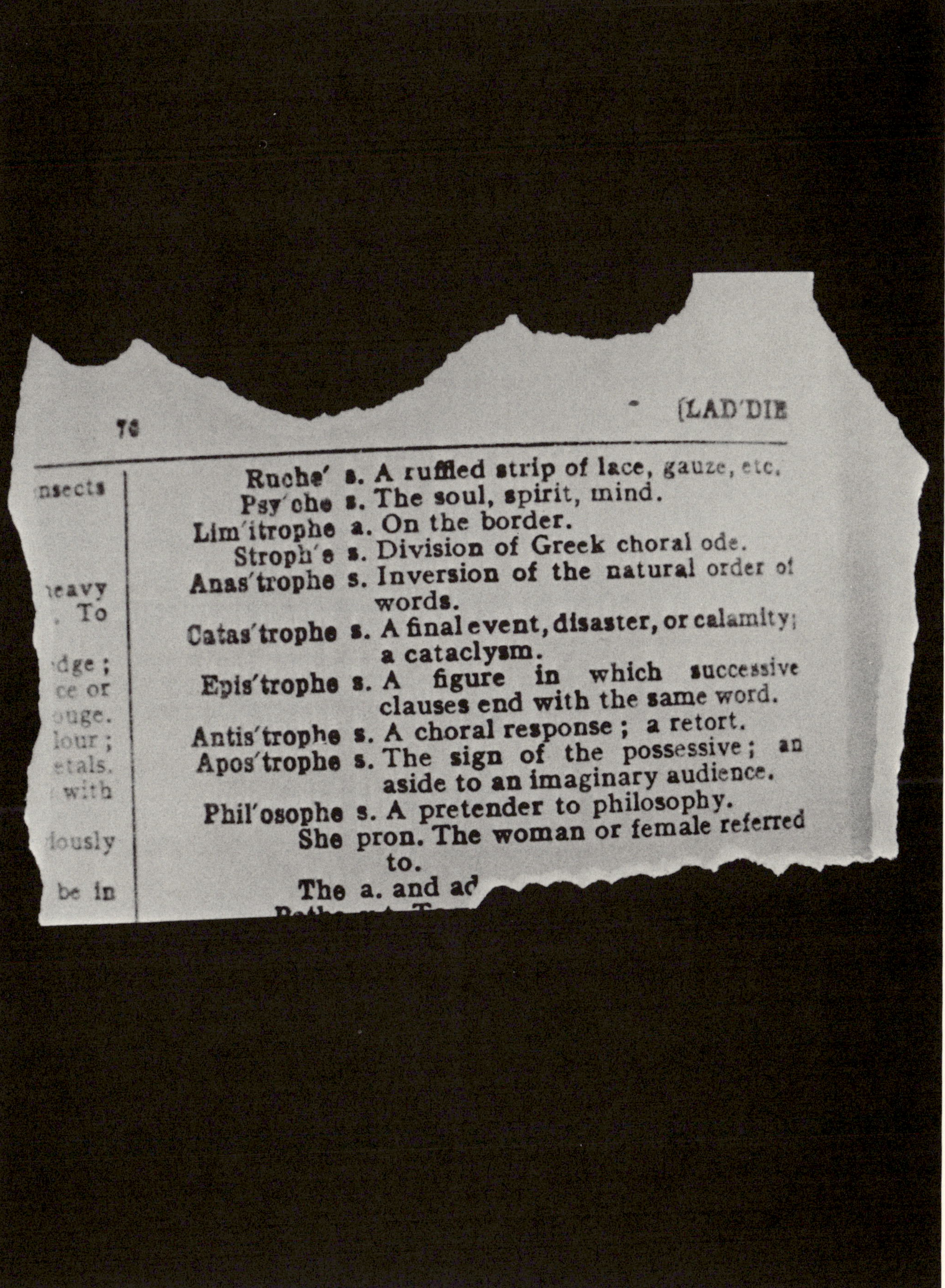

76 (LAD'DIE

Ruche' s. A ruffled strip of lace, gauze, etc.
Psy'che s. The soul, spirit, mind.
Lim'itrophe a. On the border.
Stroph'e s. Division of Greek choral ode.
Anas'trophe s. Inversion of the natural order of words.
Catas'trophe s. A final event, disaster, or calamity; a cataclysm.
Epis'trophe s. A figure in which successive clauses end with the same word.
Antis'trophe s. A choral response; a retort.
Apos'trophe s. The sign of the possessive; an aside to an imaginary audience.
Phil'osophe s. A pretender to philosophy.
She pron. The woman or female referred to.
The a. and ad

Fig 2 The Theory

This week in The THES

CATASTROPHE THEORY

Professor René Thom, creator of "catastrophe theory," talks about its application to fields as diverse as embryology, psychology, neurophysiology and social behaviour.

He discusses recent trends in the development of the theory, his own particular interest in its application to developmental biology and its relationship with areas of philosophy such as structuralism.

He also warns of the limitations of its use in predicting future events.

"Many people are putting too much hope in the theory."

"Catastrophe theory could be very useful as a way of modelling all sorts of psychological activities."

"For me the basic interest of catastrophe theory is that it is a theory of analogy. It is the first theory since Aristotelian logic which really deals with the problem of analogy."

THE TIMES
Higher Education
SUPPLEMENT

On sale at newsagents, price 12p

Fig 1 The Apostrophe

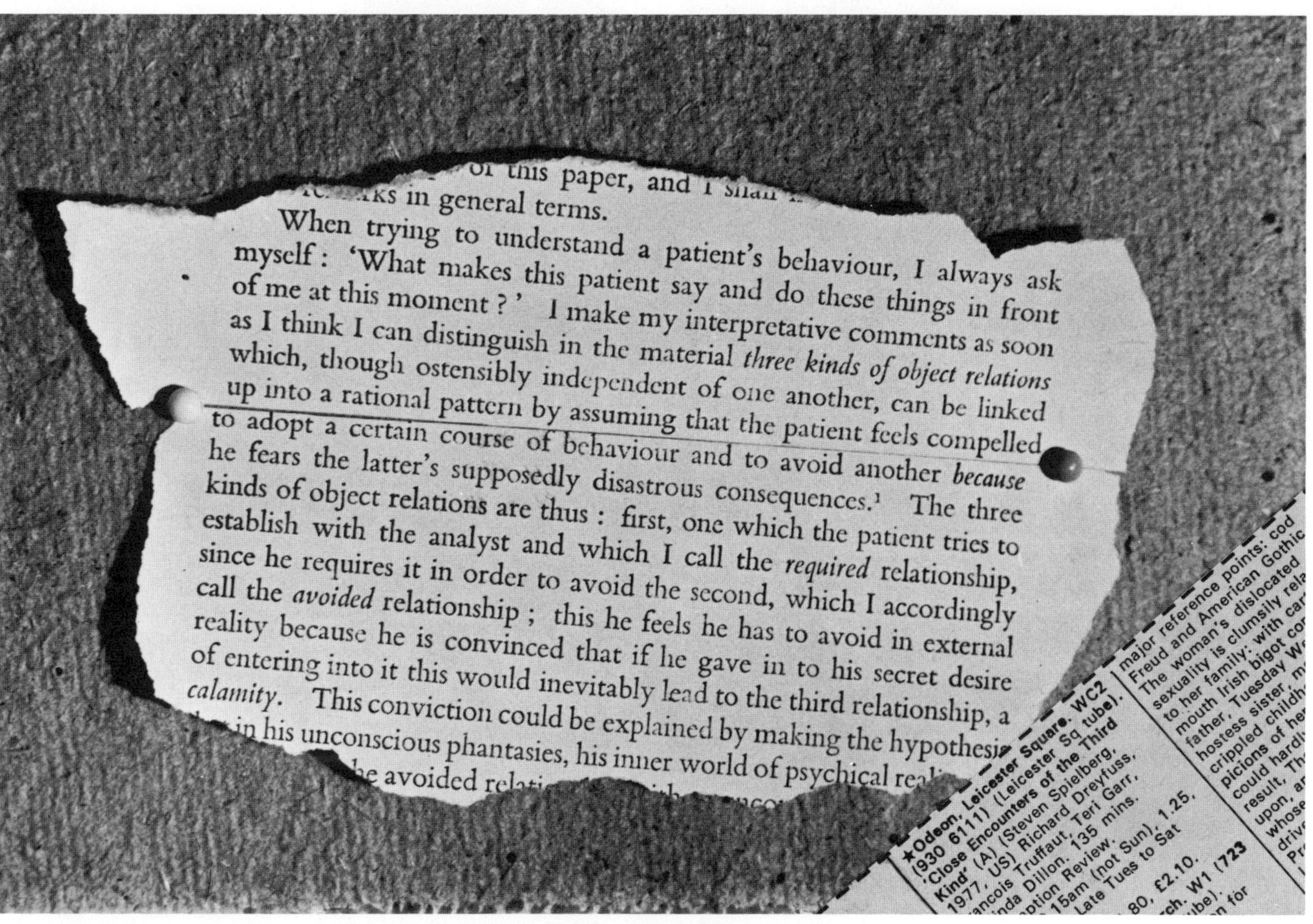

Fig 2 The Theory

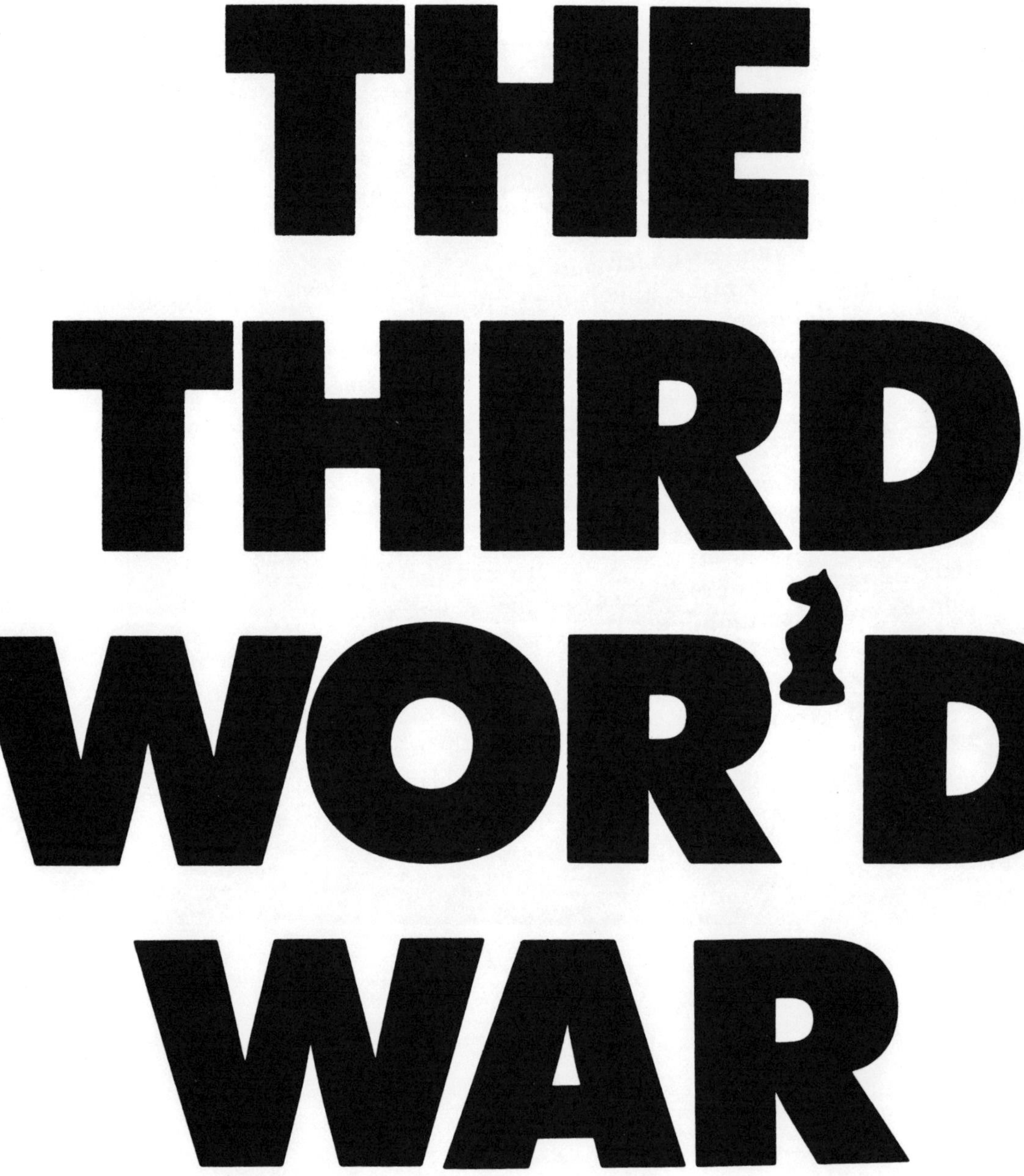

THE

THIRD

WOR'D

WAR

Fig 1 The Apostrophe

THE MISSING INK

Fig 2 The Theory

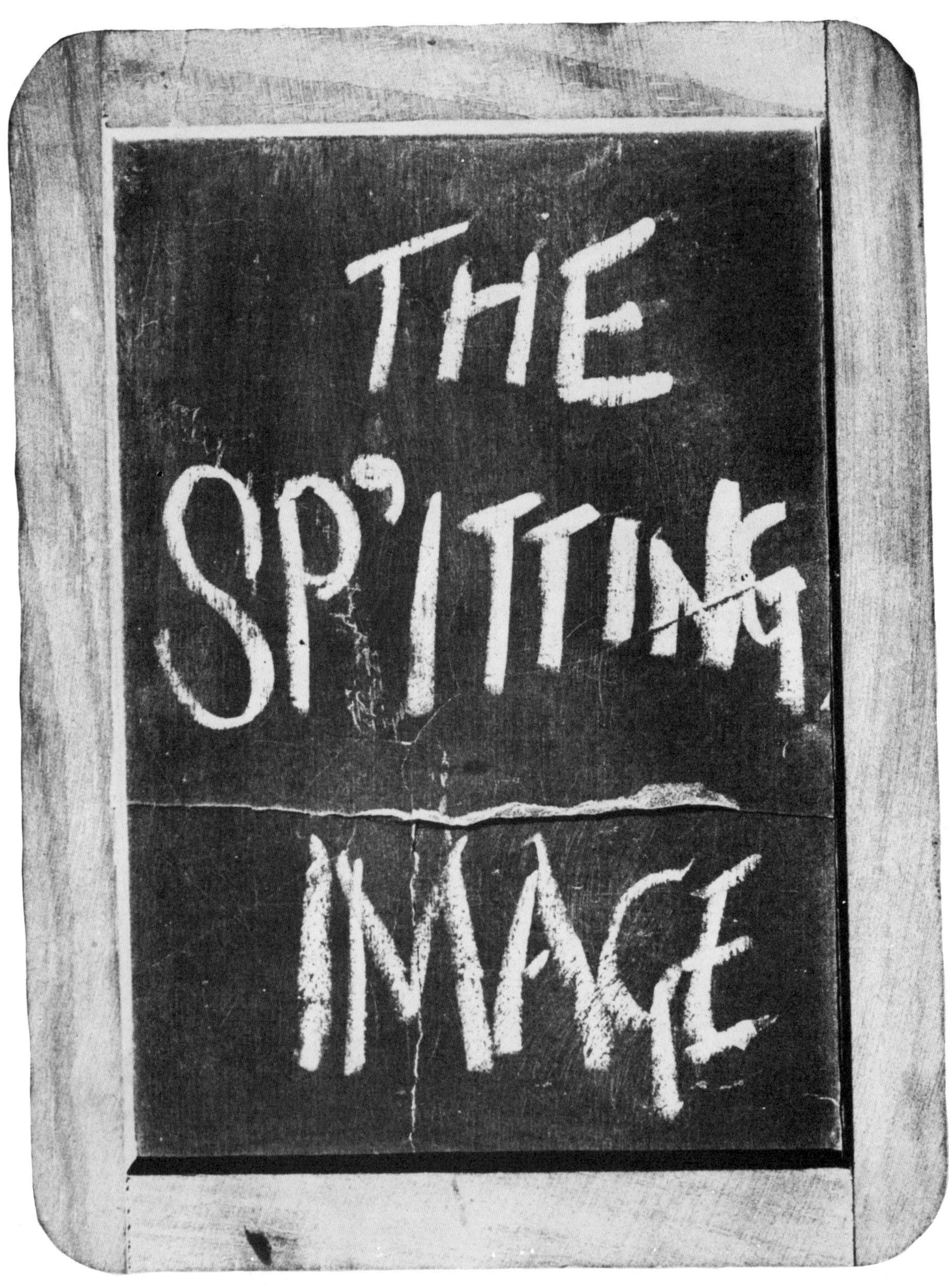

Fig 1 The Apostrophe

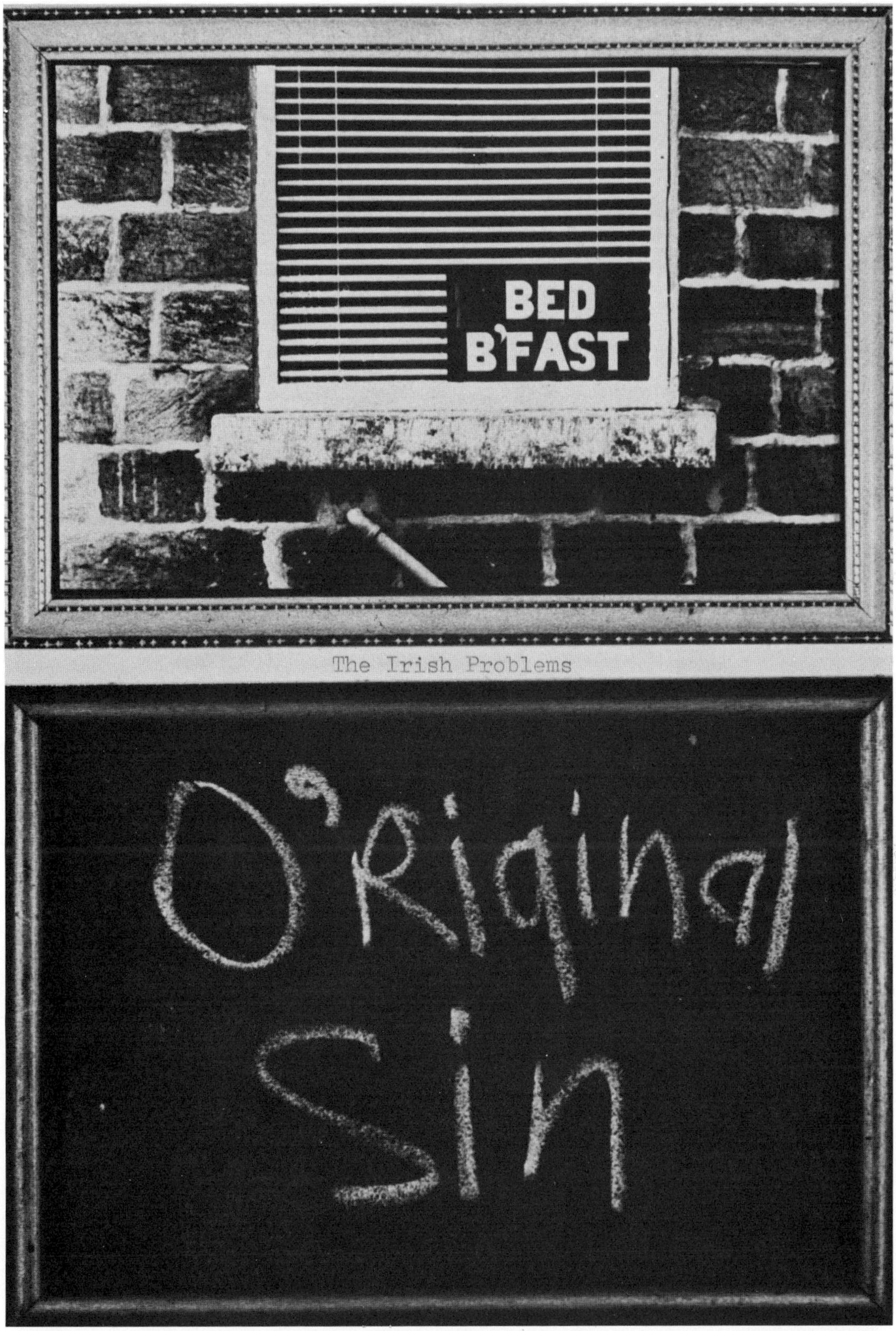

BED
B'FAST

The Irish Problems

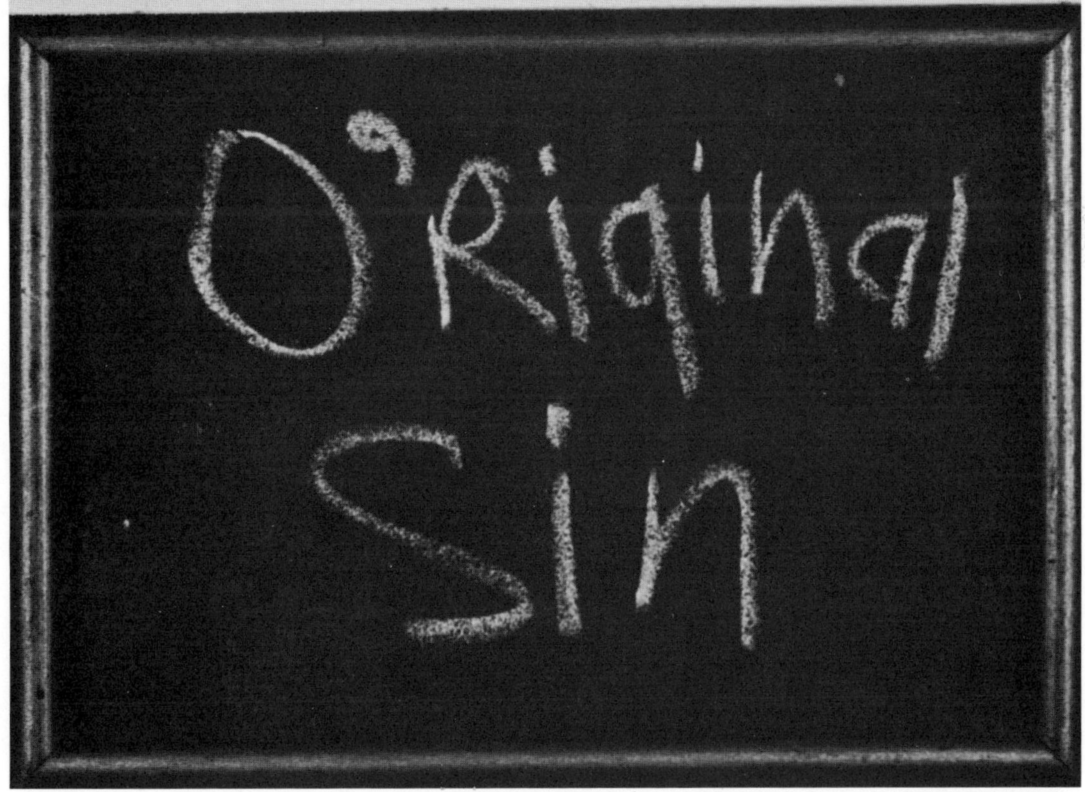

Fig 2 The Theory

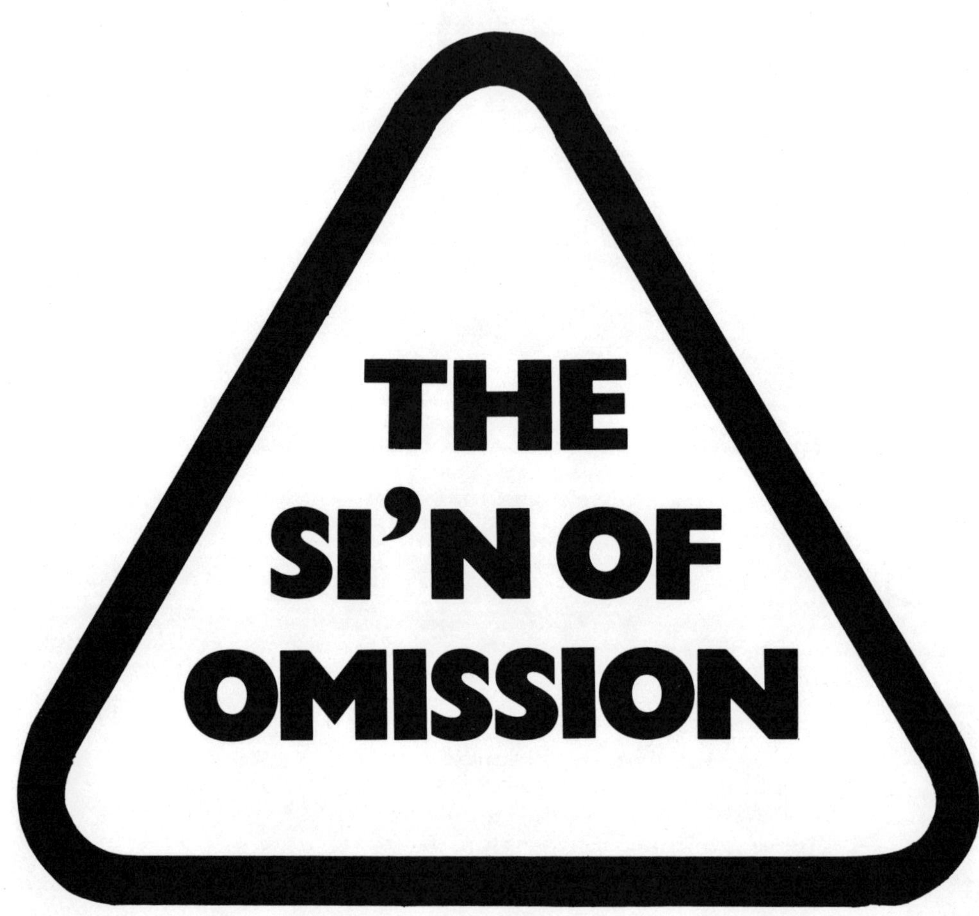

Fig 1 The Apostrophe

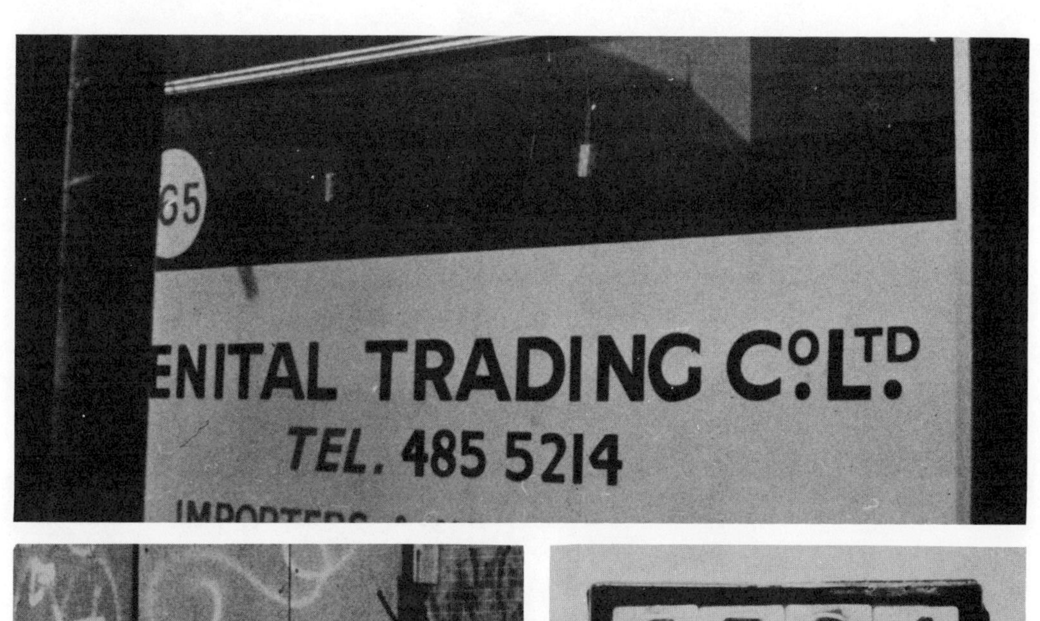

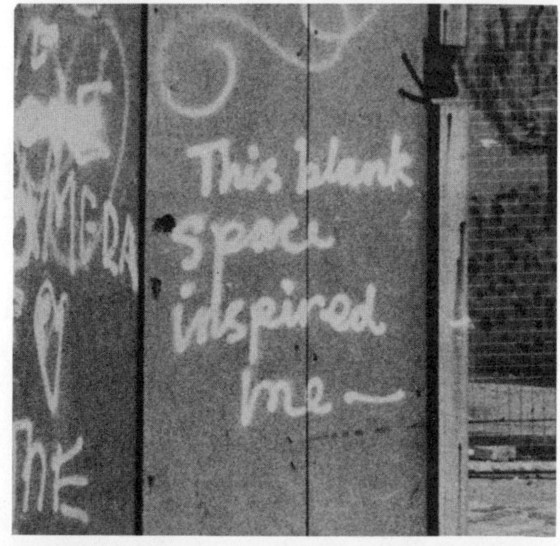

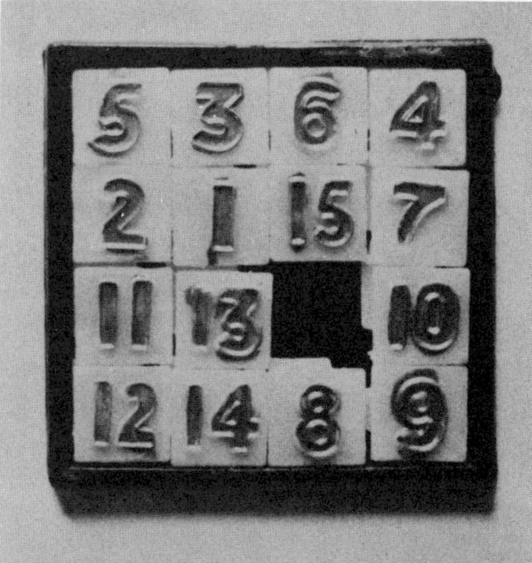

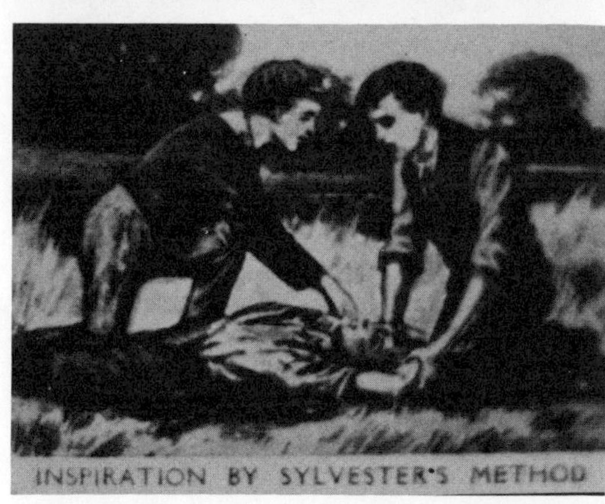

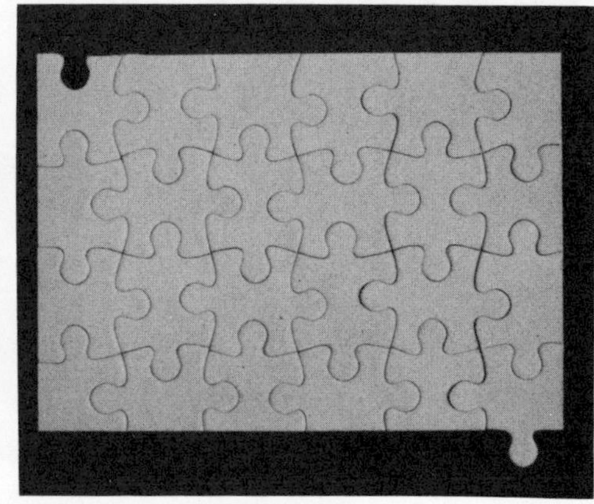

Fig 2 The Theory

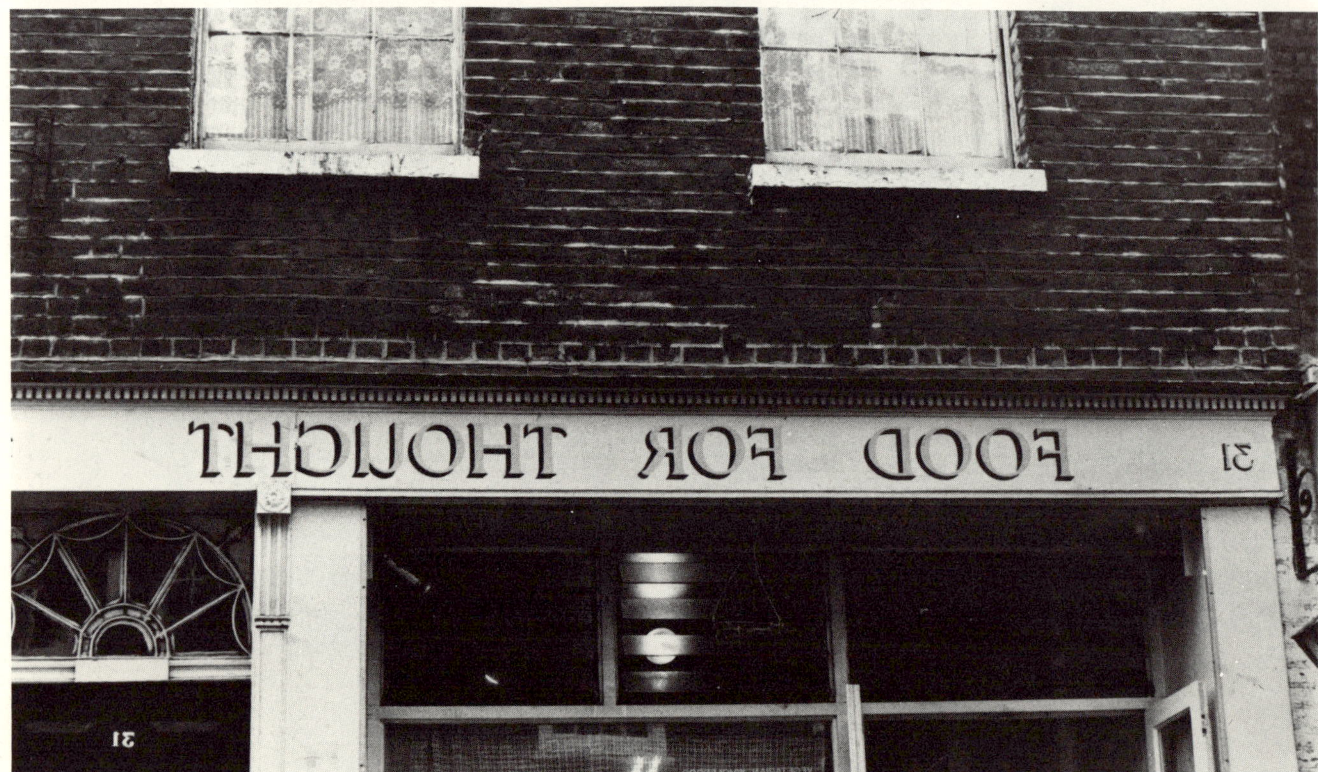

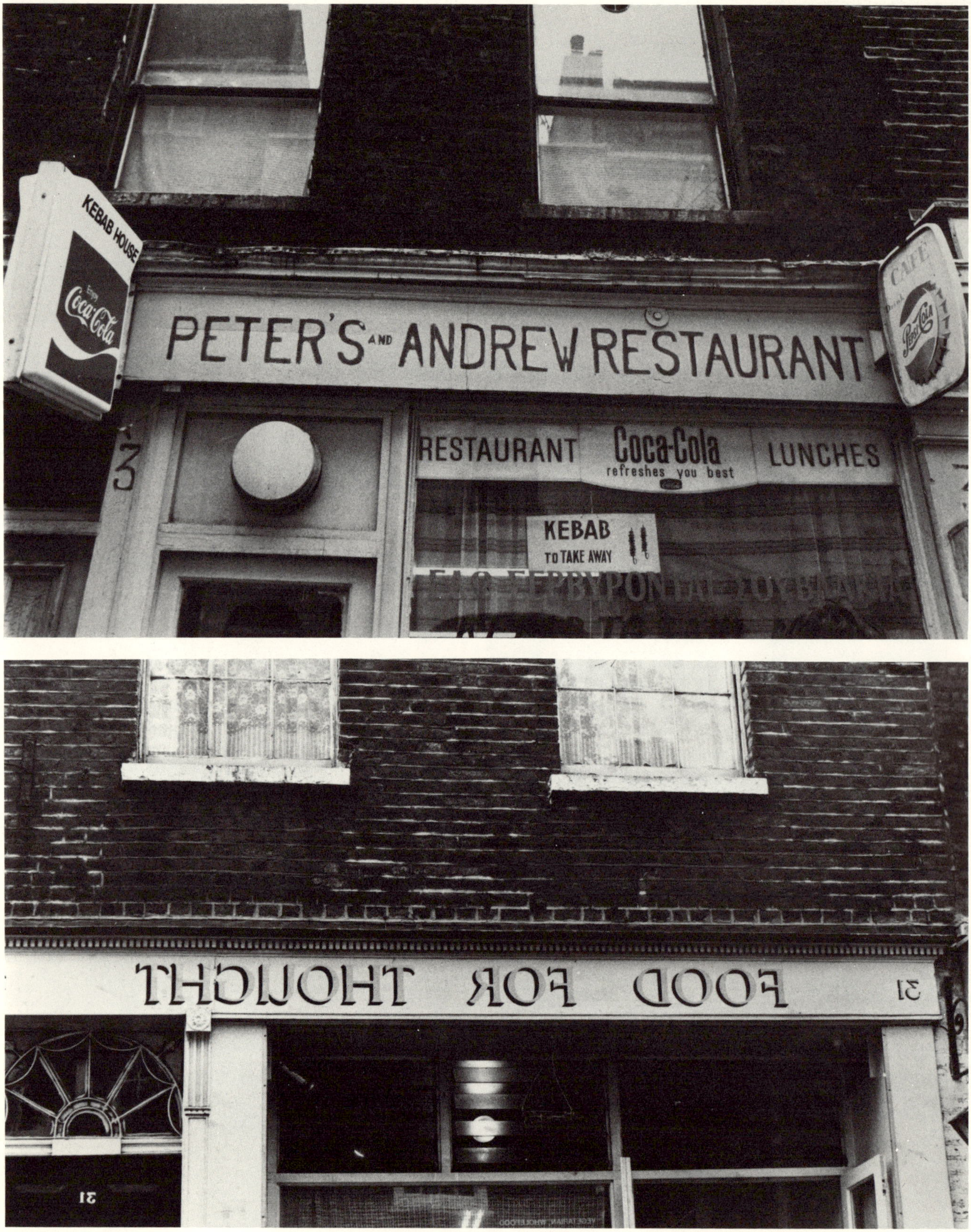

Fig 1 The Apostrophe

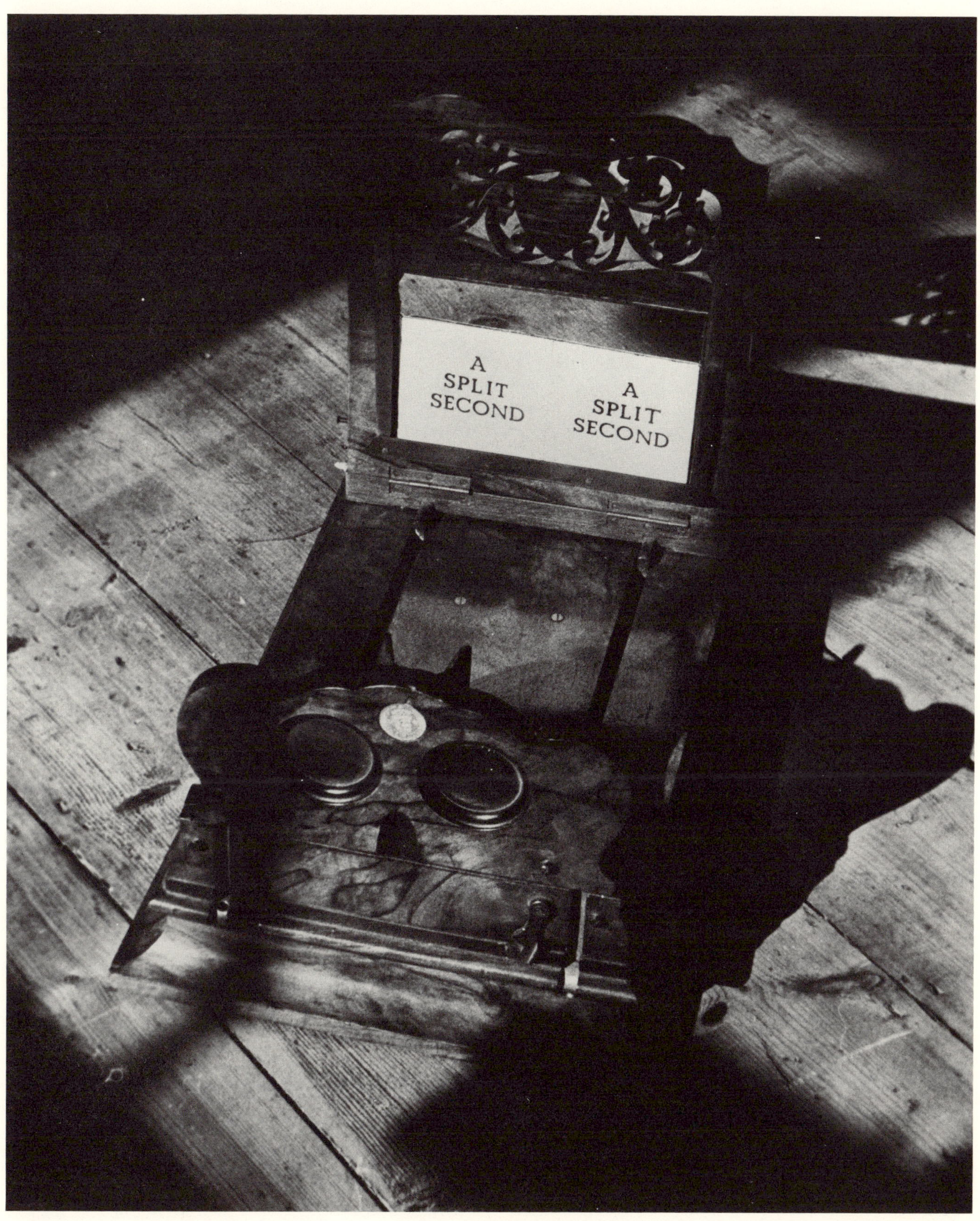

Fig 2 The Theory

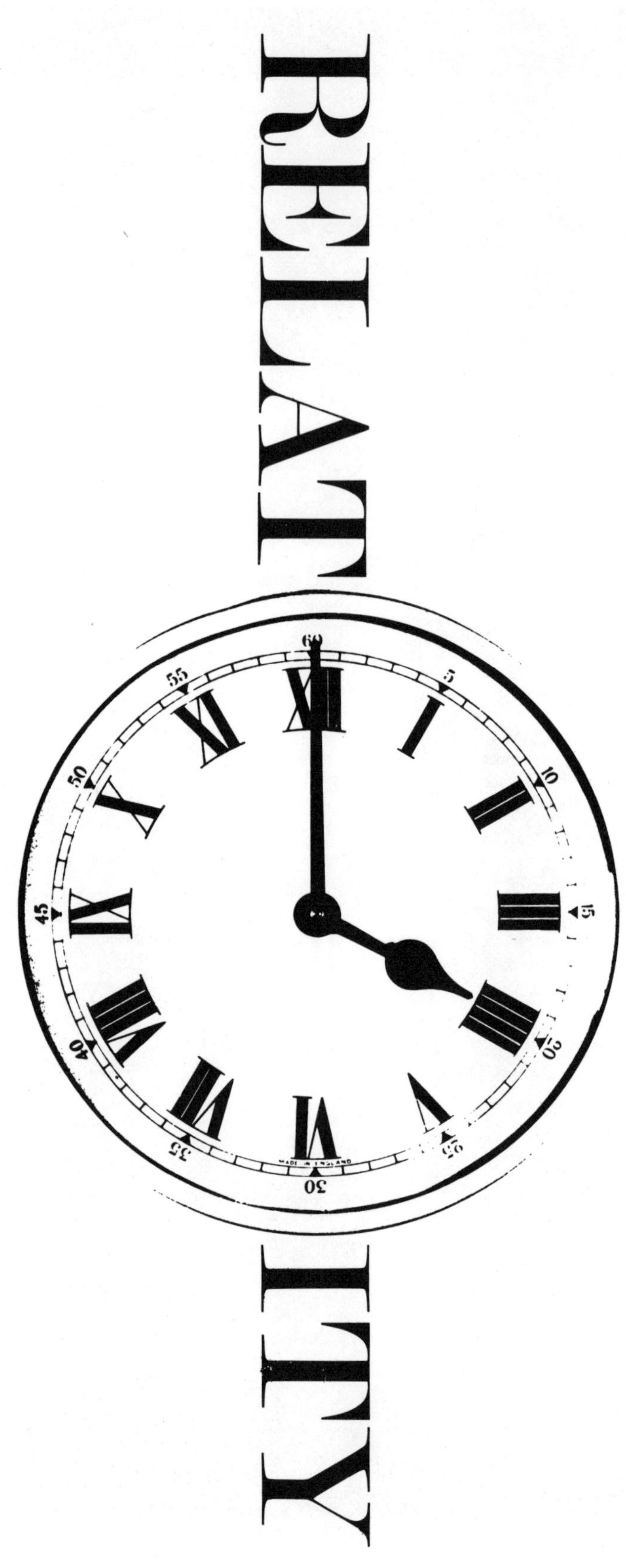

The space/time continuum

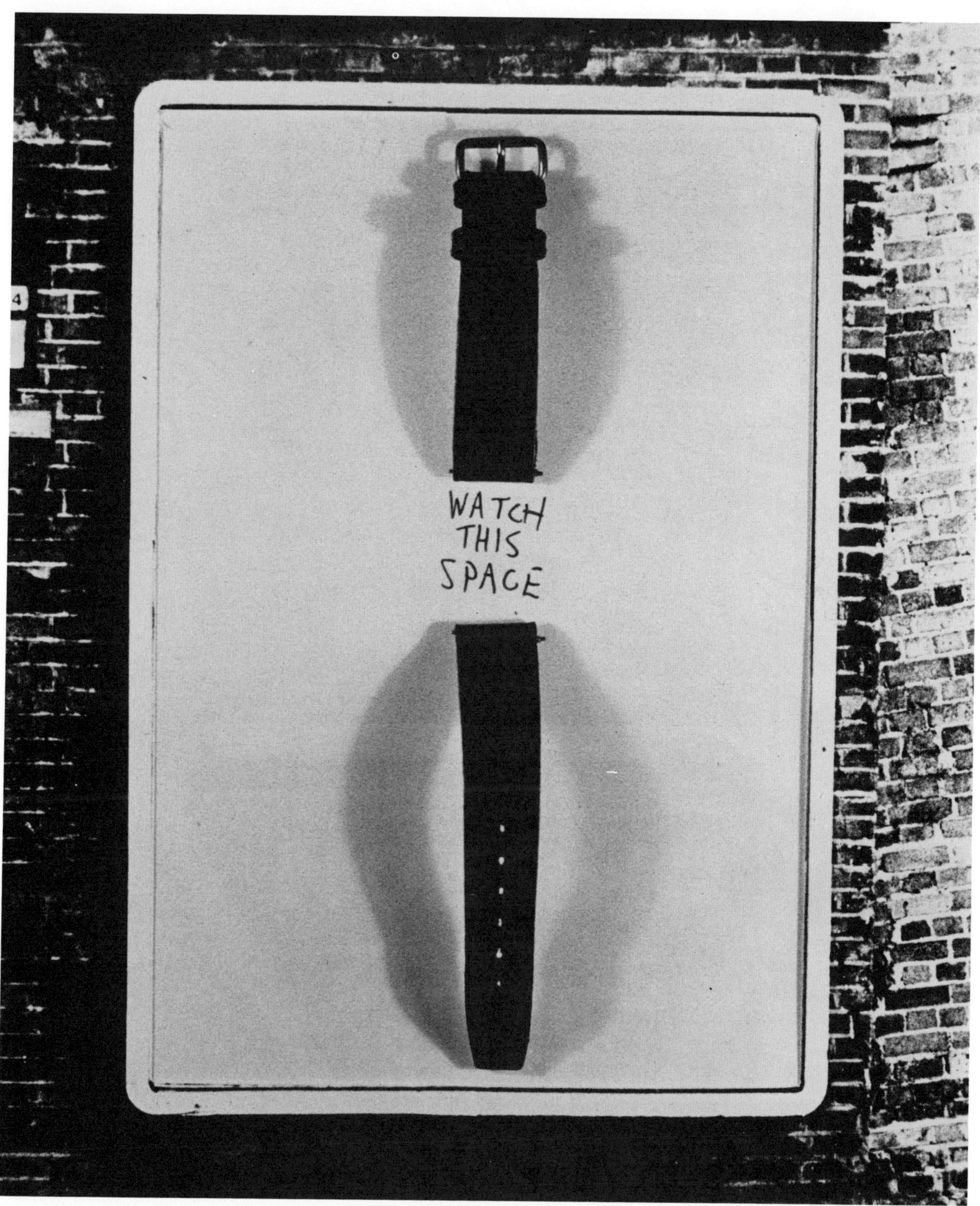

The medium/message continuum

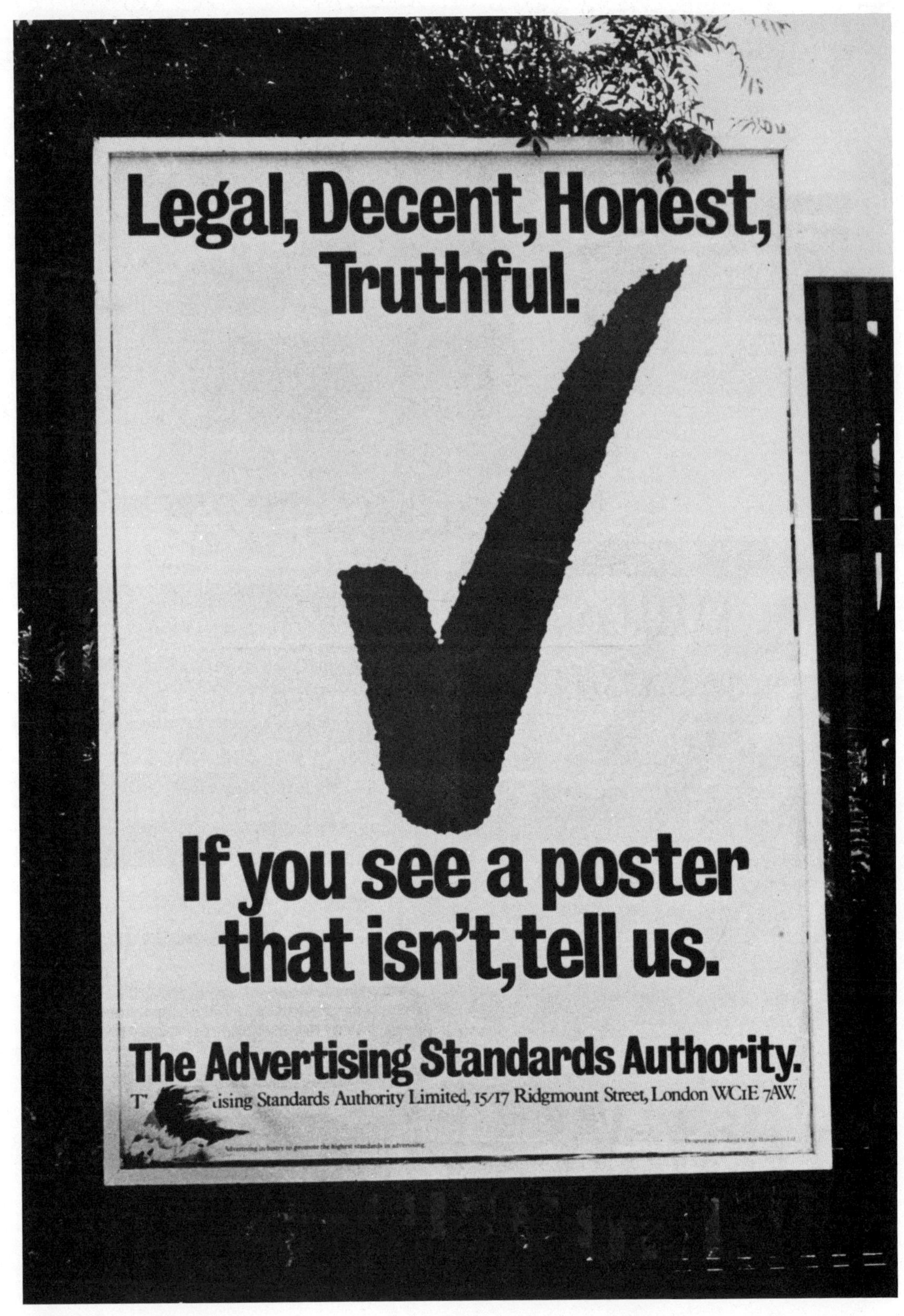
Legal, Decent, Honest, Truthful.
If you see a poster that isn't, tell us.
The Advertising Standards Authority.
ising Standards Authority Limited, 15/17 Ridgmount Street, London WC1E 7AW.

Tick

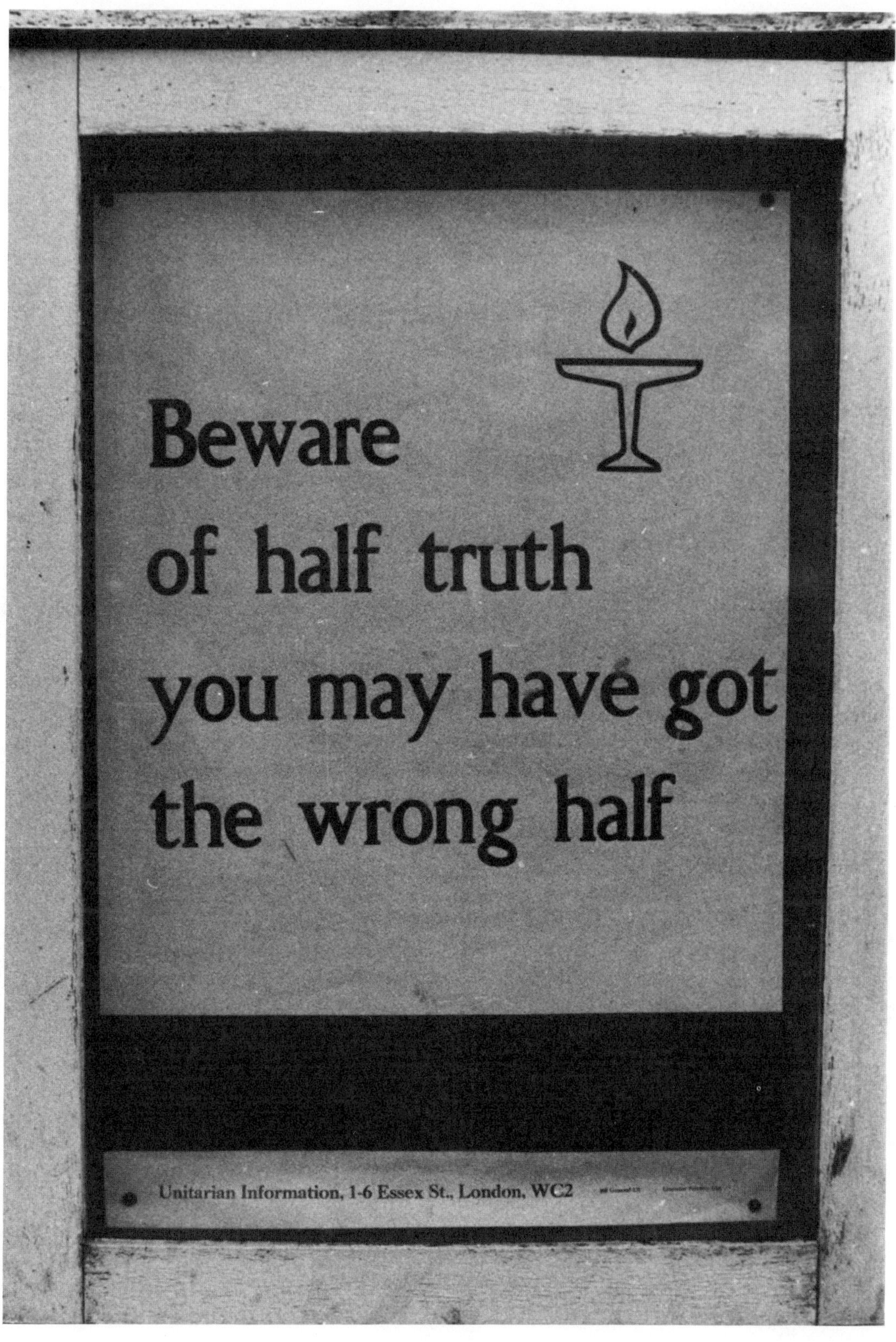
Beware
of half truth
you may have got
the wrong half
Unitarian Information, 1-6 Essex St., London, WC2

Tock

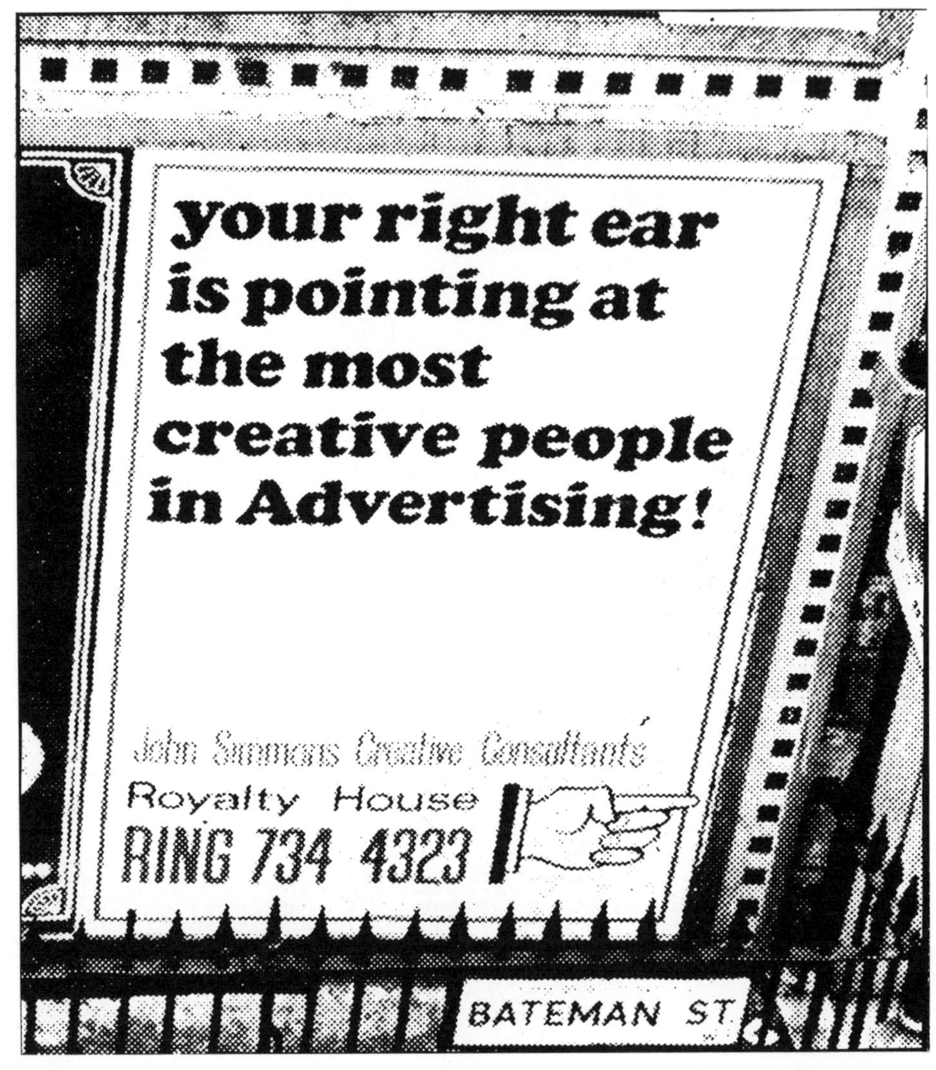
your right ear
is pointing at
the most
creative people
in Advertising!
John Simmons Creative Consultants
Royalty House
RING 734 4323
BATEMAN ST

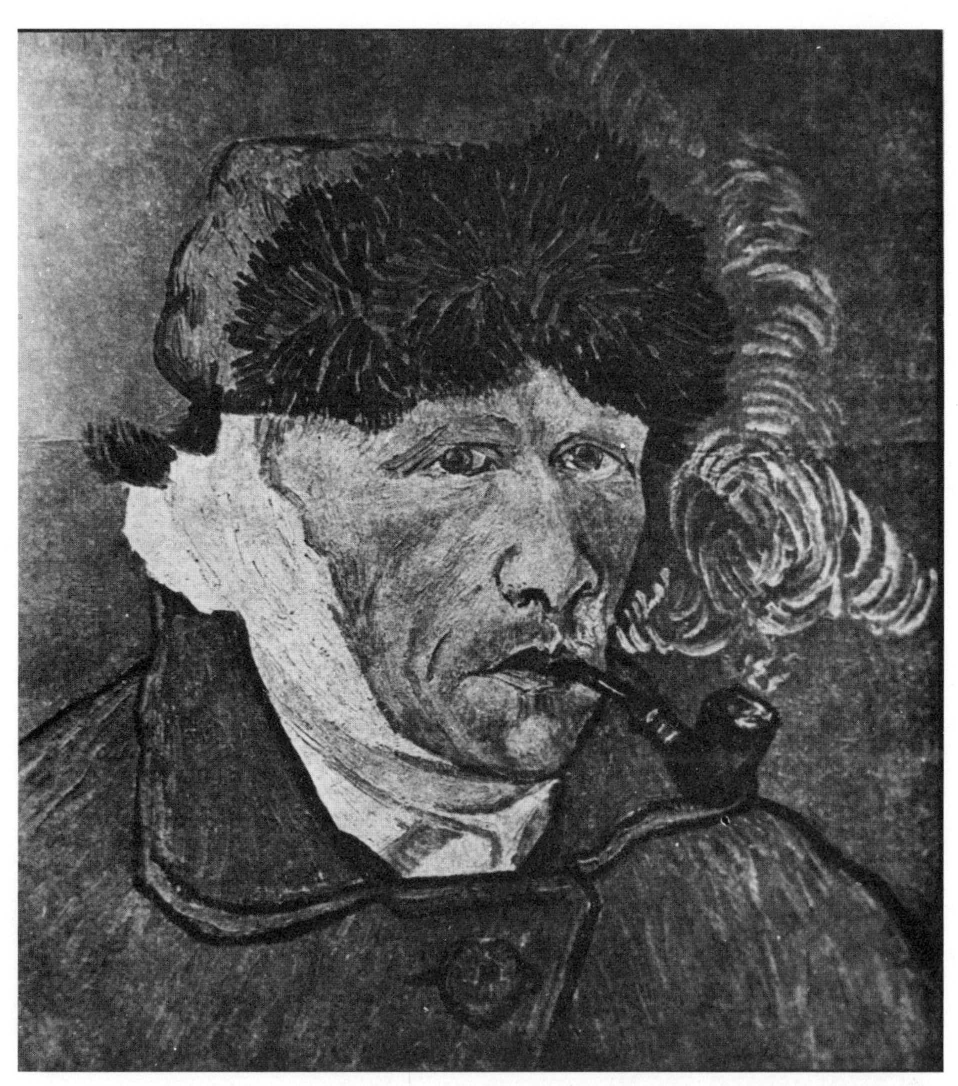

EFFECTS OF HABIT ; CORRELATED VARIATION ; INHERITANCE.

Changed habits produce an inherited effect, as in the period of the flowering of plants when transported from one climate to another. With animals the increased use or disuse of parts has had a more marked influence ; thus, I find in the domestic duck that the bones of the wing weigh less and the bones of the leg more, in proportion to the whole skeleton, than do the same bones in the wild duck ; and this change may be safely attributed to the domestic duck flying much less, and walking more, than its wild parents. The great and inherited development of the udders in cows and goats in countries where they are habitually milked, in comparison with these organs in other countries, is probably another instance of the effects of muse. Not one of our domestic animals can be named which has not in some country drooping ears ; and the view, which has been suggested that the drooping is due to disuse of the muscles of the ear, from the animals being seldom much alarmed, seems probable.

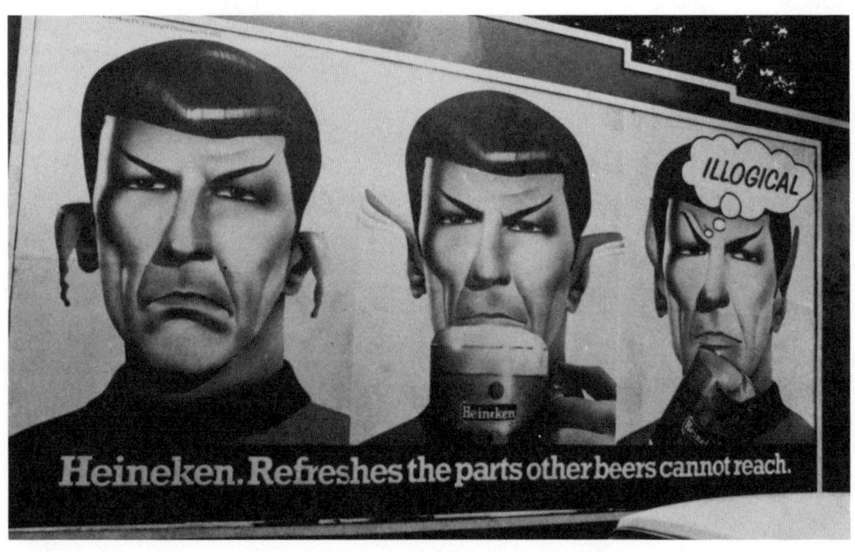

External logic

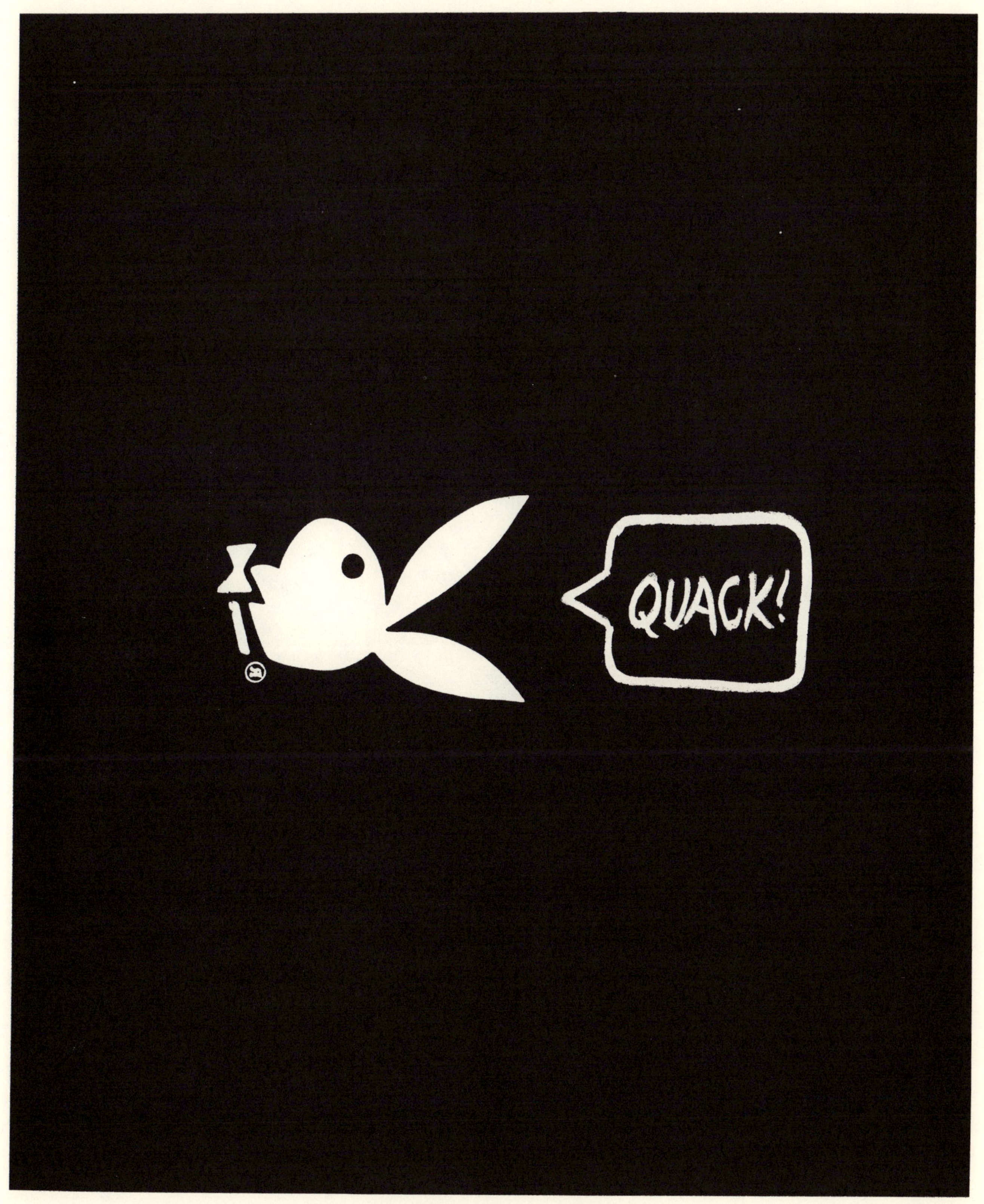

The doctor of philosophy

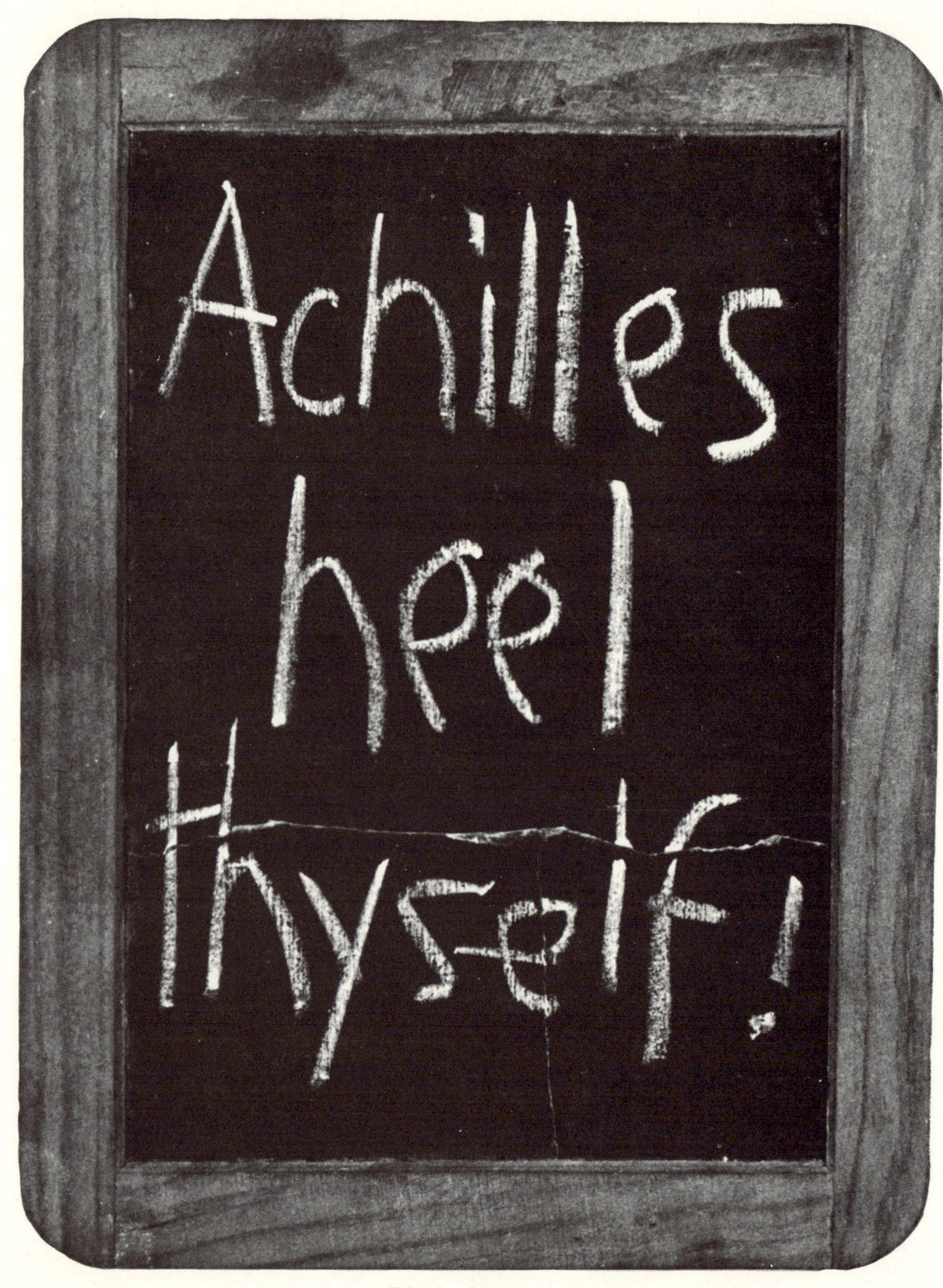

Fig 1 Mono

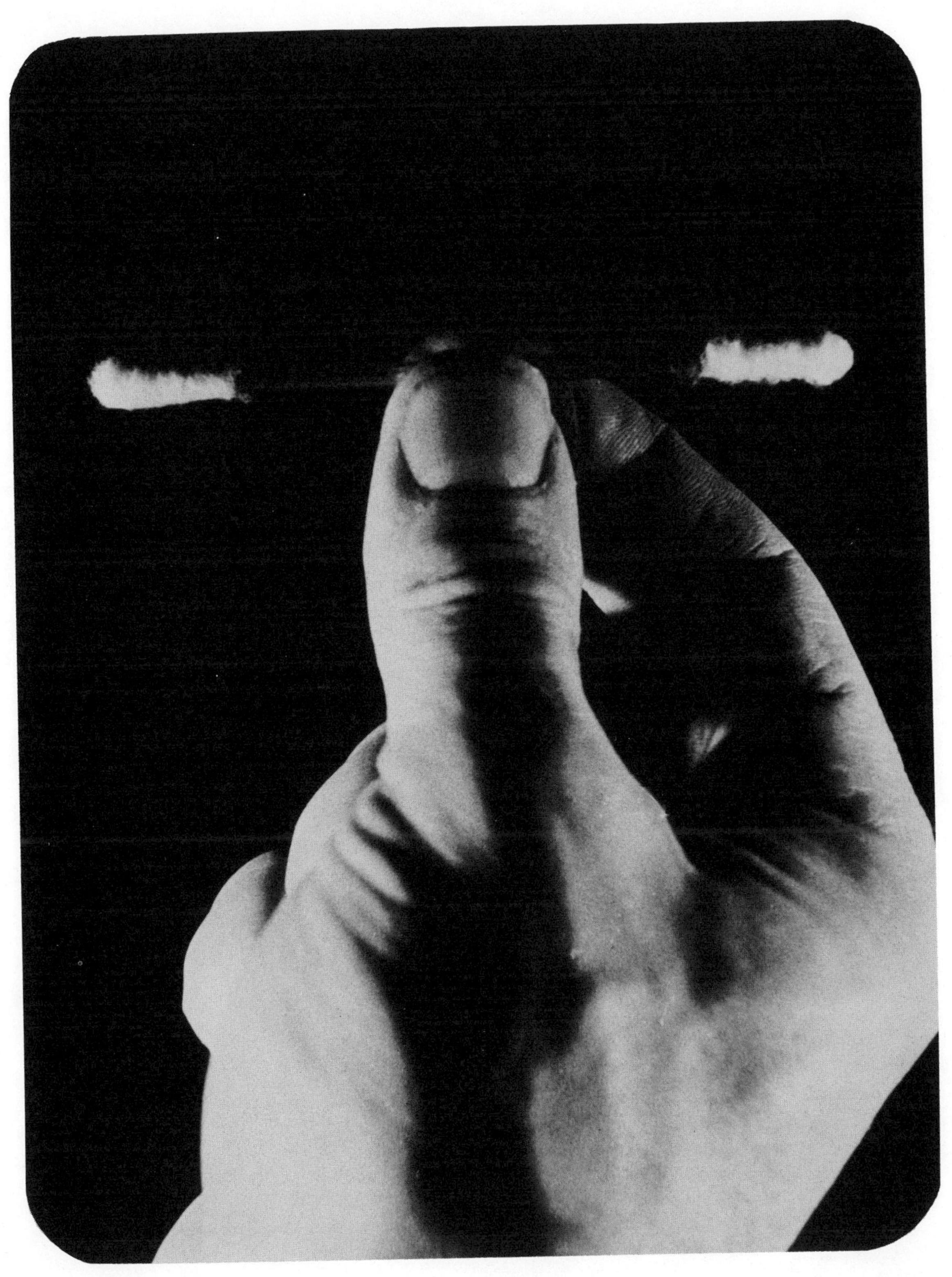

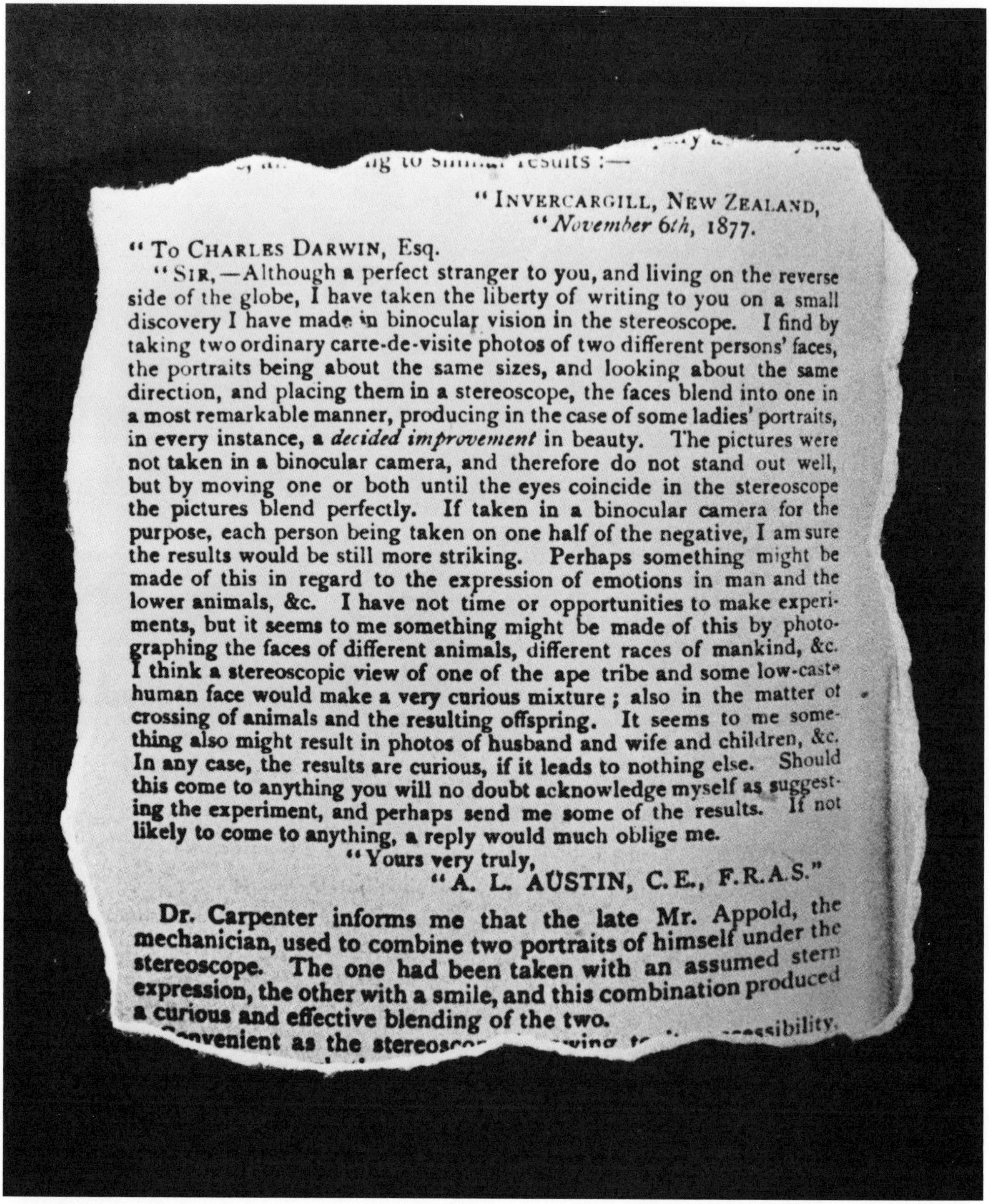

… results :—

"INVERCARGILL, NEW ZEALAND,
"*November 6th*, 1877.

"To CHARLES DARWIN, Esq.

"SIR,—Although a perfect stranger to you, and living on the reverse side of the globe, I have taken the liberty of writing to you on a small discovery I have made in binocular vision in the stereoscope. I find by taking two ordinary carte-de-visite photos of two different persons' faces, the portraits being about the same sizes, and looking about the same direction, and placing them in a stereoscope, the faces blend into one in a most remarkable manner, producing in the case of some ladies' portraits, in every instance, a *decided improvement* in beauty. The pictures were not taken in a binocular camera, and therefore do not stand out well, but by moving one or both until the eyes coincide in the stereoscope the pictures blend perfectly. If taken in a binocular camera for the purpose, each person being taken on one half of the negative, I am sure the results would be still more striking. Perhaps something might be made of this in regard to the expression of emotions in man and the lower animals, &c. I have not time or opportunities to make experiments, but it seems to me something might be made of this by photographing the faces of different animals, different races of mankind, &c. I think a stereoscopic view of one of the ape tribe and some low-caste human face would make a very curious mixture; also in the matter of crossing of animals and the resulting offspring. It seems to me something also might result in photos of husband and wife and children, &c. In any case, the results are curious, if it leads to nothing else. Should this come to anything you will no doubt acknowledge myself as suggesting the experiment, and perhaps send me some of the results. If not likely to come to anything, a reply would much oblige me.

"Yours very truly,
"A. L. AUSTIN, C.E., F.R.A.S."

Dr. Carpenter informs me that the late Mr. Appold, the mechanician, used to combine two portraits of himself under the stereoscope. The one had been taken with an assumed stern expression, the other with a smile, and this combination produced a curious and effective blending of the two.

…nvenient as the stereosco… …ccessibility,

1877

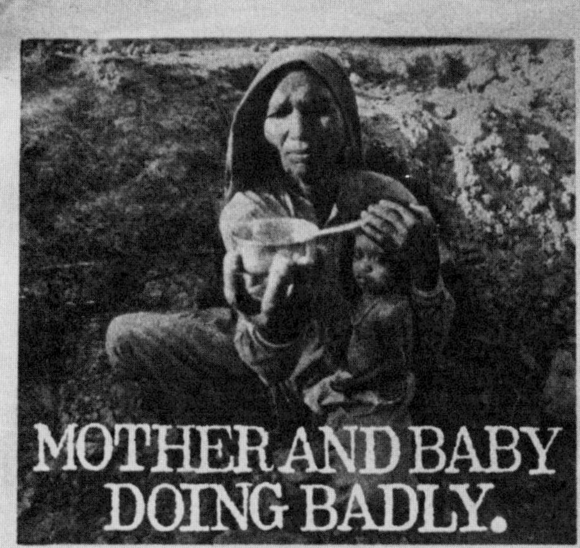

Imagine yourself in this situation.

You have two older children and a baby. You work nine hours a day in the blazing heat of the Indian sun, carrying 50lb loads of earth on your head. At the end of the day you get 10p, which will buy one pint of milk, a pound of rice and a few lentils. Not surprisingly your baby is suffering from malnutrition.

Desperate? Yes. Hopeless? No. Oxfam has shown that misery like this can be defeated.

We finance mobile creches for working mothers' children in Bombay. Nutritional and vaccination centres in Ethiopia. Family planning clinics in Delhi. Schools for handicapped children in Peru. We train local health workers in St. Vincent. And much more.

Need we add that it costs money? Your money? Just ½% of your income (£1 a month if you earn £2,400) could help change the lives of mothers and babies in sixty different countries.

FEED <u>ALL</u> THE FAMILY.

This form is simply an instruction to your bank to pay regularly whatever sum you choose to Oxfam's work. You can of course cancel it at any time by contacting your bank.

To: The Manager Date .... 19 ......

Bank Name ....

Bank Address ....

....

Please pay Oxfam £ .... every month/year*

starting on .... (date) until further notice.

Name (Block letters please) ....

Address ....

STM6/6/0

Signature .... P.O. GIRO 2002000

When completed this form should be sent not to your bank but to: Guy Stringer, Room 59, Oxfam, Oxford.

Thank you. *Delete where applicable

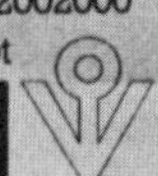

OXFAM

40

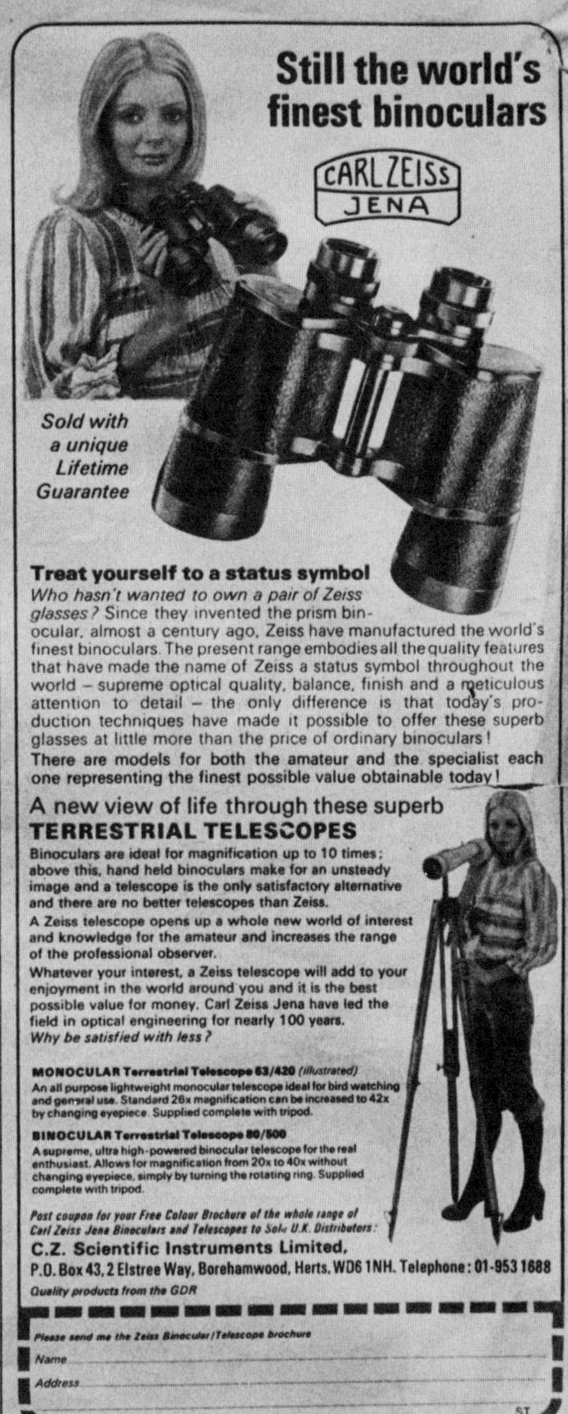

1977

If the pictures presented to the two eyes are quite different (or if the difference between the viewing positions of an object is so great that the corresponding features fall well outside the range where fusion is possible) a curious and highly distinctive effect occurs. Each eye in turn rejects its picture, or part of its picture, so that continuous fluctuation takes place. Parts of each picture are successively combined and rejected, in various ways. This is known as 'retinal rivalry'. Rivalry also occurs if different colours are presented to the two eyes, though fusion into mixture colours can occur for short periods.

An effect known as the Stroop effect studied so far entirely in the laboratory, illustrates a universal problem in scientific observation—conflict when the same object gives rise in the same person to two conflicting decisions. In the standard laboratory paradigm a colour word, say "BLUE" is shown to the person but written in some other coloured ink; he has to name the colour of the ink. As one can well imagine his response is slowed down (Stroop effect) and it can even be wrong because of the interference from the word information.

Viewed from the top the human brain looks something like the kernel of a walnut: it is in *two halves*, the right hemisphere and the left hemisphere. Because of a curious developmental quirk, all the functions of one side of the body are controlled by signals sent out by the opposite hemisphere; for instance, the left hemisphere guides the right hand, and the right hemisphere the left hand. In addition, the two hemispheres appear to have different functions, this information coming mainly from observing brain-injured patients. Speech, for example, is sited in the left hemisphere, while the ability to manipulate spatial problems is located in the right hemisphere. (This is for right-handed people; for left-handers it is sometimes a little more complicated.) Now we know that analytical processes (including logic and speech) are generated in the left hemisphere, and intuitive processes (including body movement as in skiing, and "artistic" talents) are found in the right hemisphere. In other words, sequential information processing occurs in the left hemisphere and simultaneous processing in the right.

'A first step is to introduce two technical terms to assist us in distinguishing from [each other] what Dr Johnson called the *two ideas* that any metaphor, at its simplest, gives us. Let me call them the tenor and the vehicle. . . . At present we have only some clumsy descriptive phrases with which to separate [the two halves – or members – of a metaphor]. "The original idea" and "the borrowed one"; "what is really being said or thought of" and "what it is compared to"; "the underlying idea" and "the imagined nature"; "the principal subject" and "what is resembles"; or, still more confusing, simply "the meaning" and "the metaphor", or "the idea" and "its image".
'How confusing these must be', he continues, 'is easily seen. . . . We need the word "metaphor" for the whole double unit.'

[The conception of metaphor] – as a mere putting together (or juxtaposition) of two things to see what will happen – is a contemporary fashionable aberration, which takes an extreme case as the norm. . . . This is André Breton, the leader of the French Super-Realists stating the doctrine very plainly: "To compare two objects, as remote from [each other] in character as possible, or by any other method [to] put them together in [an abrupt] and striking fashion, this remains the highest task to which poetry can aspire" . . .

the 25 poorest nations on earth, with a *per capita* income of only £71 a year.
This juxtaposition of conspicuous waste and starvation of basic services explains why many countries decided to ignore invitations to attend the festivities or at most to send low-level diplomatic representatives.

The Hatter opened his eyes very wide on hearing this; but all he *said* was, "Why is a raven like a writing-desk?"

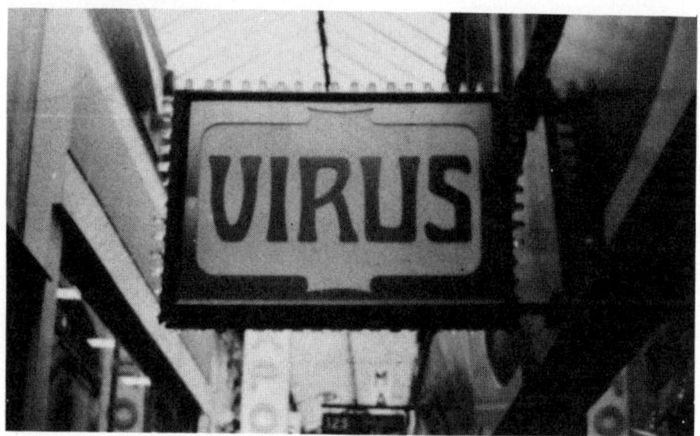

Disease means bodily disease. Gould's Medical Dictionary defines disease as a disturbance of the function or structure of an organ or a part of the *body*. The mind (whatever it is) is not an organ or part of the body. Hence, it cannot be diseased in the same sense as the body can. When we speak of mental illness, then, we speak metaphorically. To say that a person's mind is sick is like saying that the economy is sick or that a joke is sick. When metaphor is mistaken for reality and is used for social purposes, then we have the makings of myth. The concepts of mental health and mental illness are mythological concepts, used strategically to advance some social interests and to retard others, much as national and religious myths have been used in the past.

The germ of an idea

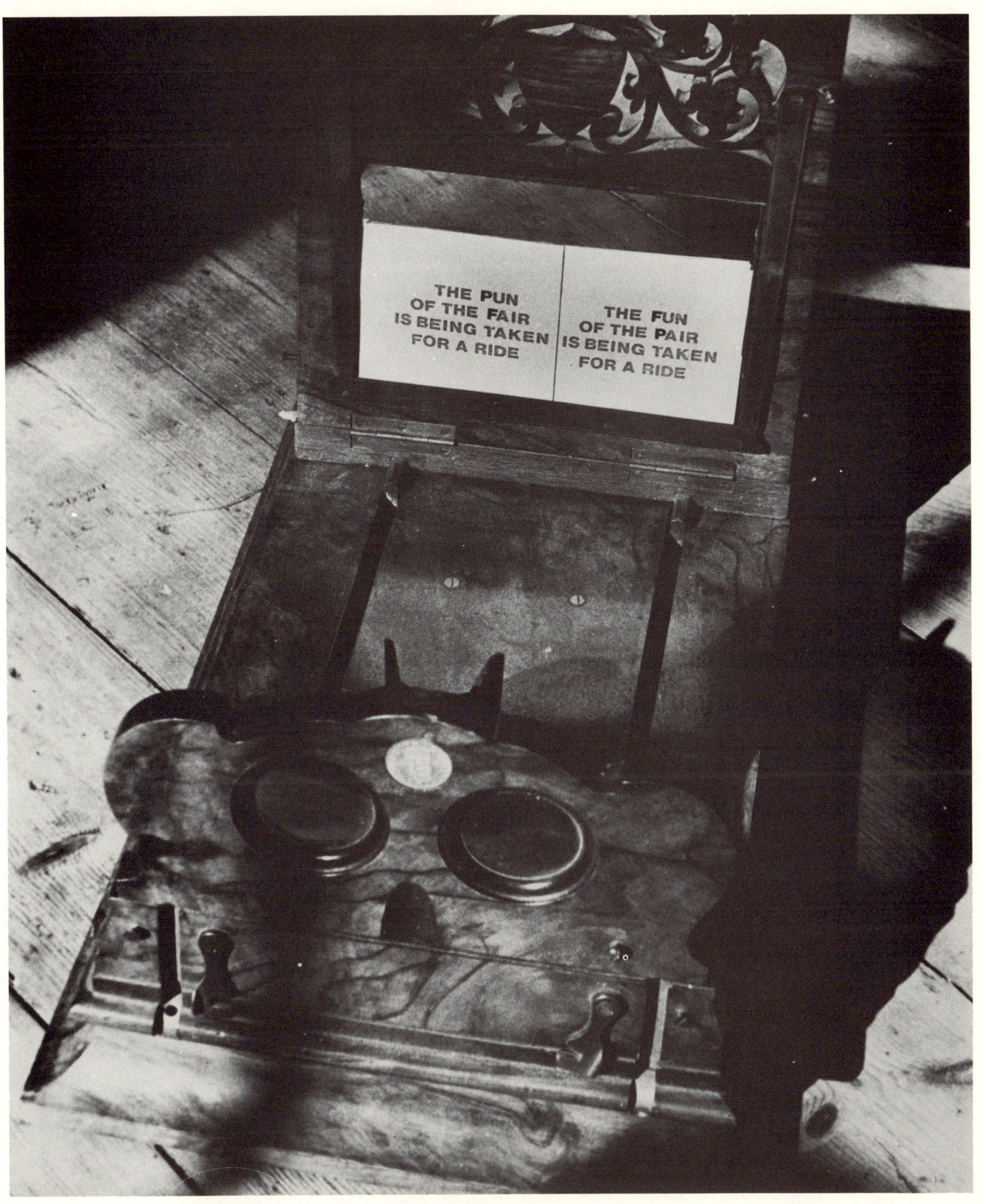

In-depth analysis

And Milton punned-punned even in the bare and virile *Samson Agonistes,* where, at least once, there occurs a weighty and effective pun-by-etymology; Delilah is, in Samson's words.

'That specious monster, my accomplished snare.'

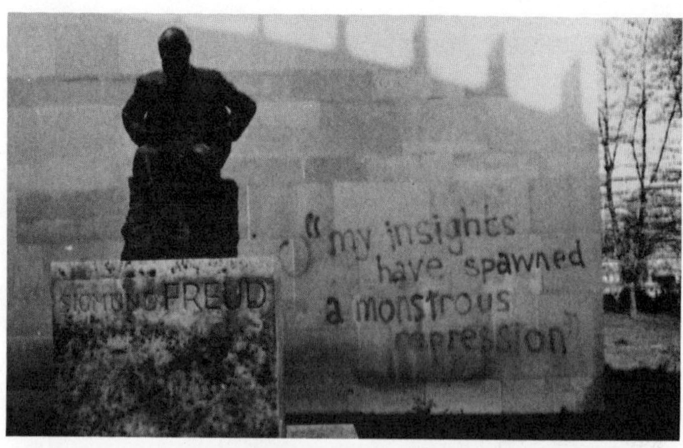

The old stereoscopic system works very well (give or take some mild eyestrain) and makes the stunning underwater sequences and the creature itself extremely effective. The film's ultra-low budget and stilted cast ensure some pretty funny moments but its overall beauty and pathos never seemed stronger. If this one works

I would extend my argument to the broader realms of language. At what point do I give up trying to teach the correct use of the apostrophe, when the majority of adults seem to communicate effectively by misplacing it or ignoring the beast altogether? How long should I keep plugging away at differences between "I" and "Me" or "Like" and

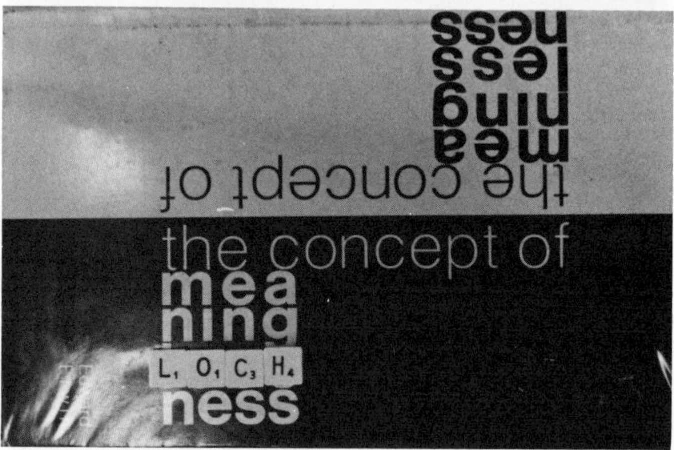

cogito ogre sum

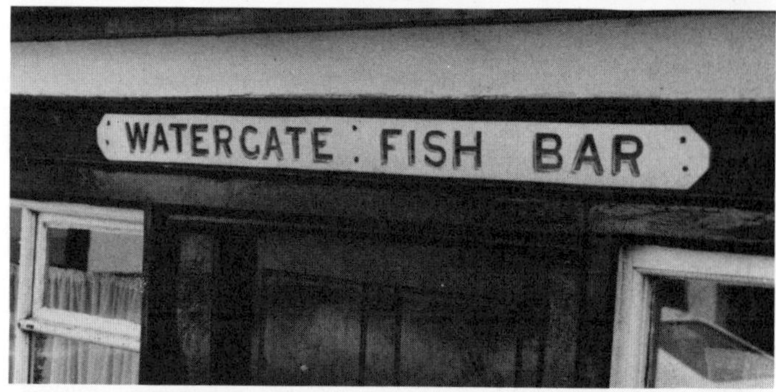

If a succession of dollops of water are placed so that each one overlaps the preceding one to form a chain, then the water always flows through this chain to end up in the original position. This implies that a chain of successive connected images will always lead back to the original image, no matter how far it is extended. This also implies that one pattern can lead directly to another which at first sight seems very remote unless one knows the sequence that connects the two.

Nu, or Nun, in Egyptian mythology, the personification of CHAOS or the Ocean from whom all things arose. He is depicted as a man partially immersed in water supporting the beings of his creation.

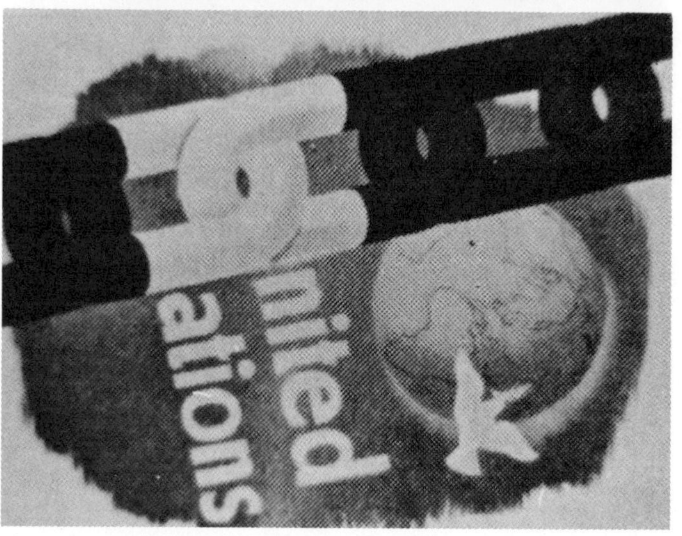

Nu is the word most frequently used (aside from '*oy*' and the articles) in speaking Yiddish. And with good reason: *Nu* is the verbal equivalent of a sigh, a frown, a grin, a grunt, a sneer. It is an expression of amusement or recognition or uncertainty or disapproval. It can be used fondly, acidly, tritely, belligerently.

Nu is a qualification, an emphasizer, an interrogation, a caster of doubt, an arrow of ire. It can convey pride, deliver scorn, demand response. When used in tandem, as *nu-nu,* it carries another cargo of nuances.

Here are a score of shadings of this two-lettered miracle

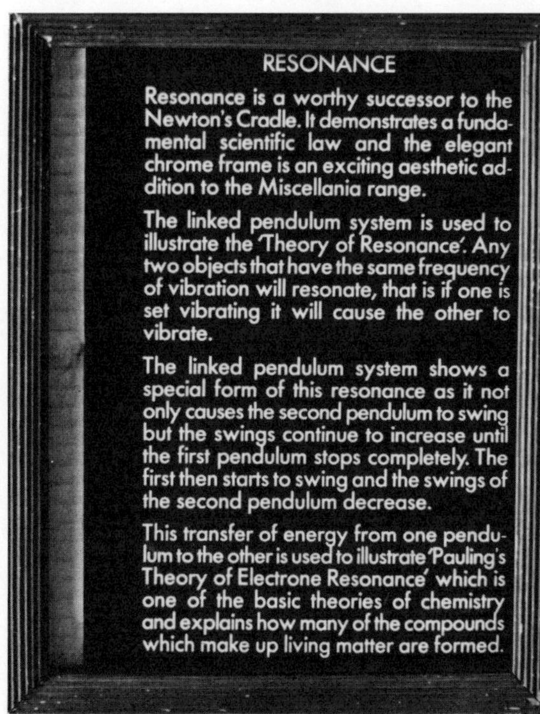

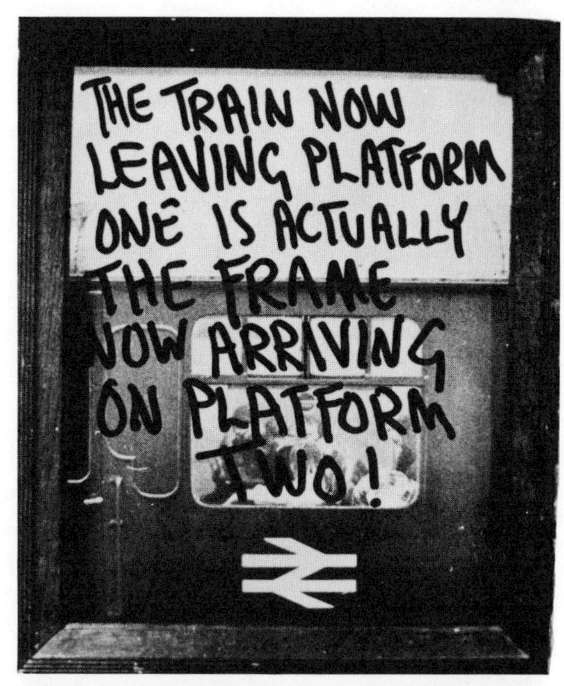

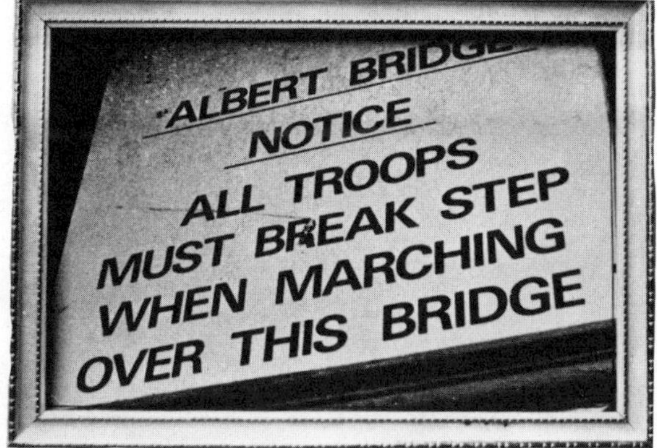

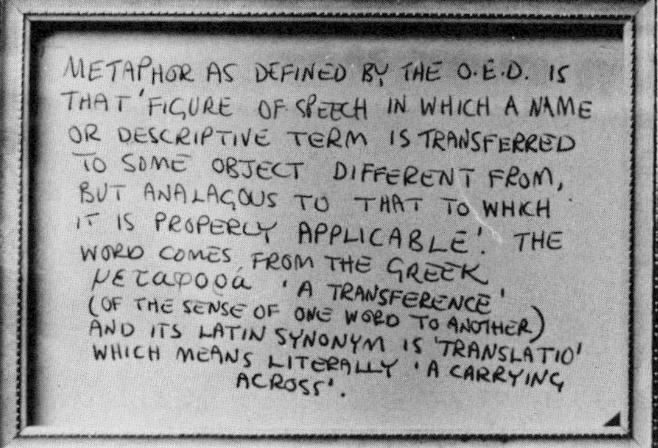

Frames of cross reference

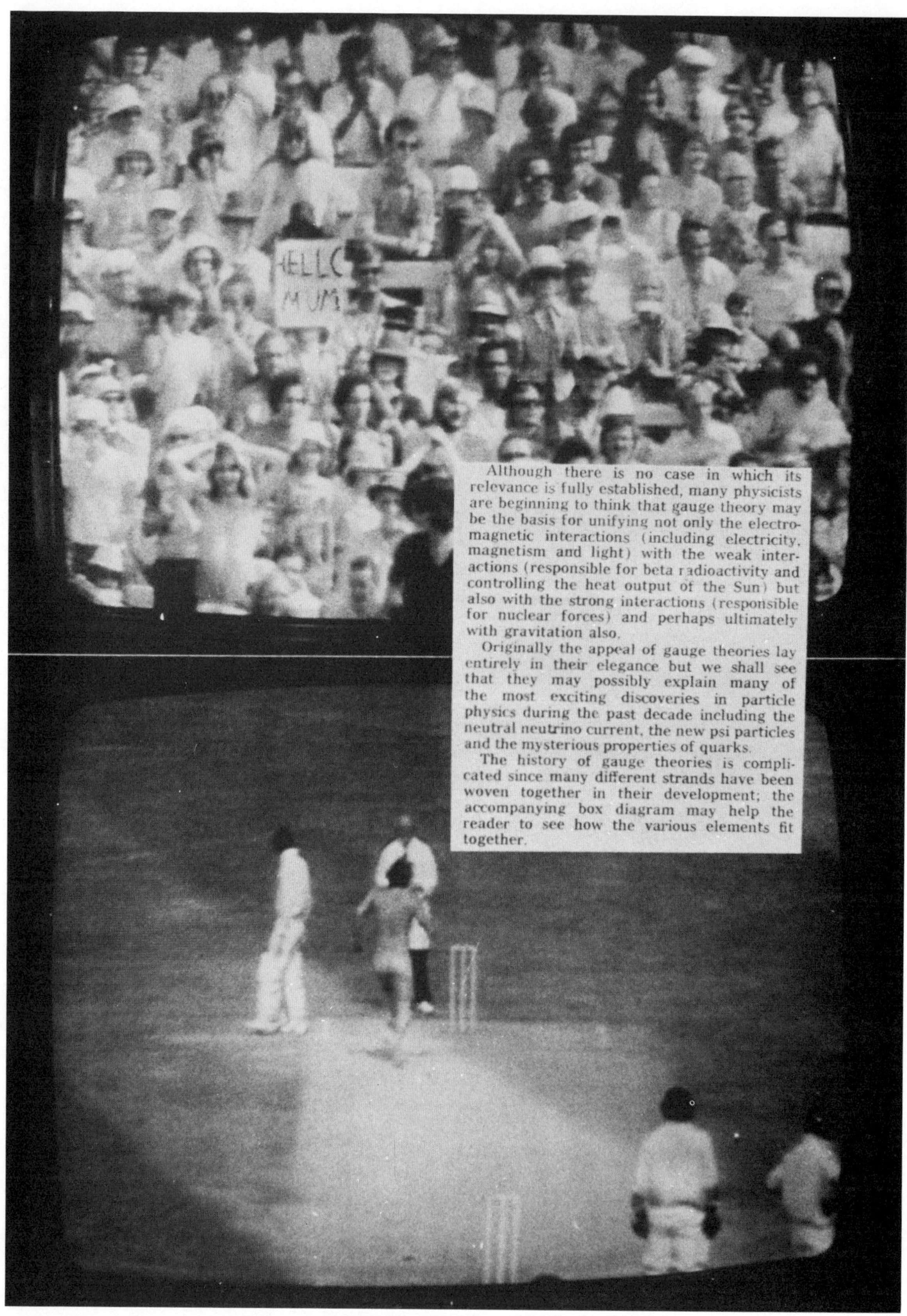

Although there is no case in which its relevance is fully established, many physicists are beginning to think that gauge theory may be the basis for unifying not only the electromagnetic interactions (including electricity, magnetism and light) with the weak interactions (responsible for beta radioactivity and controlling the heat output of the Sun) but also with the strong interactions (responsible for nuclear forces) and perhaps ultimately with gravitation also.

Originally the appeal of gauge theories lay entirely in their elegance but we shall see that they may possibly explain many of the most exciting discoveries in particle physics during the past decade including the neutral neutrino current, the new psi particles and the mysterious properties of quarks.

The history of gauge theories is complicated since many different strands have been woven together in their development; the accompanying box diagram may help the reader to see how the various elements fit together.

Box diagrams

HOW, WHEN AND WHERE

One player goes out, and the rest pick on a word with several meanings, or, if you like, word sound with several spellings. For example, *plain* and *plane*. The one not in the secret is then called back, and is allowed to ask each player in turn the same three questions. And they in their replies should mix up the various meanings of the chosen word. Like this:

John: How do you like it?
Joan: Up in the air.
John: When do you like it?
Joan (thinking of the tool)*:* When I'm putting up a bookshelf.
John: Where do you like it?
Joan (thinking of the opposite of patterned): On the wallpaper.

The crucial feature of the gauge theories was the way in which they confronted, head-on, the issue of the consistency of the laws of nature throughout space-time. They therefore promised to be an important part of any key to the universe. In particular, the gauge theories related one piece of the cosmic wallpaper to another, by considering how local events were connected with distant events.

Joan (thinking of the opposite of patterned): On the wallpaper.
John (no wiser yet): How do you like it?
Jocelyn: Sharp.
John: When do you like it?
Jocelyn (thinking of flat land): When I'm doing a long walk.
John: Where do you like it?
Jocelyn (thinking of the tree): In the garden.
And so on. John has three guesses, and pays a forfeit if he fails to get the word.

'gauge theory

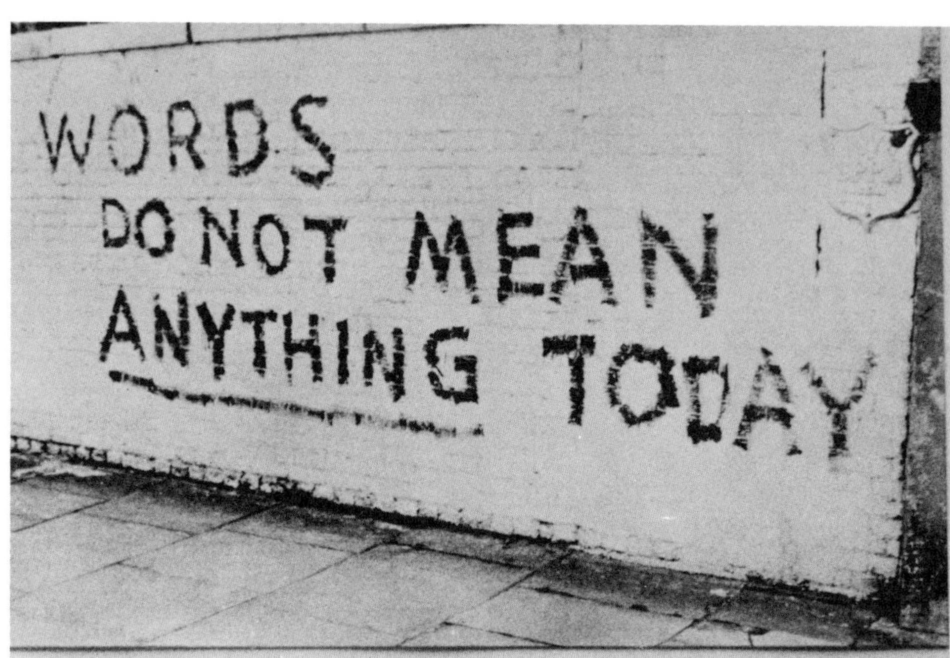

If we interpret "meaningless" as "a priori false," then the negation of a meaningless statement will be true. For example, if "Virtue is square" is meaningless, then its negation, "Virtue is not square," is true. Thus, we can preserve the rule that the negation of a false statement is true and, conversely, that the negation of a true statement is false. Further, talk of meaningless statements will not force us to abandon the so-called law of the excluded middle (which says that all statements are either true or false).

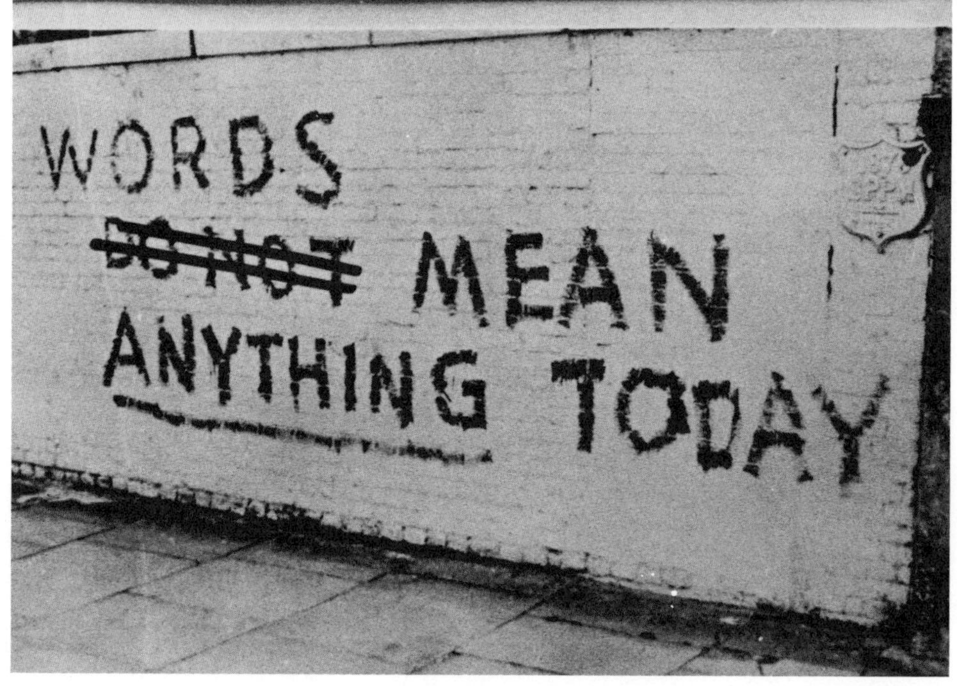

Vice is versa

*

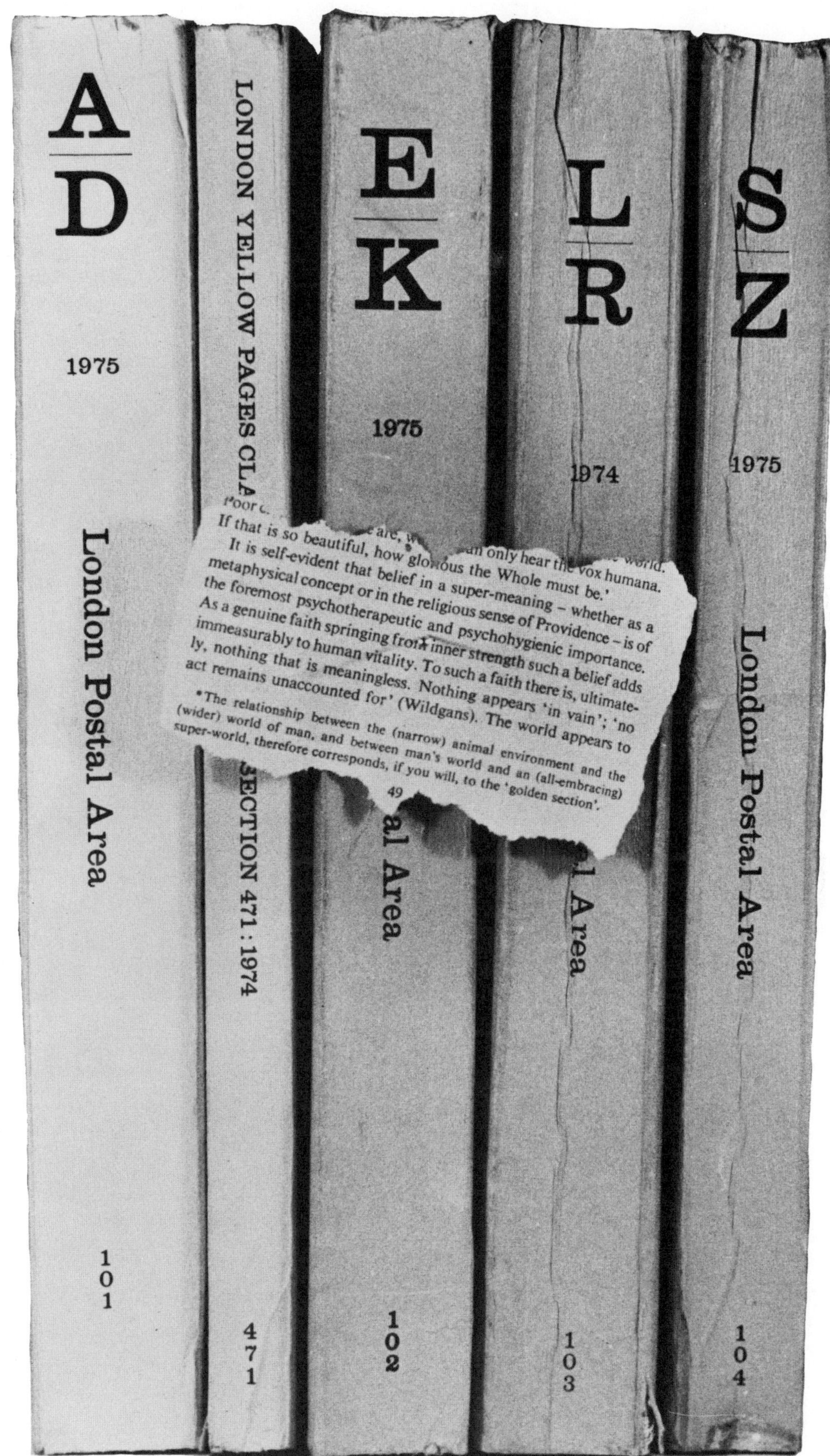

**The Golden Section*

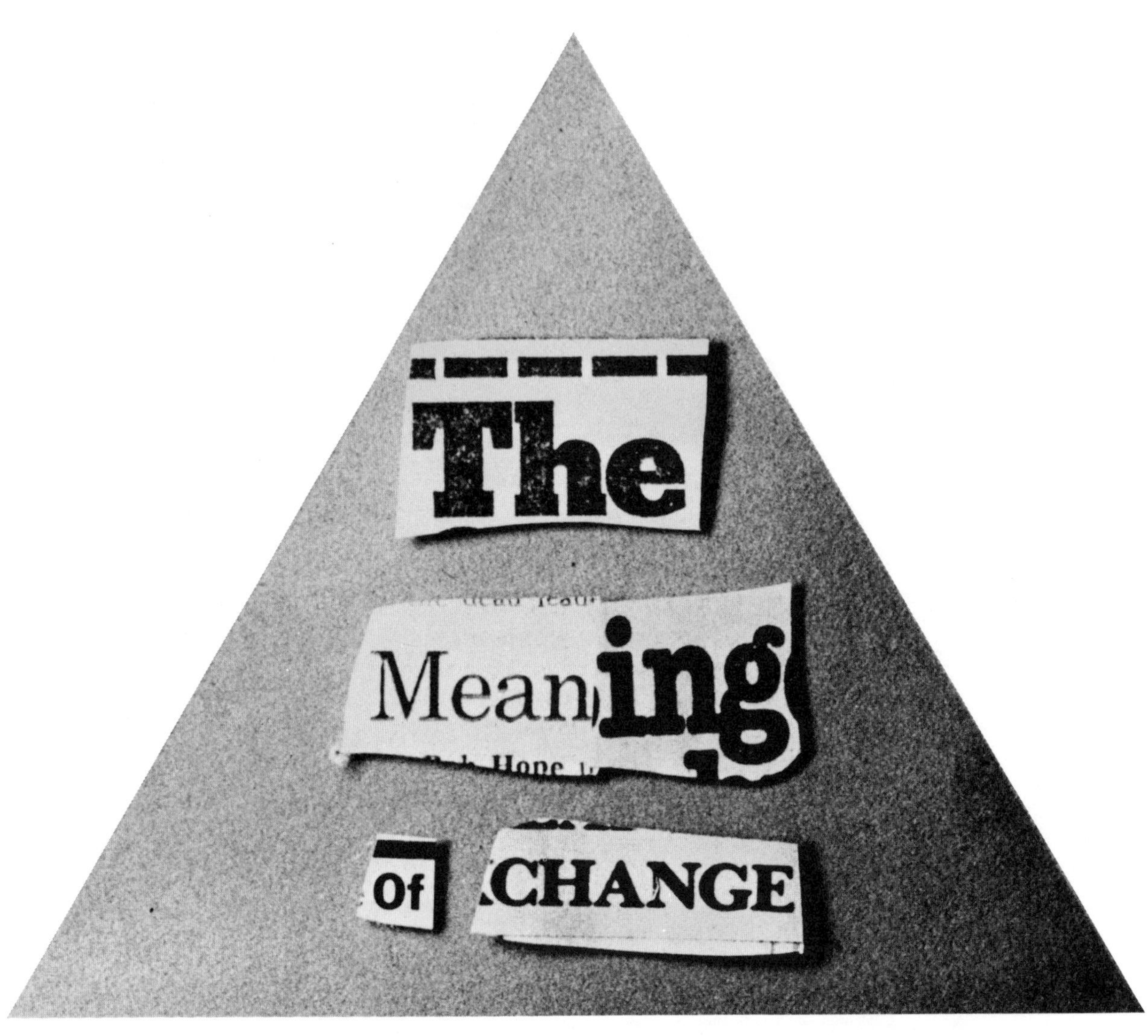
The
Meaning
Of CHANGE

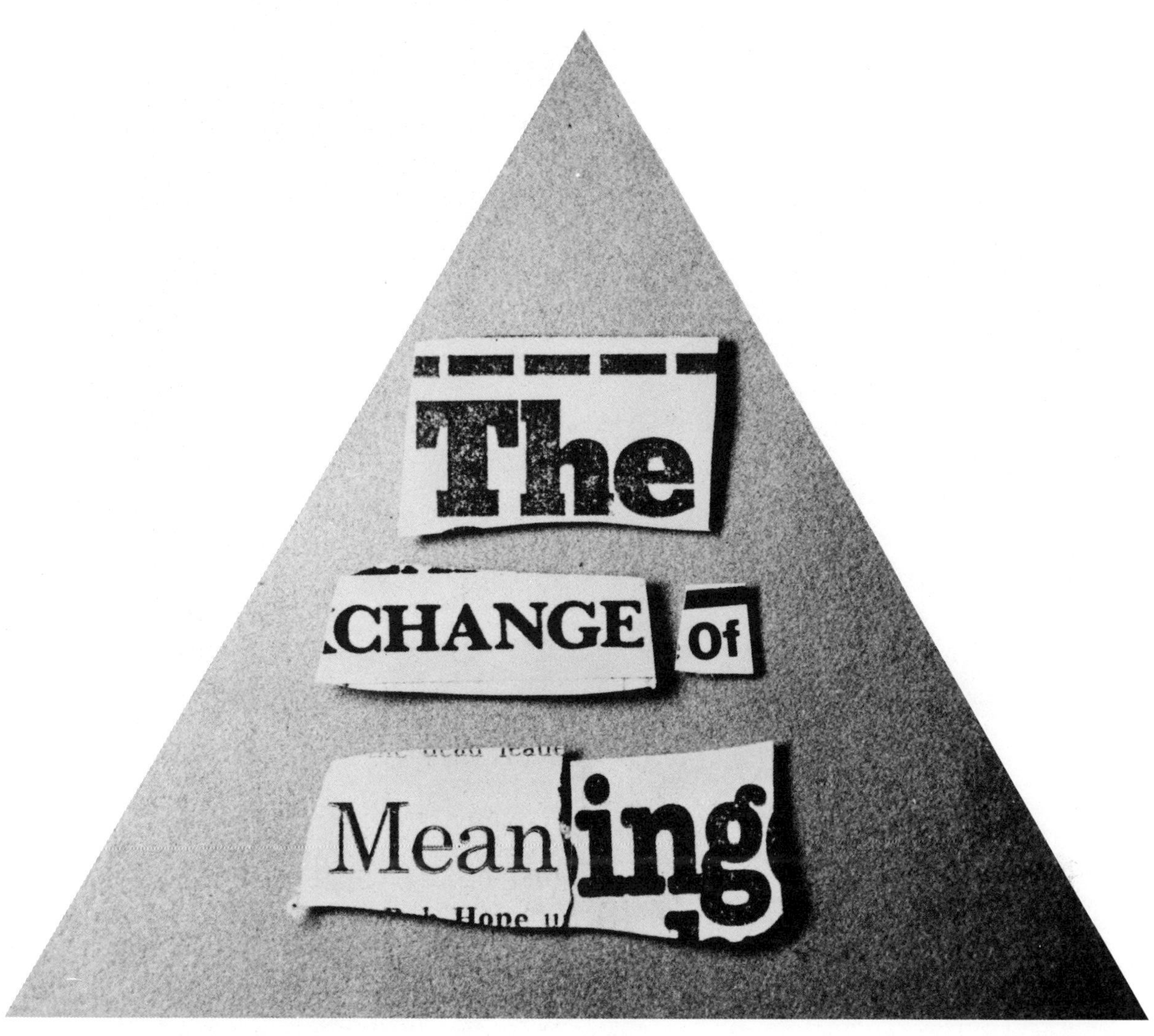
The
CHANGE of
Meaning

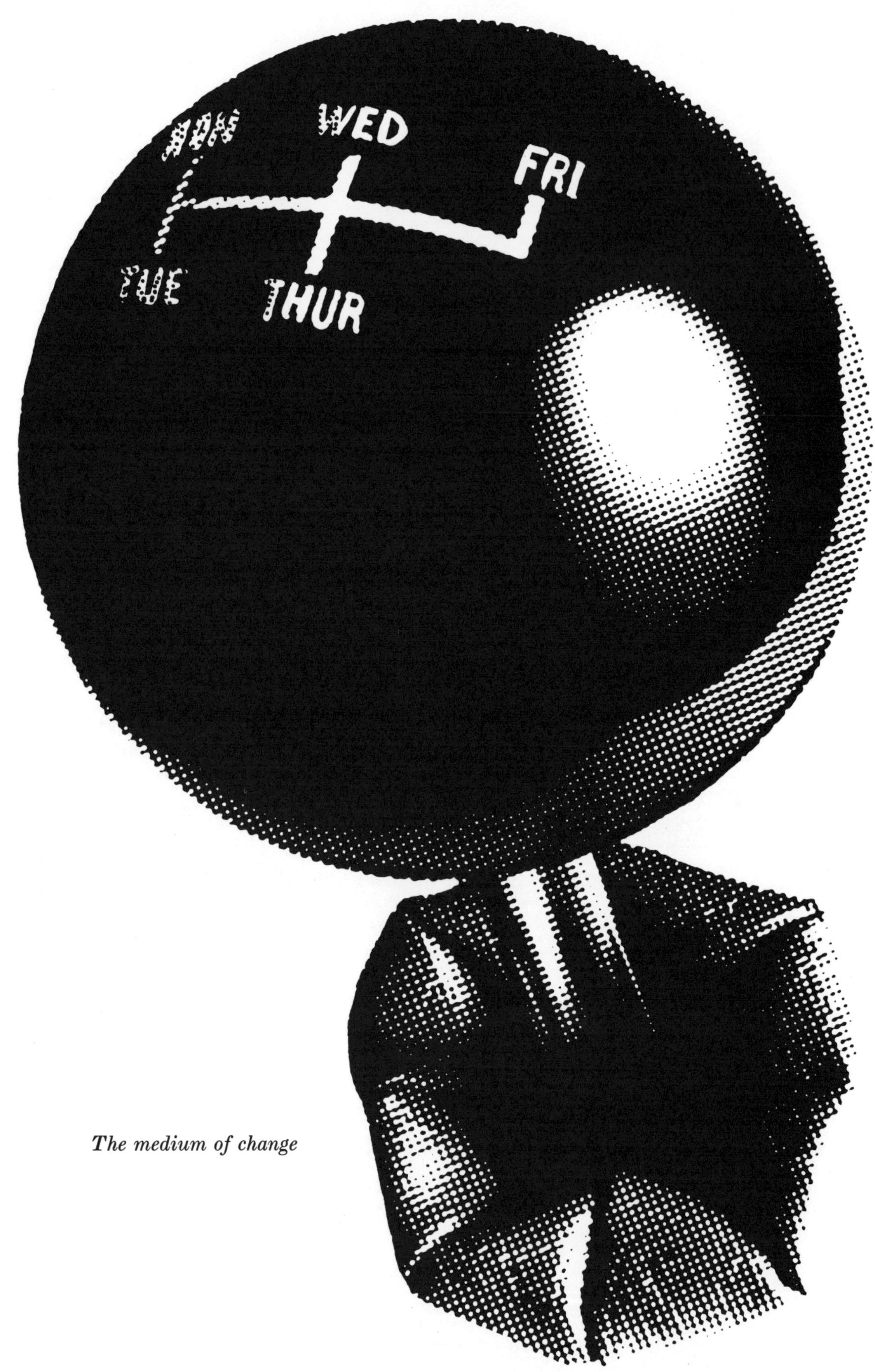

The medium of change

cepted by a double-concave eyepiece
re·frac·tion (ri frak′shən) *n.* [LL. *refractio*] 1. the bending of a ray or wave of light, heat, or sound, as it passes obliquely from one medium to another of different density, in which its speed is different, or through layers of different density in the same medium 2. *Astron.* the bending of the rays of light from a star or planet, greatest when the star or planet is lowest in the sky, so that it seems higher than it really is 3. *Optics a)* the ability of the eye to refract light entering it, so as to form an image on the retina *b)* the measuring of the degree of refraction of an eye
refractive index *same as* INDEX OF REFRACTION
re·frac·tom·e·ter (rē′frak täm′ə tər) *n.* an instrument for measuring refraction, as of the eye

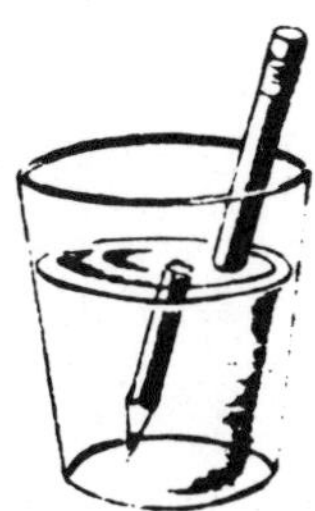

ILLUSION CAUSED BY REFRACTION

DOCTOR — THERE'S A FLY IN MY SOUP!

One trifle—which seems so, but which, like a dead fly, spoils the ointment—is the danger of placing the emphasis, or stress of voice, on the small word in a sentence. Thus, I have heard it read, 'God *is* love.' These three monosyllables are capable of three different emphases. If we say '*God* is love,' we imply that, above all other beings, God is love. If we say 'God is *love*,' we imply that, above all other, and greater than all other, attributes of God, stands forth His glorious attribute of love. But if we lay the false emphasis on the auxiliary word 'is' and say 'God *is* love,' we imply that someone has asserted the contrary—someone has said 'God is *not* love': and you who believe that He is love, who know that He is love, stand up as His follower and disciple, and contradict this maligner of God's character, and insist that 'God is love.'

This false emphasis on the auxiliary verb might be exemplified by many instances. Two of the most common among the clergy are: ☞

The change of medium

A PENGUIN BOOK
The Medium is the Massage
Marshall McLuhan
Quentin Fiore
An Inventory of Effects

IS

IAN LEE
MY IDEA OF A
N VEL

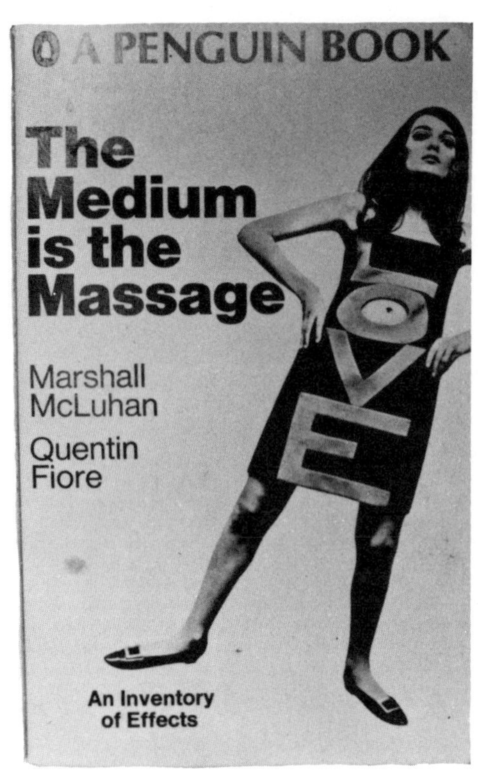

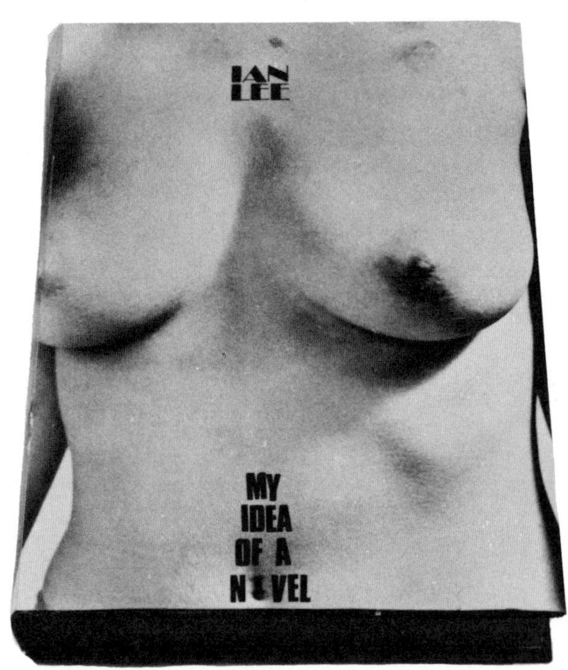

Seeing

language
in the
strictest
sense of
the word

is

language in
the widest
sense of
the word

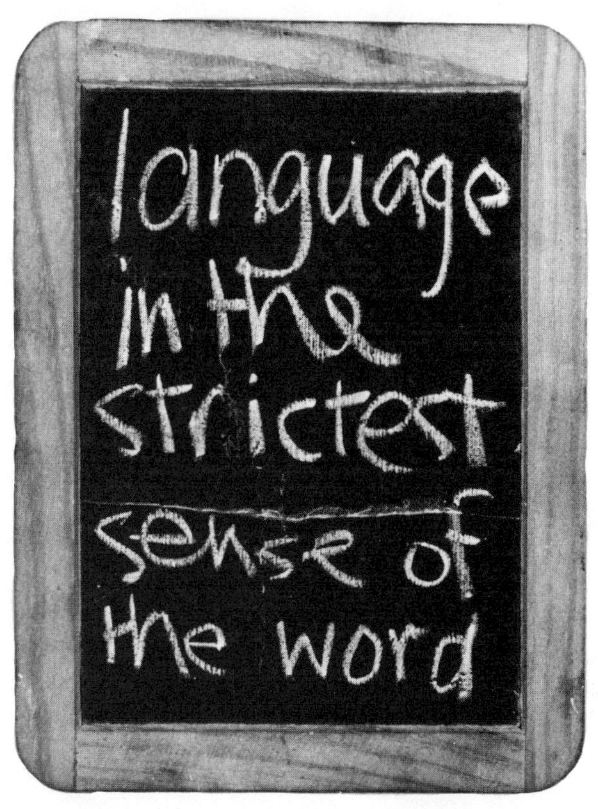

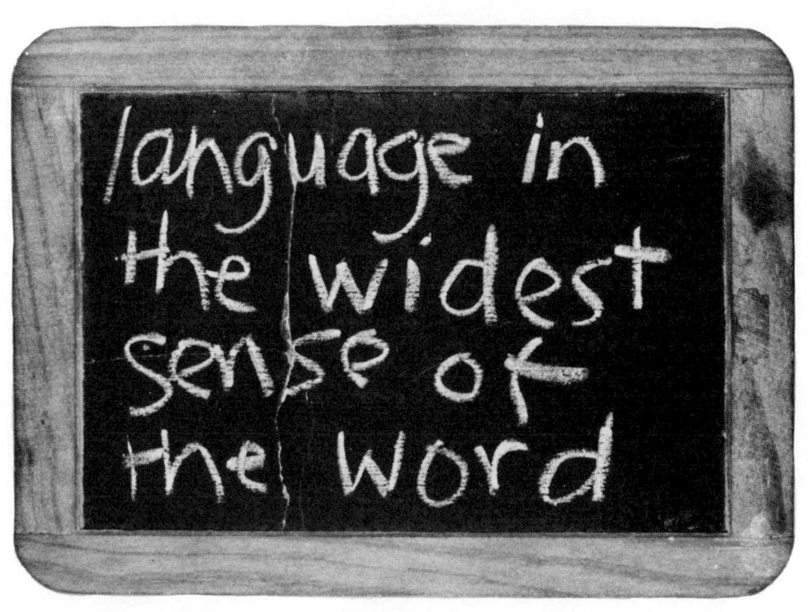

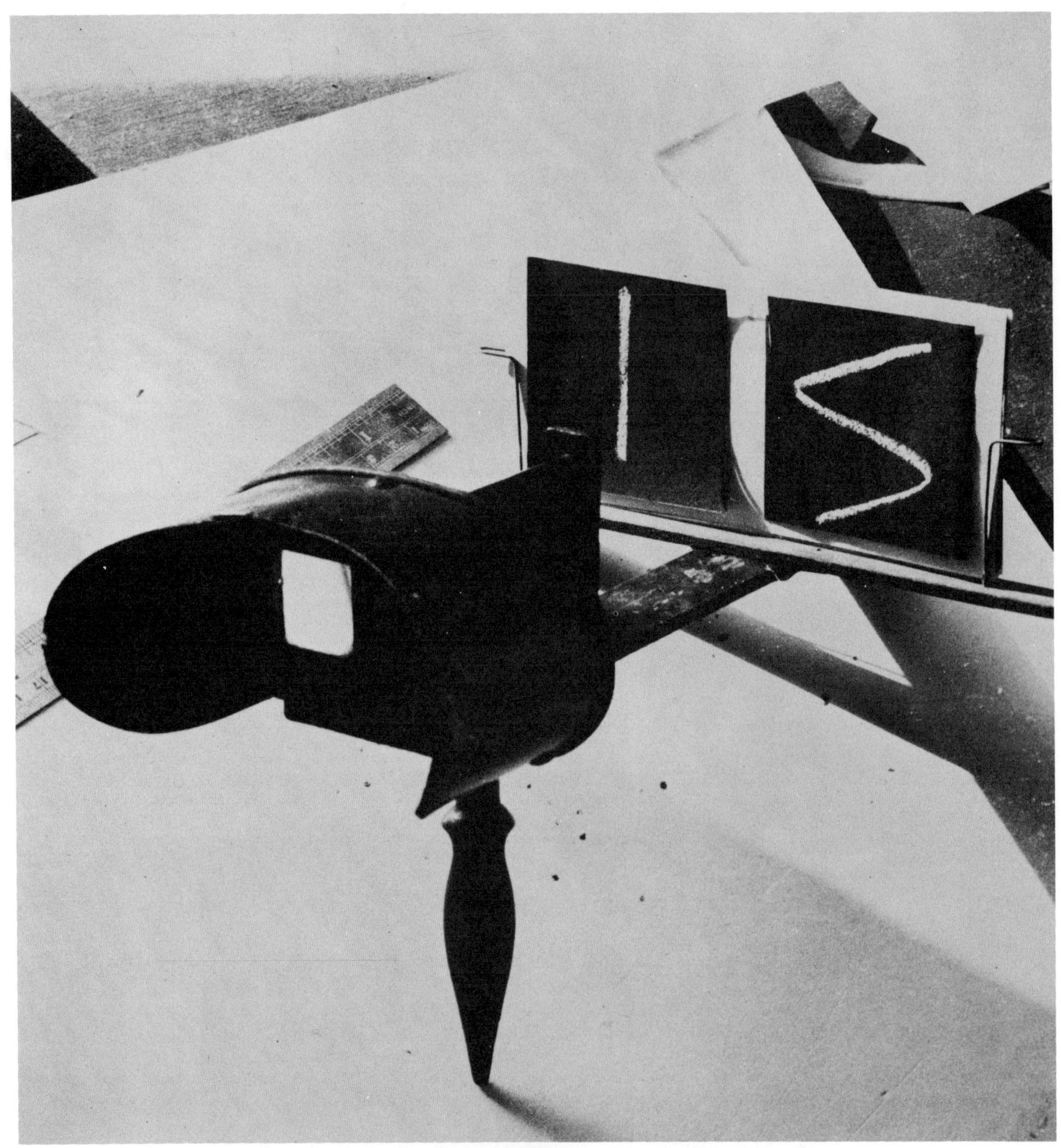

The medium

wave motion
A science ex
from the
LEEDS CITY MUSEUM
SAT. 15th NOV. 1975 to SAT. 10th JAN. 1976
OPENING HOURS

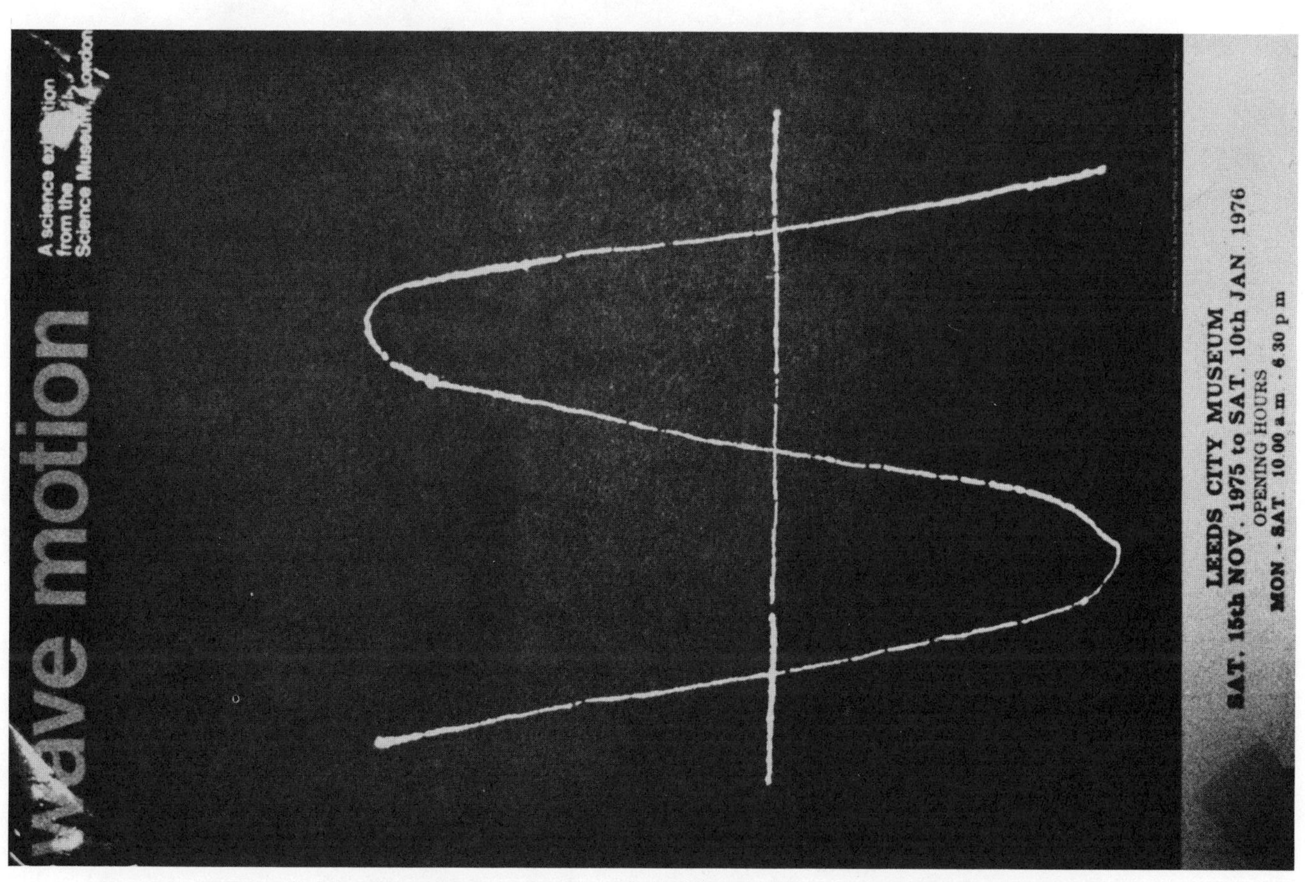

The message

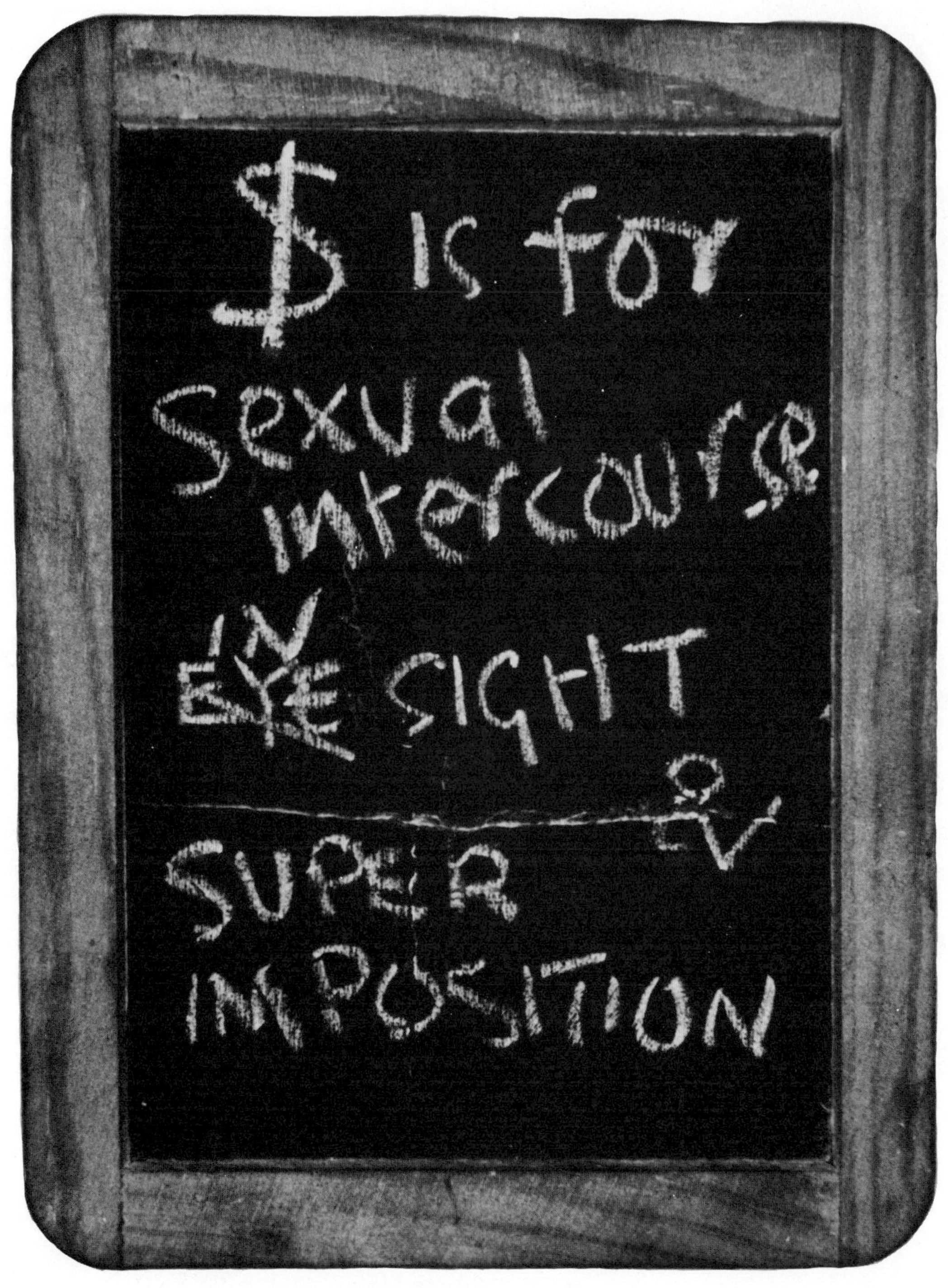

Symbol Ism

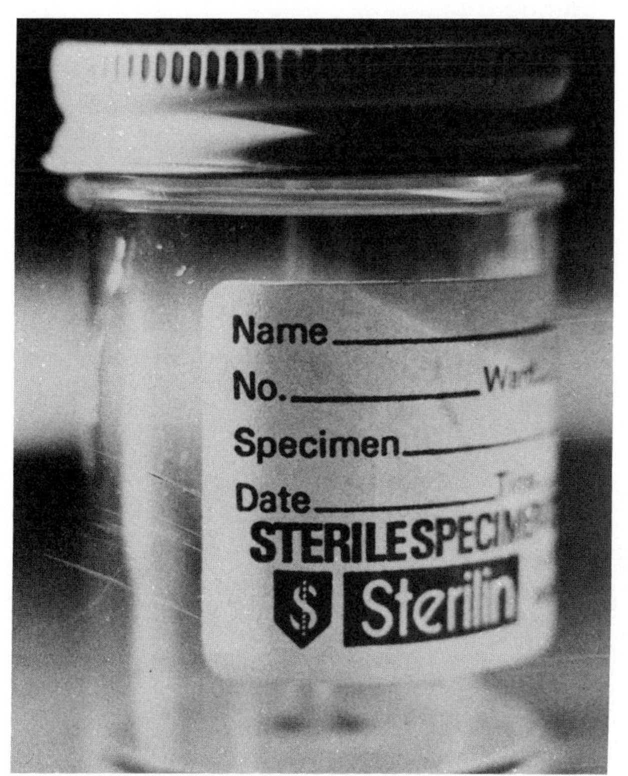

'ISMS

a dictionary of words ending in -ISM -OLOGY, and -PHOBIA

with some similar terms arranged in subject order

2nd edition

SI chology

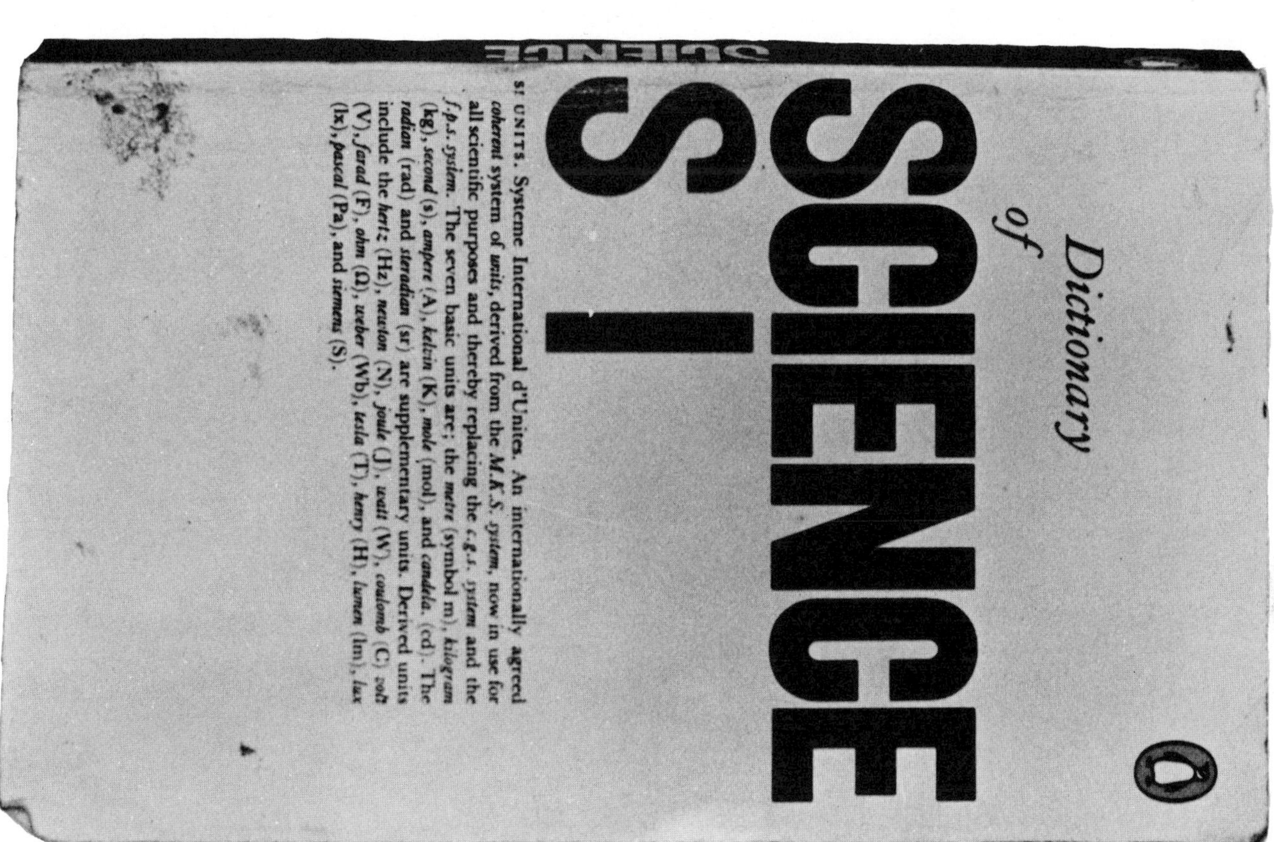
Dictionary of SCIENCE

SI

SI UNITS. Systeme International d'Unites. An internationally agreed *coherent* system of *units*, derived from the *M.K.S. system*, now in use for all scientific purposes and thereby replacing the *c.g.s. system* and the *f.p.s. system*. The seven basic units are: the *metre* (symbol m), *kilogram* (kg), *second* (s), *ampere* (A), *kelvin* (K), *mole* (mol), and *candela* (cd). The *radian* (rad) and *steradian* (sr) are supplementary units. Derived units include the *hertz* (Hz), *newton* (N), *joule* (J), *watt* (W), *coulomb* (C) *volt* (V), *farad* (F), *ohm* (Ω), *weber* (Wb), *tesla* (T), *henry* (H), *lumen* (lm), *lux* (lx), *pascal* (Pa), and *siemens* (S).

CLIFFORD, WILLIAM Body and Mind. The Facts of Consciousness.	1845-1879	66
DARWIN, CHARLES Natural Selection.	1809-1882	78
DOSTOEVSKY, FYODOR M. Pushkin.	1821-1881	100
FREUD, SIGISMUND The Psychology of Errors.	1856-	115
GALTON, SIR FRANCIS Crime and Insanity. The Herd Spirit. Early Sentiments.	1822-1911	125

Inner Space

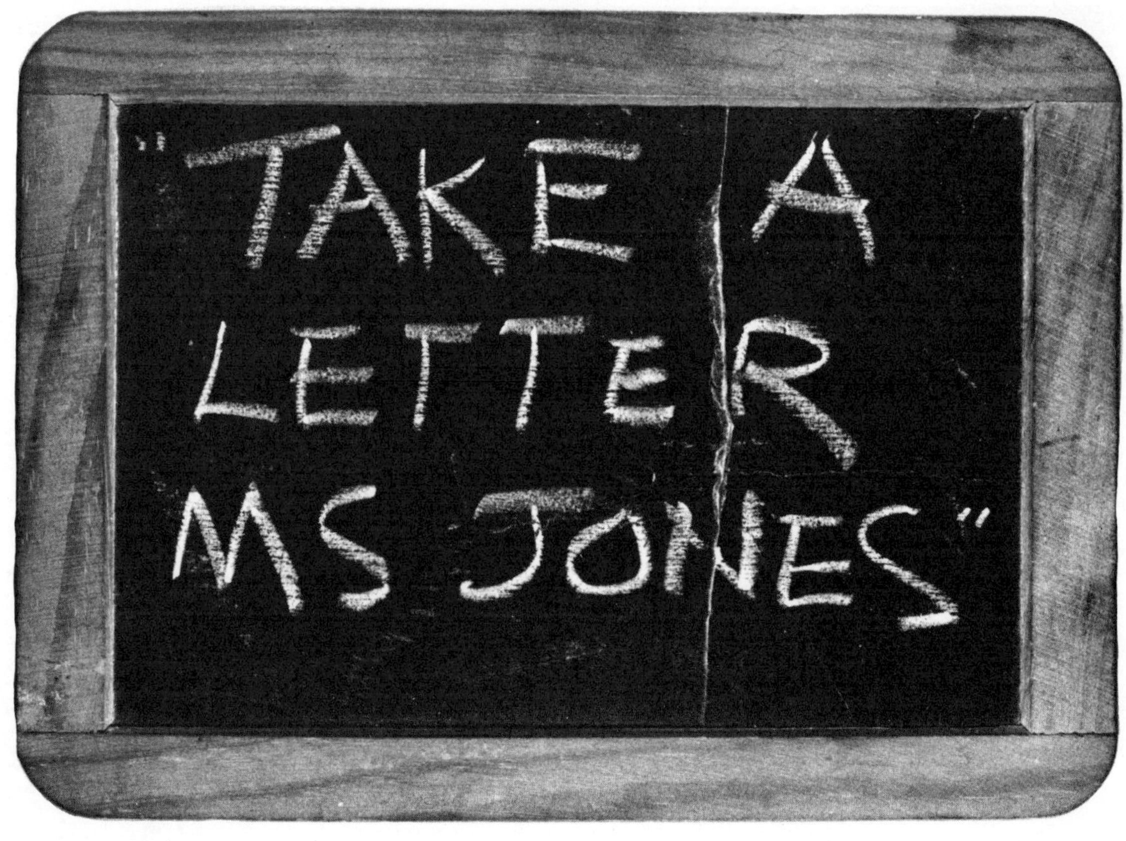

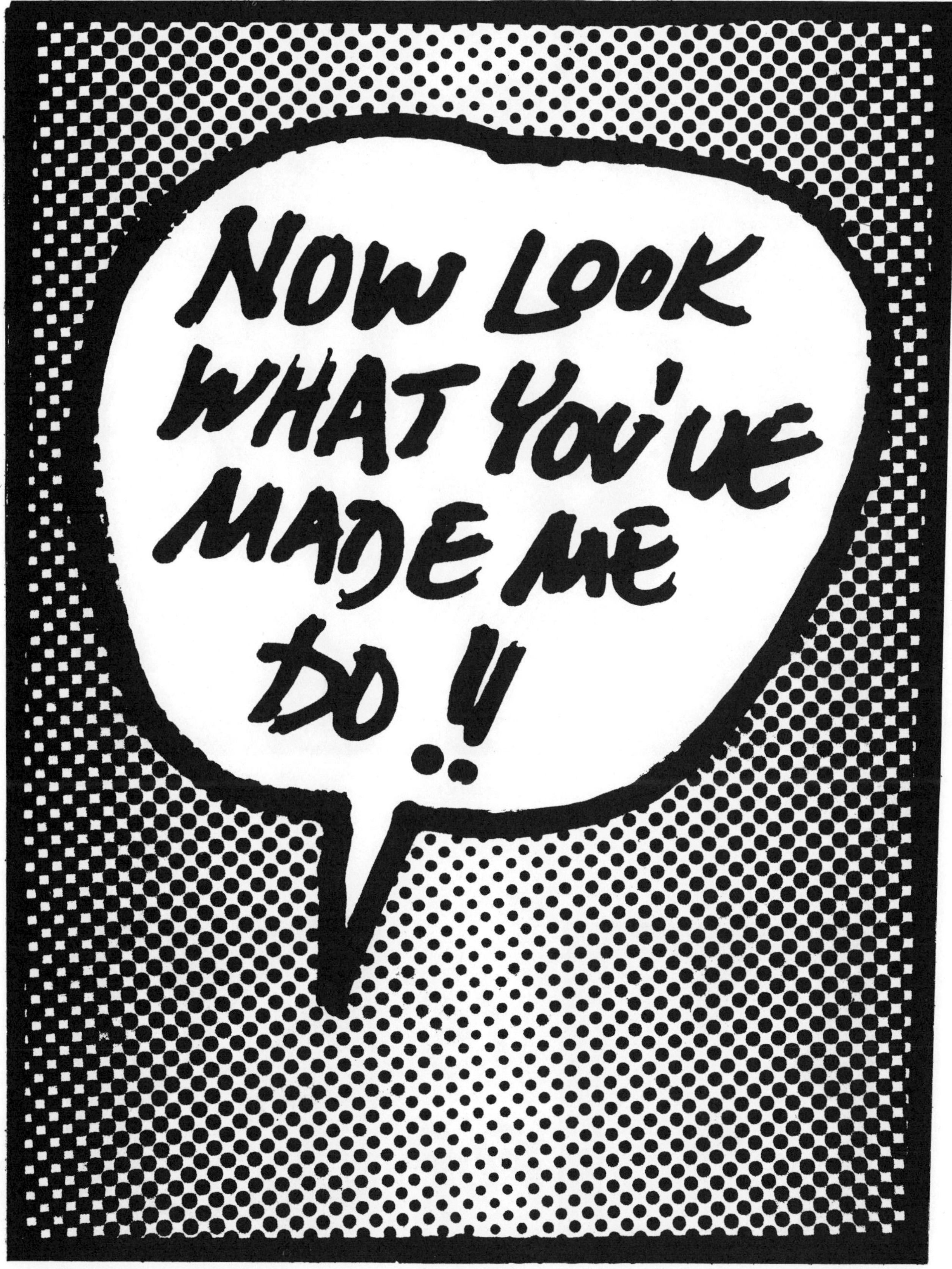

Dear SR

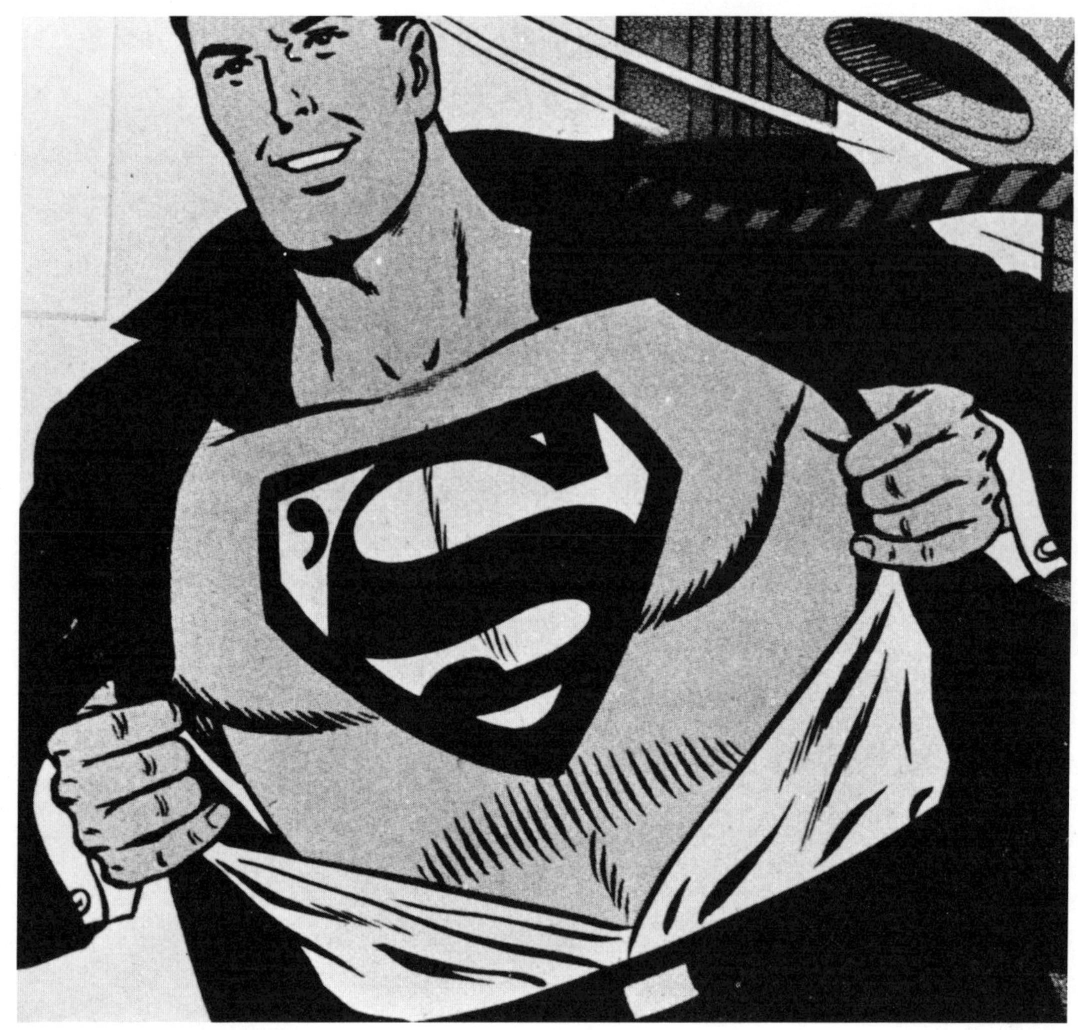

Stimulus

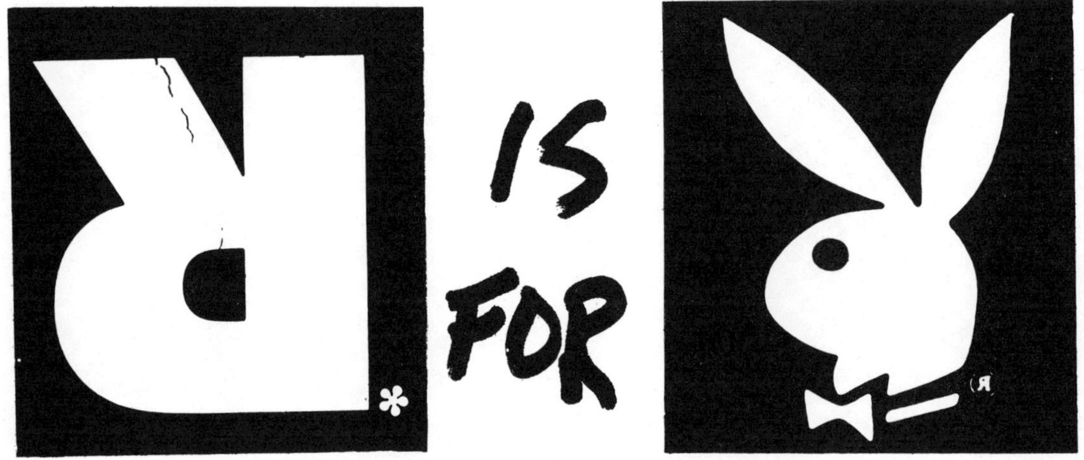

Response

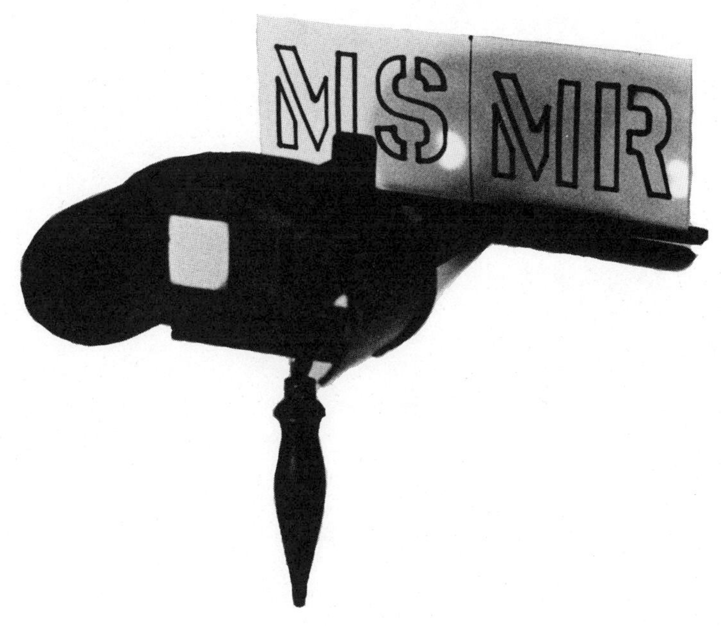

S is for Ship

In such complex activity, then, we can see that what we really have is a series of S-R connections. The phenomenon of connecting a series of such S-R units is known as *chaining*, a process that should be apparent in any complex activity. We might note that there are a

… up into bit… behavio… ment th… terms of stimulus an… pro-

response'. The theory is based on the atomistic concepts of the last century, which have been abandoned in all other branches of contemporary science. Its basic assumptions – that all activities of man, including language and thought, can be analysed into elementary S-R units – were originally founded on the physiological concept of the reflex arc. The new-born organism came into the world equipped with a number of simple, 'unconditioned' reflexes, and … learnt and did in

R is for Relationship

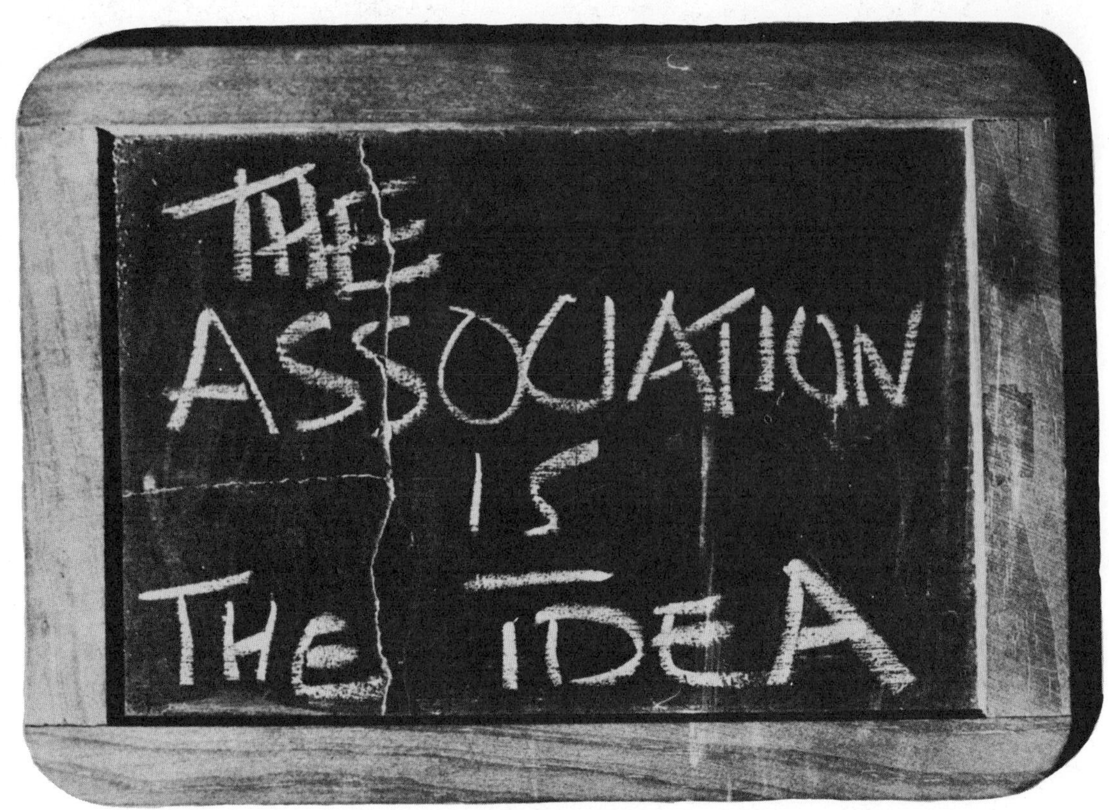

The three S's

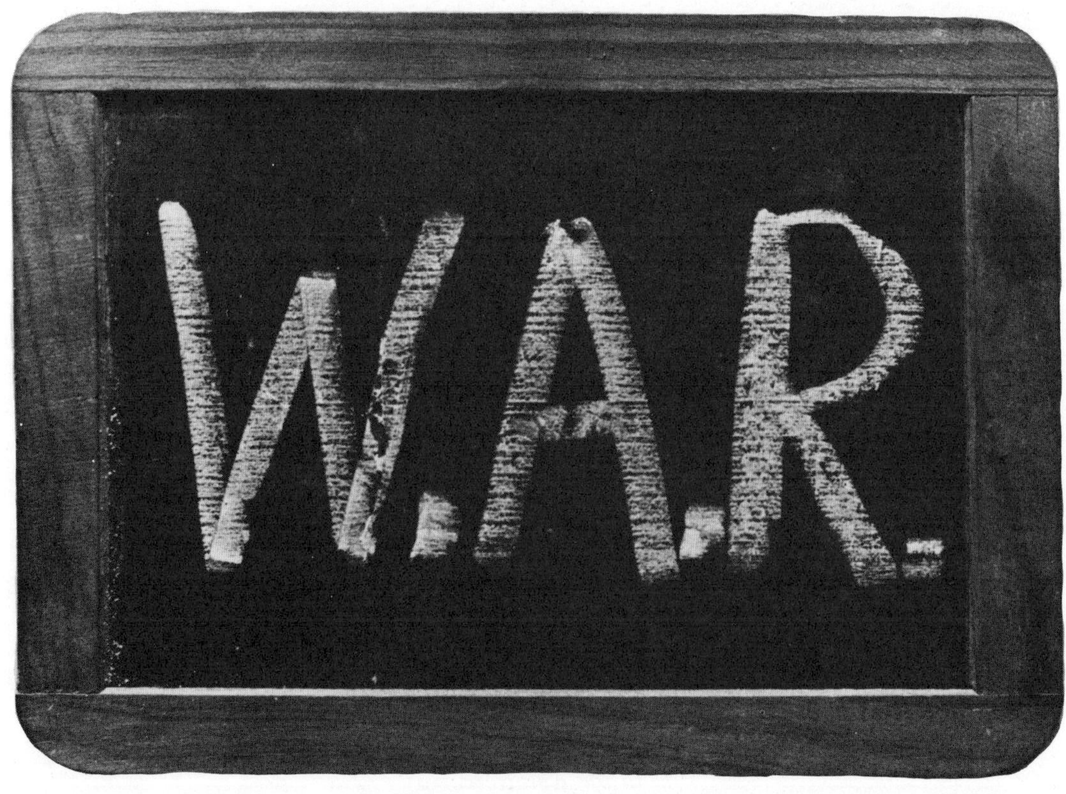

The three R's

because the latest technologies have rendered war meaningless. The hydrogen bomb is history's exclamation point. It ends an age-long sentence of manifest violence!

Furthermore, much of the meaning of spoken language is carried by the intonation, which is not directly represented in writing. (It is a fallacy to assume that punctuation indicates intonation. Most punctuation comes too late to signal anything about how the sentence should be read. Instead, intonation is signalled by meaning—once you know the meaning of a sentence you know how to articulate it.)

It was the linguistic expression, tens of thousands of years ago, of the predication either of a quality of a material substance, or of a change in that substance, that formed the framework of the grammar of the great languages of the world, and made all later developments of logical thought possible. This great step in human development produced the *Sentence*, a " two-in-one " or binary unit, which gives linguistic expression to a Subject and a Predicate, or to the idea of a substance and the idea of a related phenomenon.

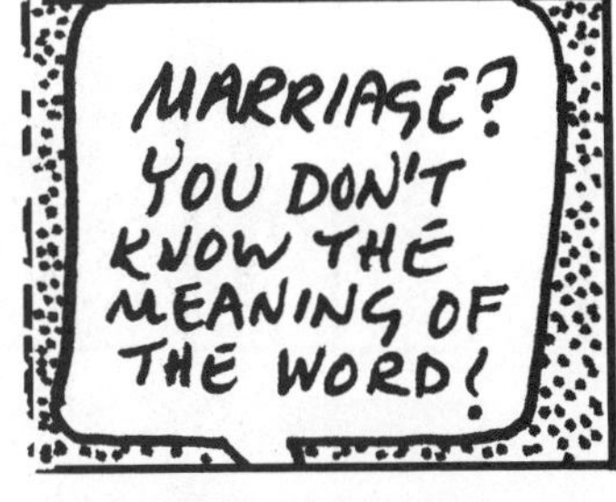

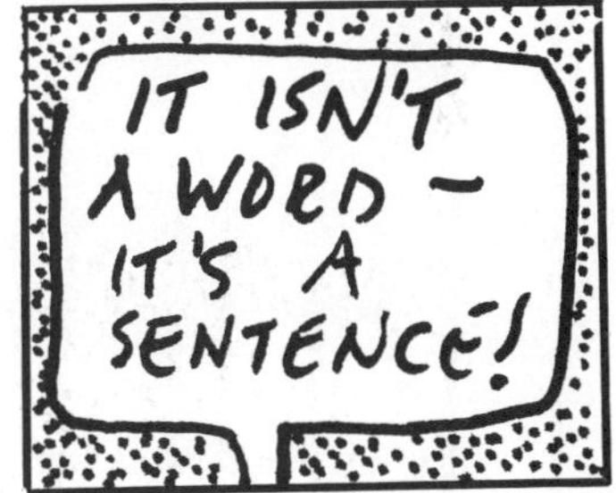

COMBINATION SIGNS AND CHARACTERS 65

[illegible]	÷	colon : and hyphen -
Dollar	$	capital S over solidus sign /
Equation	=	hyphen - and raised hyphen
Exclamation mark	!	apostrophe ' and full stop .

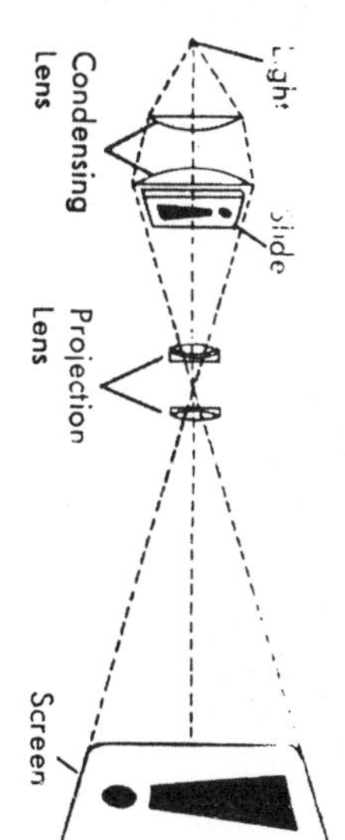

exclamation mark (!) have a similar and an interesting origin. The ! represents the Latin exclamation *Io*, which was used to signify a cry of joy. When the Latin writers wished to signify joy they wrote this word, then, so that it might not be read as a part of the verse or line, they wrote the letters one above the other, thus $\frac{I}{o}$, and this, in rapid writing, soon developed into !. The ? came

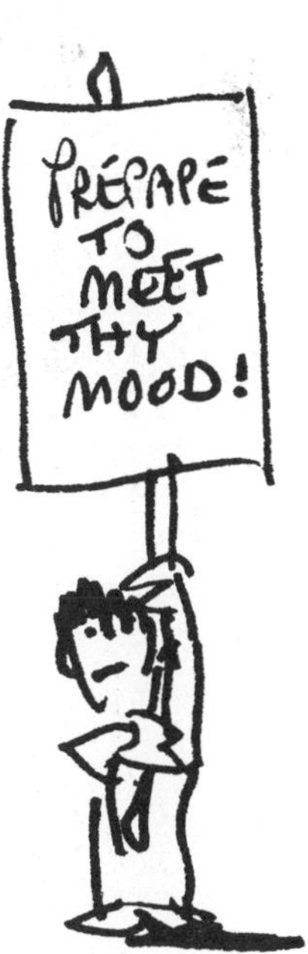

'iofeedback

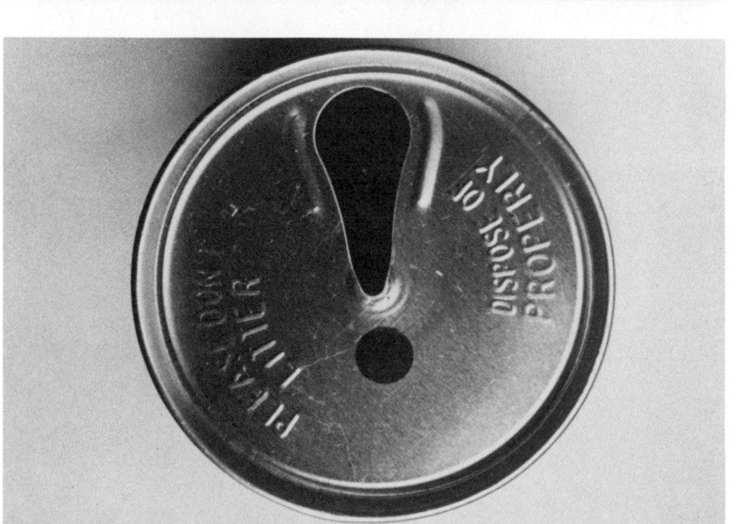

Freu–de, *f.* (-n) joy, gladness; delight, pleasure, satisfaction; enjoyment, comfort; *plötzlicher Ausbruch der –de,* transport (of joy); *mit –de* or *–den,* gladly, joyfully, with pleasure; *vor –de außer sich sein,* be beside o.s. with joy; *seine –de haben an einer S.,* take delight in a th.; *es macht mir große –de,* it gives me great pleasure;

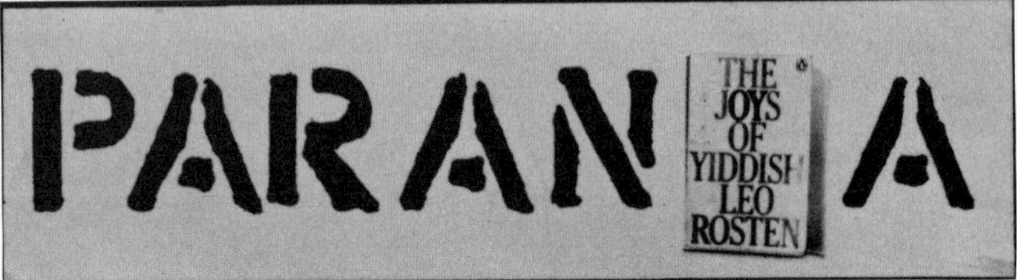

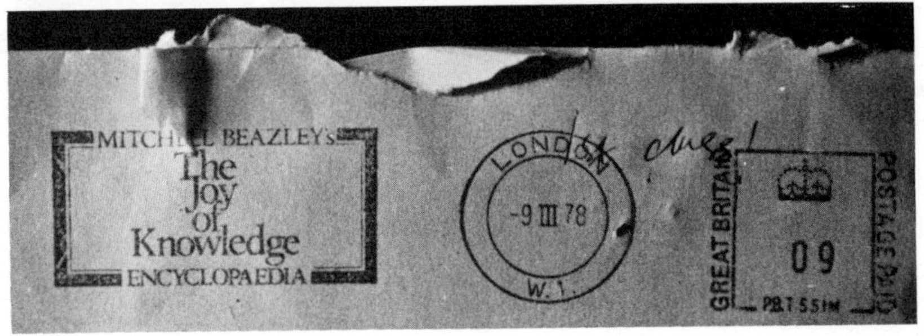

Explaining the J.O.K.E.

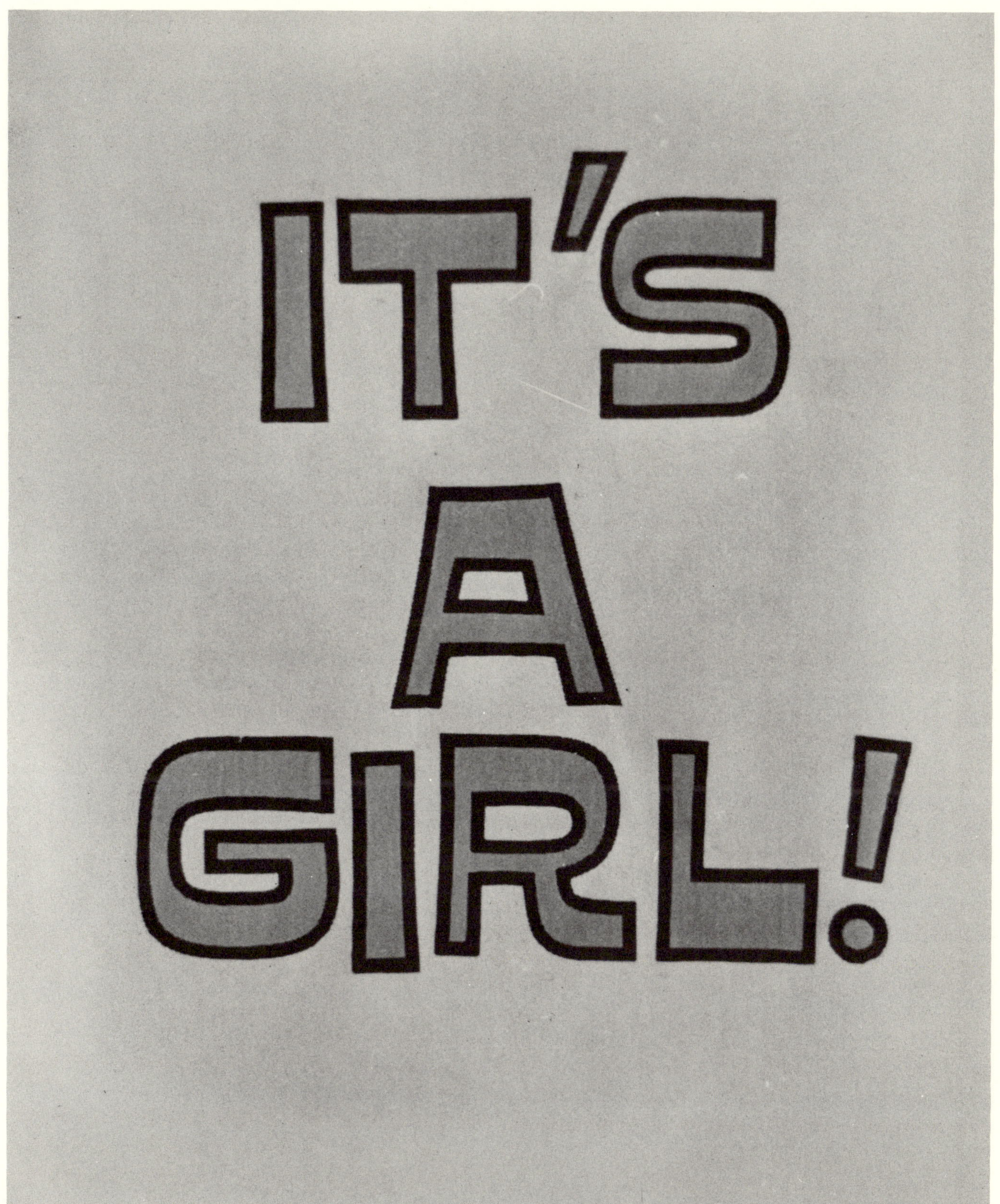

Fancy coming out with a crack like that!

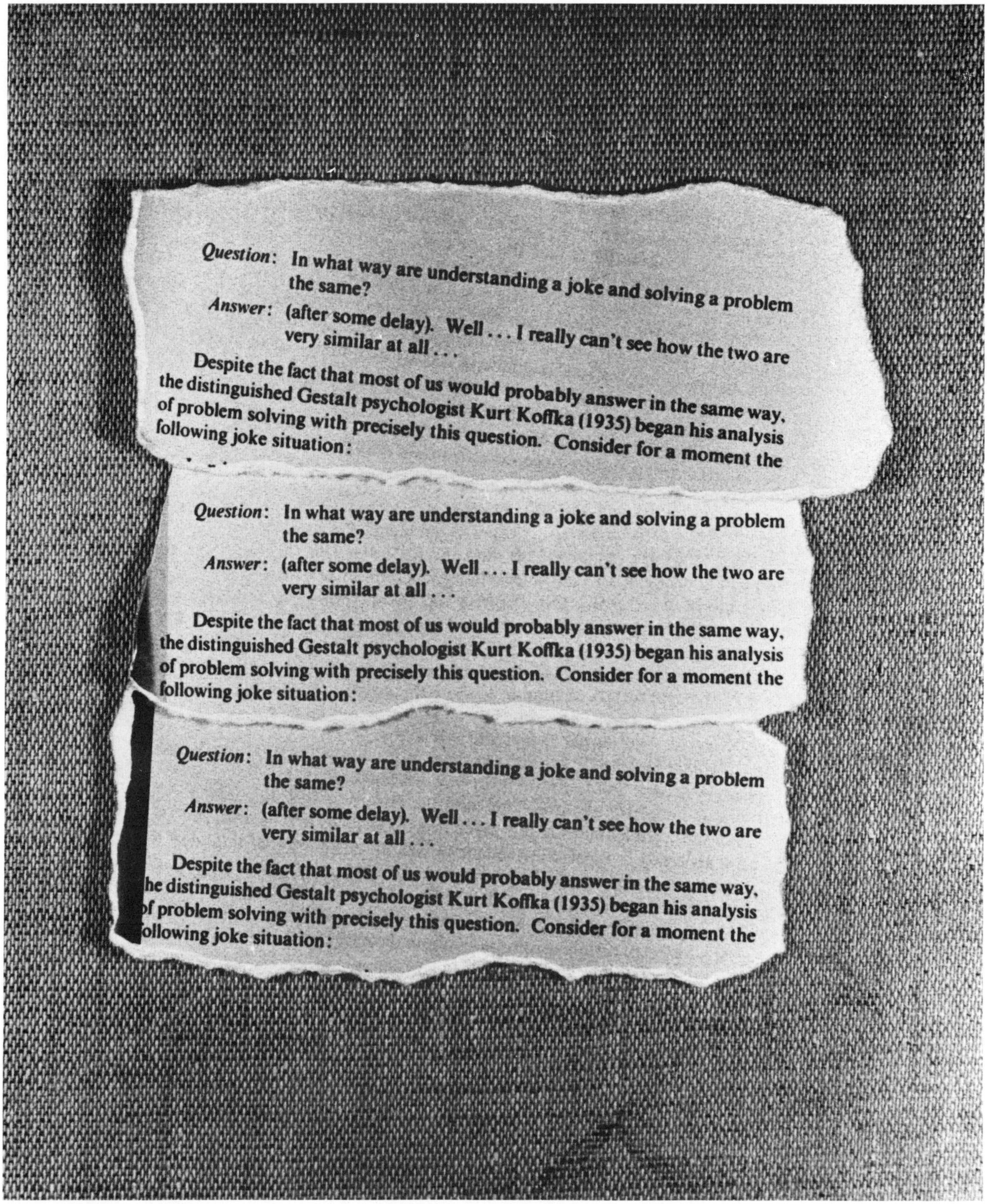

Question: In what way are understanding a joke and solving a problem the same?

Answer: (after some delay). Well . . . I really can't see how the two are very similar at all . . .

Despite the fact that most of us would probably answer in the same way, the distinguished Gestalt psychologist Kurt Koffka (1935) began his analysis of problem solving with precisely this question. Consider for a moment the following joke situation:

Question: In what way are understanding a joke and solving a problem the same?

Answer: (after some delay). Well . . . I really can't see how the two are very similar at all . . .

Despite the fact that most of us would probably answer in the same way, the distinguished Gestalt psychologist Kurt Koffka (1935) began his analysis of problem solving with precisely this question. Consider for a moment the following joke situation:

Question: In what way are understanding a joke and solving a problem the same?

Answer: (after some delay). Well . . . I really can't see how the two are very similar at all . . .

Despite the fact that most of us would probably answer in the same way, the distinguished Gestalt psychologist Kurt Koffka (1935) began his analysis of problem solving with precisely this question. Consider for a moment the following joke situation:

Funny you should ask

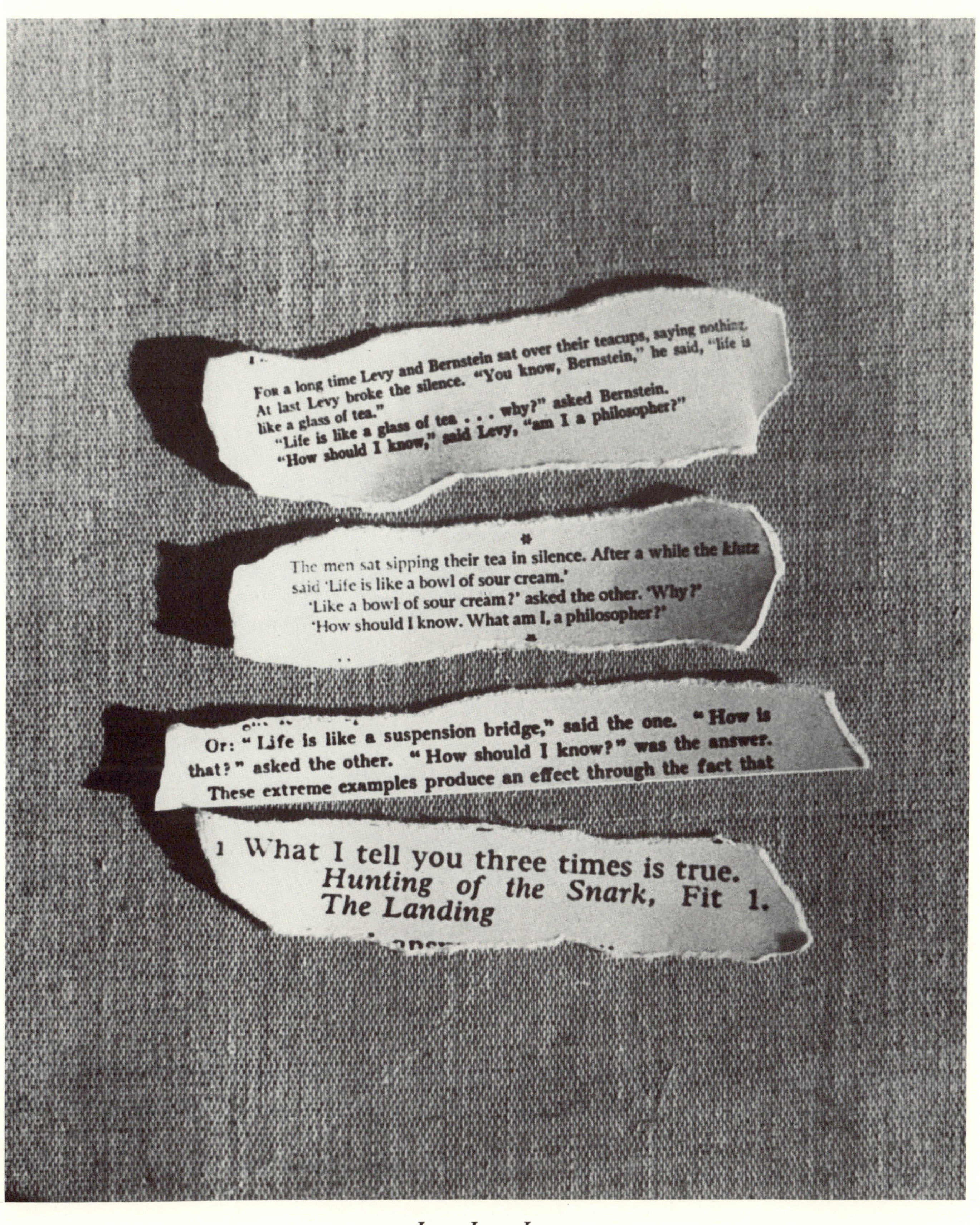

I say I say I say

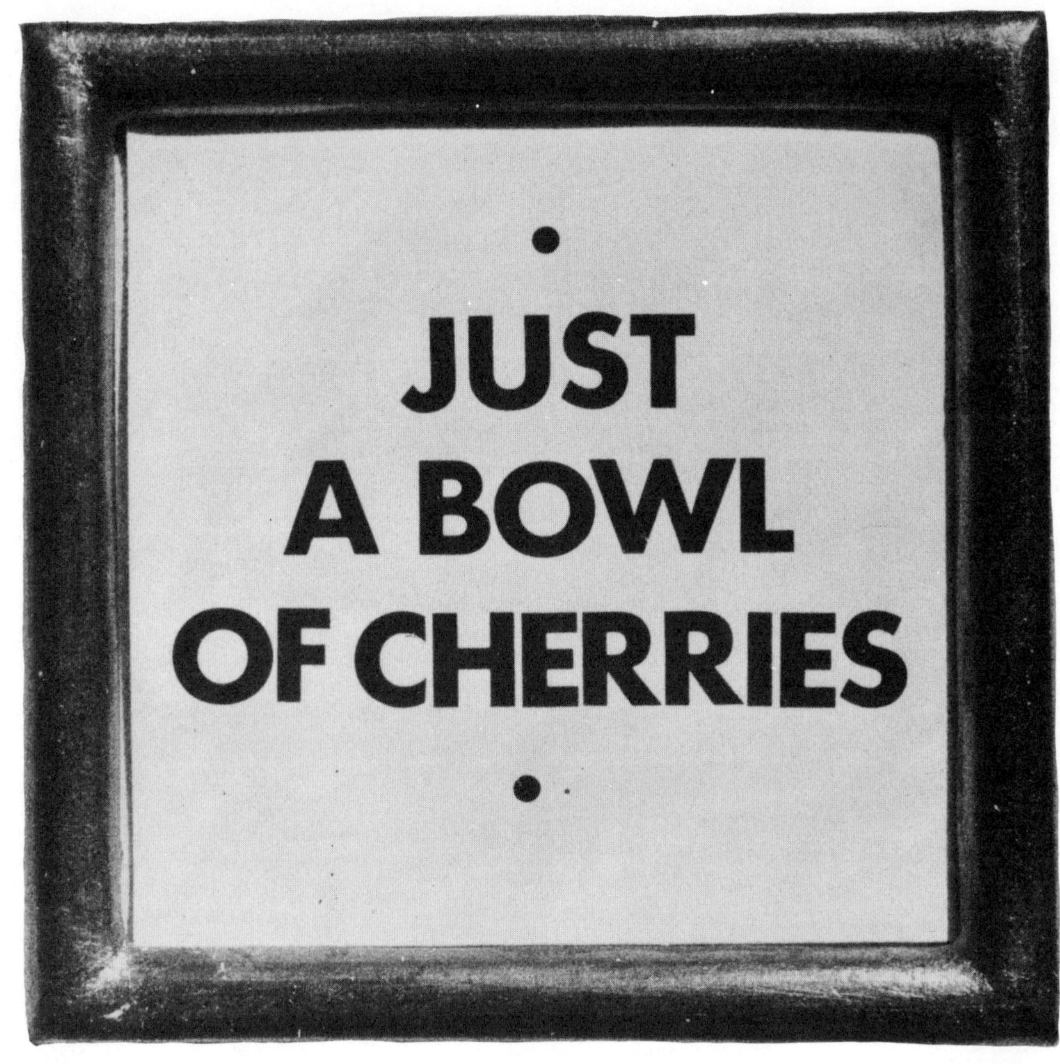

Still life

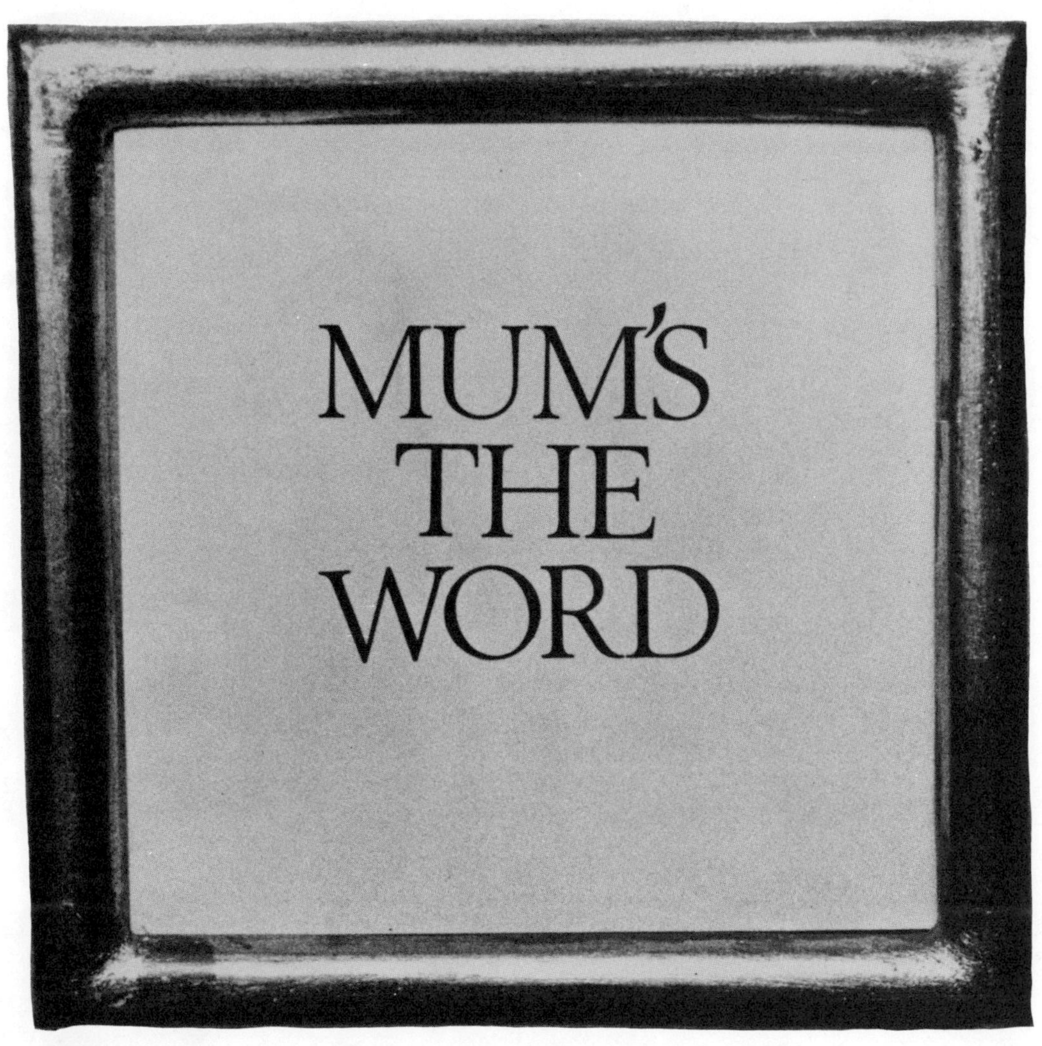

The secret of life

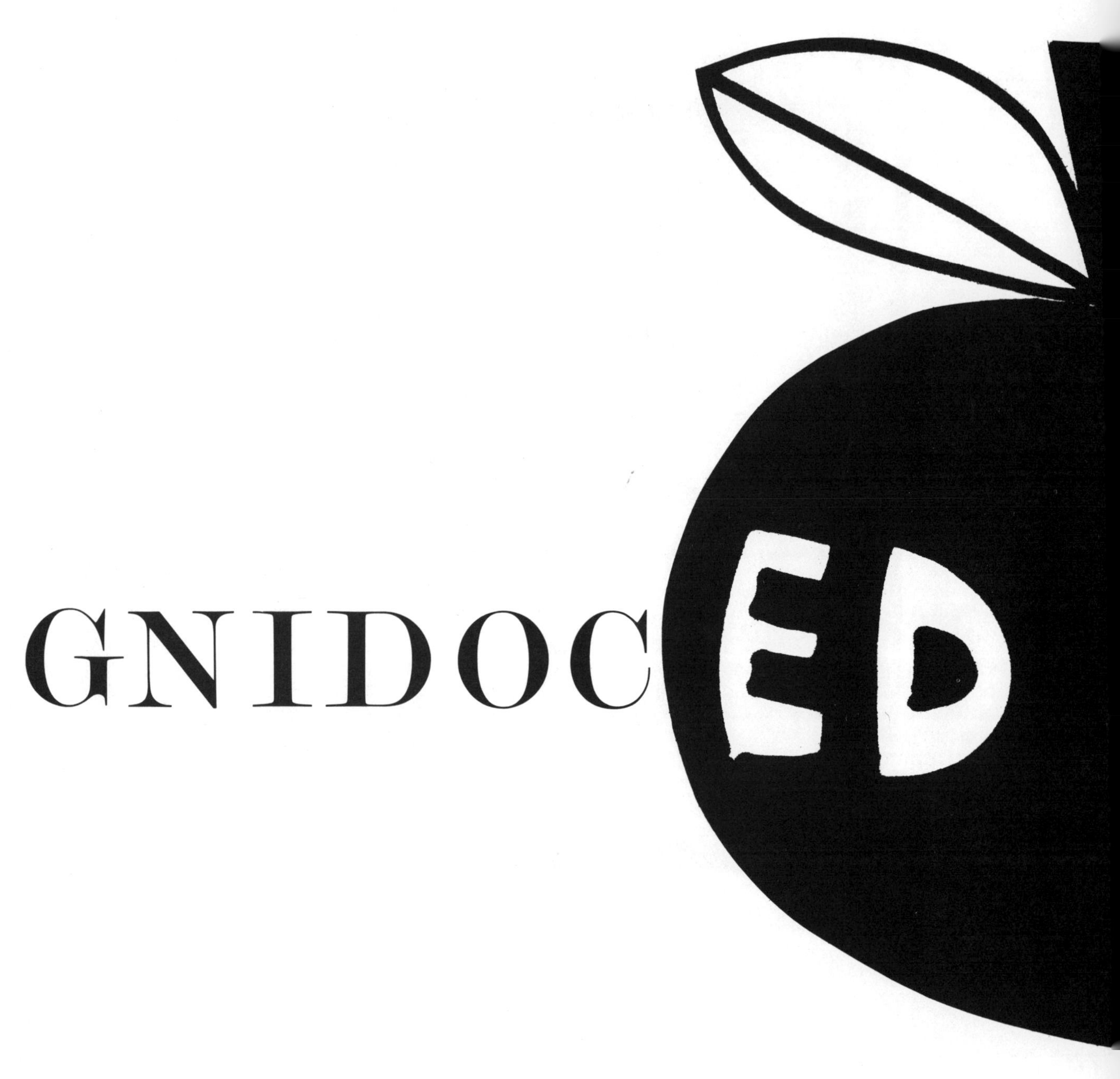

Eve deifieD

EN CODING

The genetic code

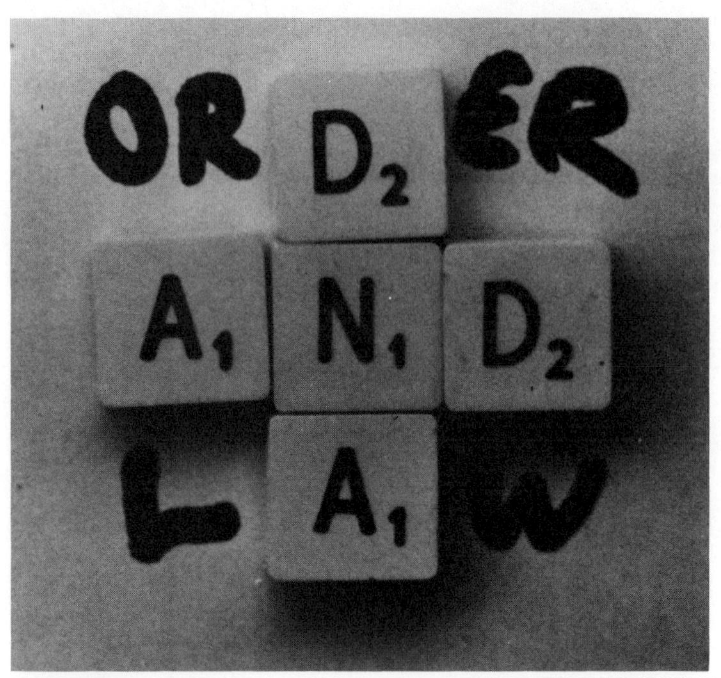

THE VERTICAL EXPRESSION
OF A HORIZONTAL DESIRE

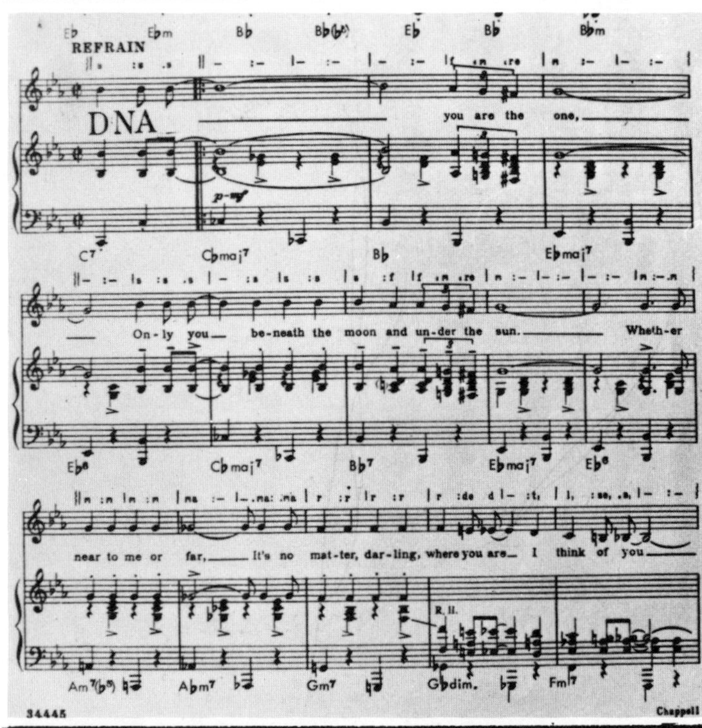

cŏlpŏrteur′ (-tėr; *also* kŏl′), n. Book-hawker, esp. one employed by society to distribute Bibles. [F]

The biology of belief

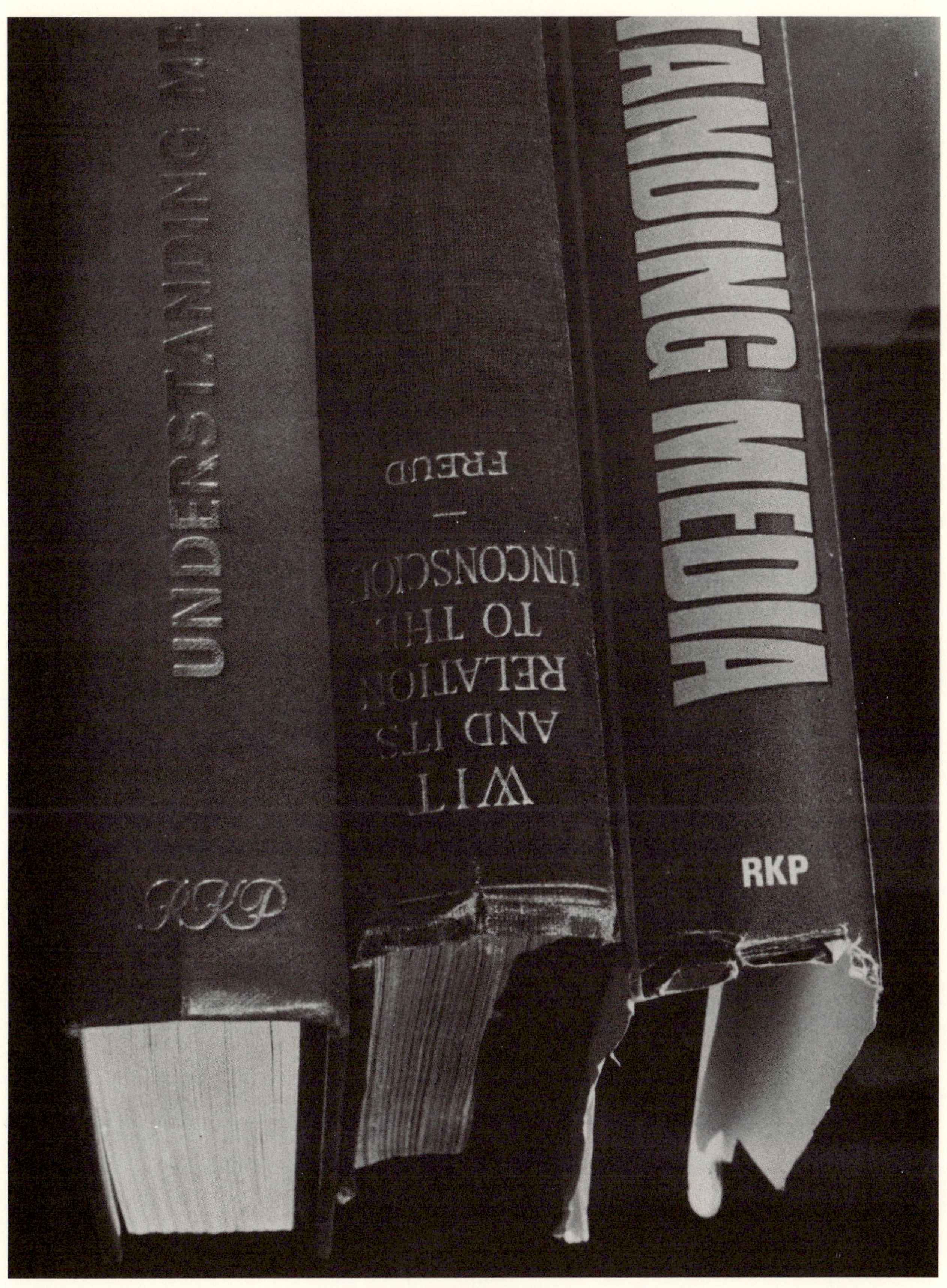

The immediate family

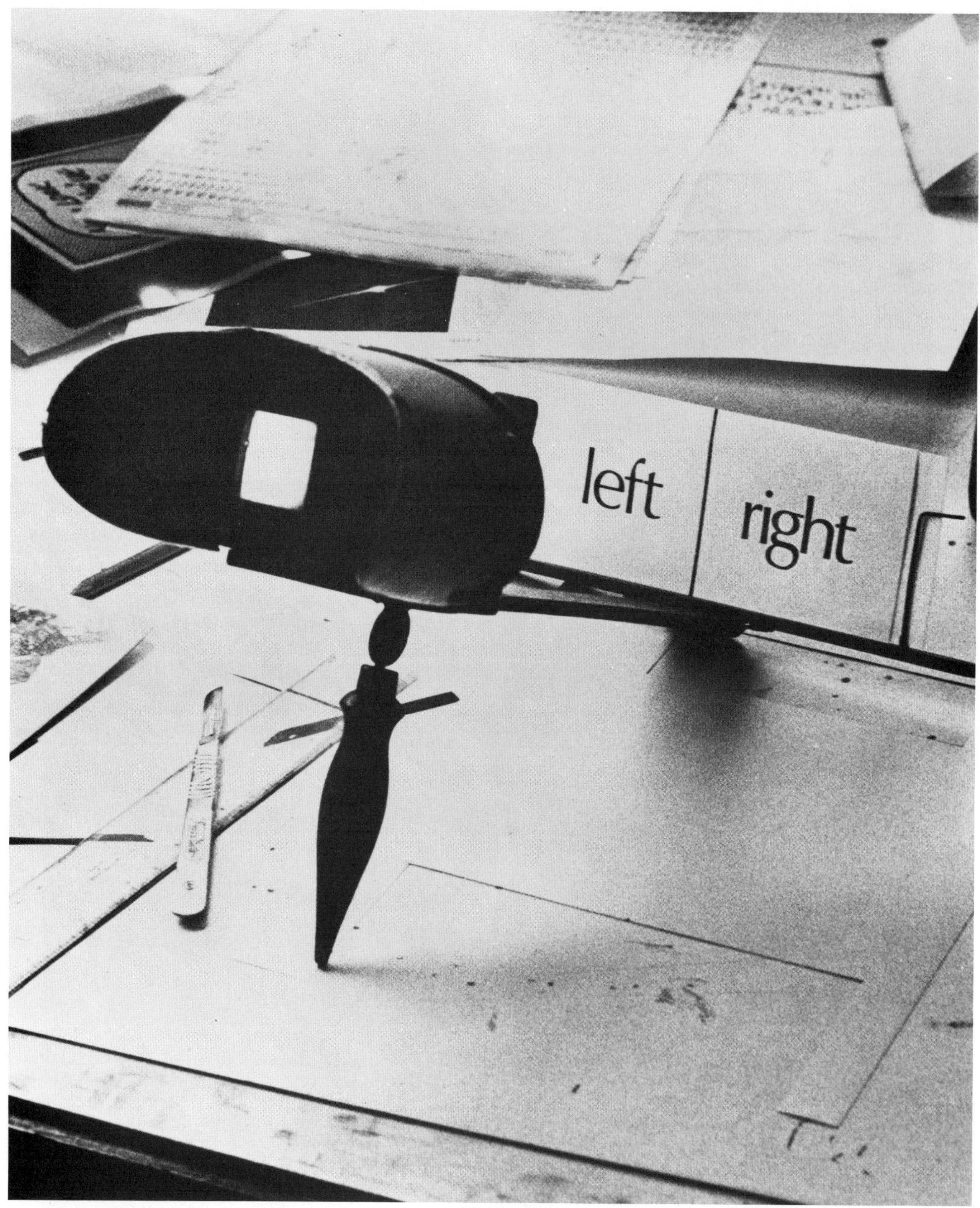

and ~~intellectual~~ sexual

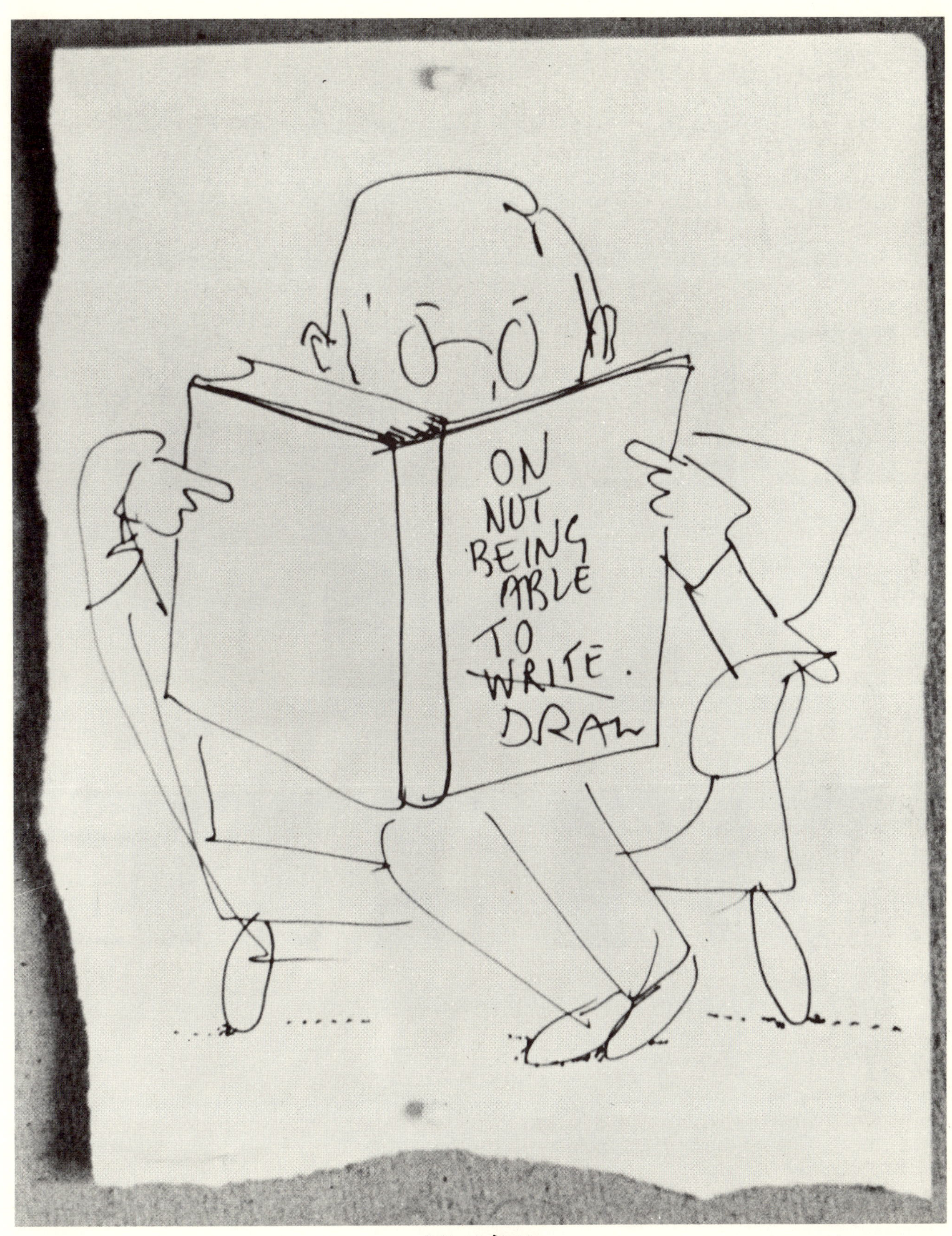

Mixed ~~media~~ marriage

BLACK AND WHITE

Grey matter

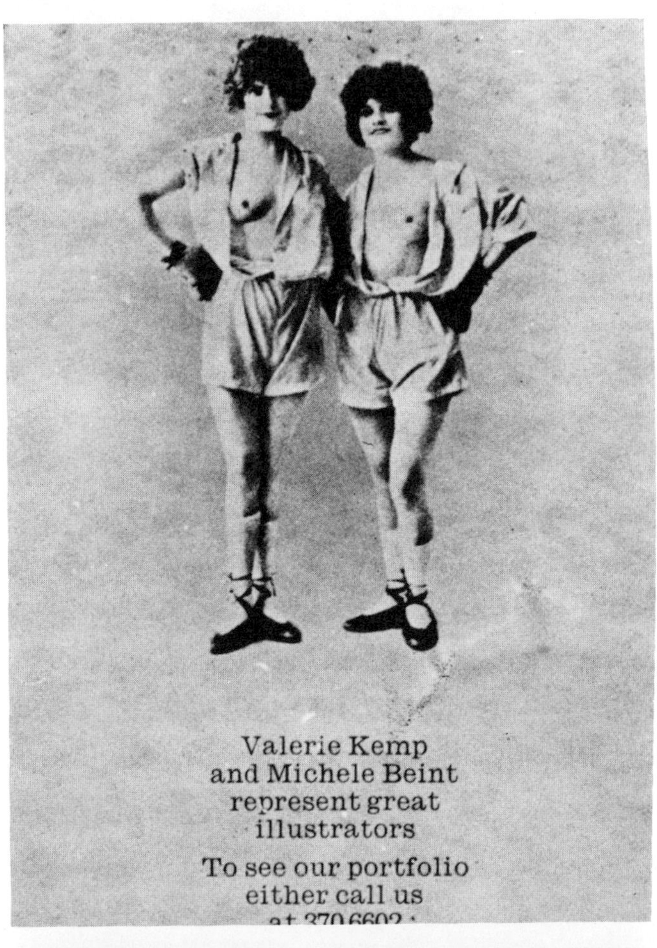

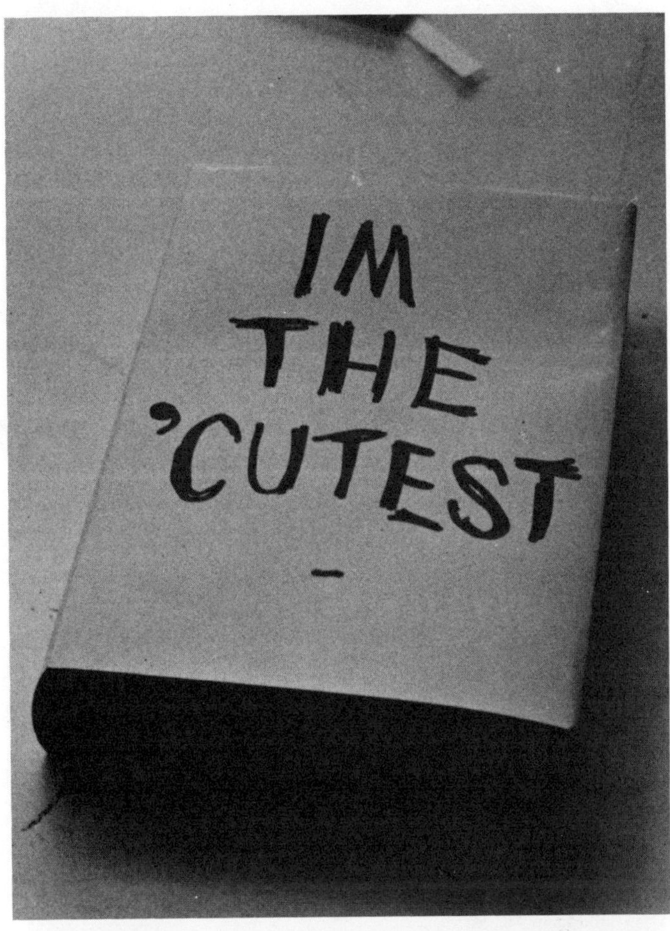

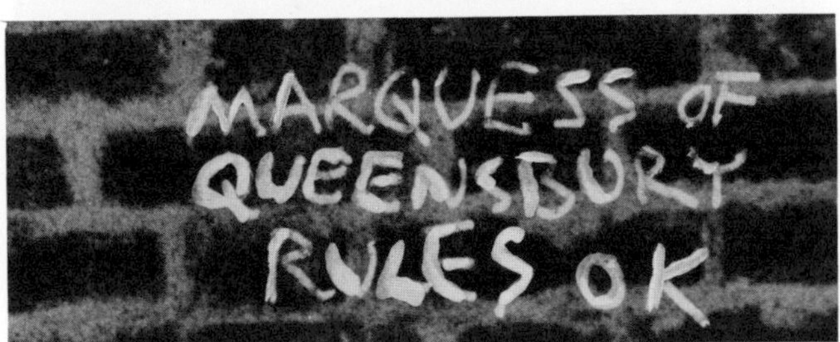

1.5 Such propositions are not to be identified with arguments, although all arguments contain propositions. Piety demands that our first example be a dull hack, hallowed by immemorial tradition. Its tedious, trite and trivial character will ensure that no one is distracted from what is being illustrated by any interest in the illustration. Later I shall deploy interesting and important examples. I hope thus to escape the dangers of boring myself and everybody else, or suggesting that the subject itself is as trifling as this first illustration.

IQ test

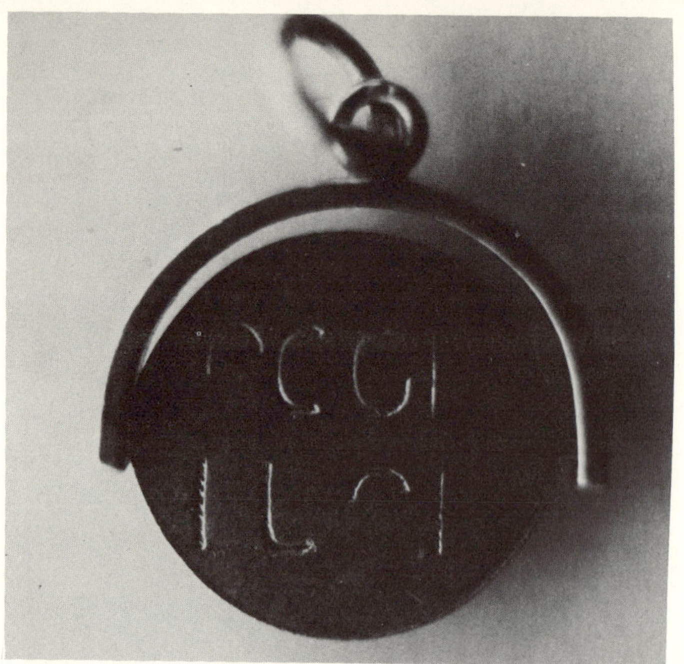

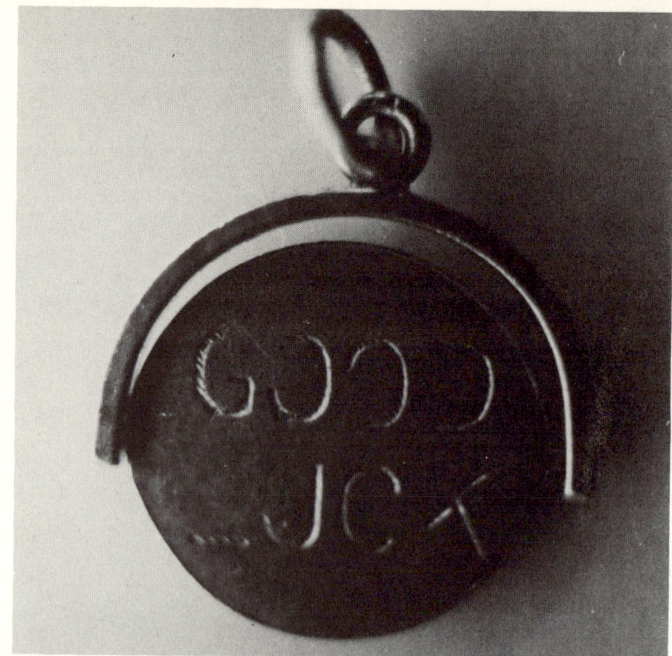

Viewed from the top the human brain looks something like the kernel of a walnut: it is in two halves, the right hemisphere and the left hemisphere. Because of a curious developmental quirk, all the functions of one side of the body are controlled by signals sent out by the opposite hemisphere; for instance, the left hemisphere guides the right hand, and the right hemisphere the left hand. In addition, the two hemispheres appear to have different functions, this information coming mainly from observing brain-injured patients. Speech, for example, is sited in the left hemisphere, while the ability to manipulate spatial problems is located in the right hemisphere. (This is for right-handed people; for left-handers it is sometimes a little more complicated.) Now we know that analytical processes (including logic and speech) are generated in the left hemisphere, and intuitive processes (including body movement as in skiing, and "artistic" talents) are found in the right hemisphere. In other words, sequential information processing occurs in the left hemisphere and simultaneous processing in the right.

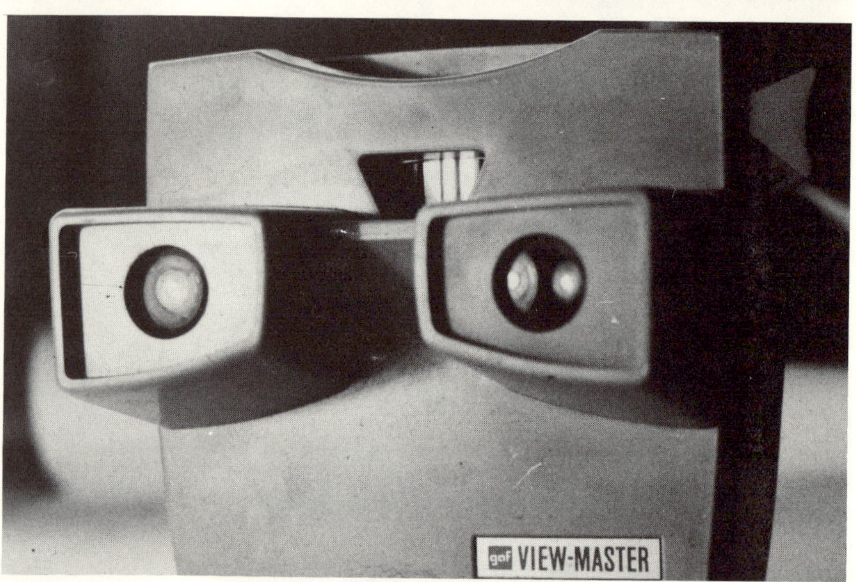

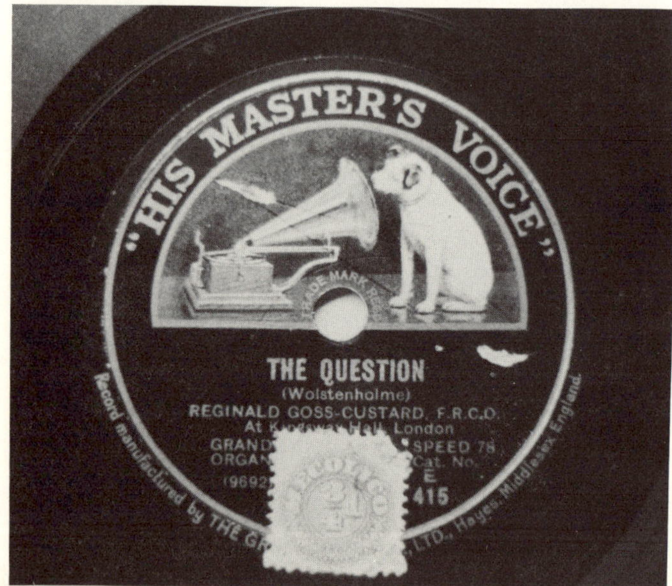

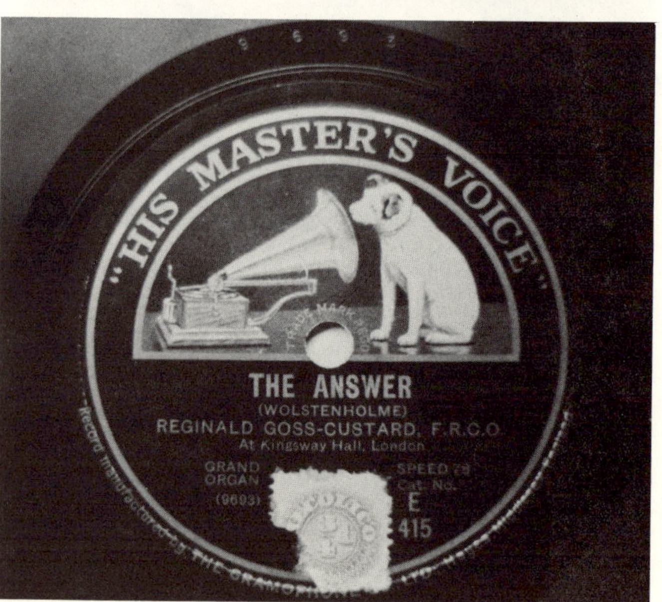

The statement on the other side is true

You could stick just about everything that's wrong with society on the back of a Green Shield Stamp.

The statement on the other side is false

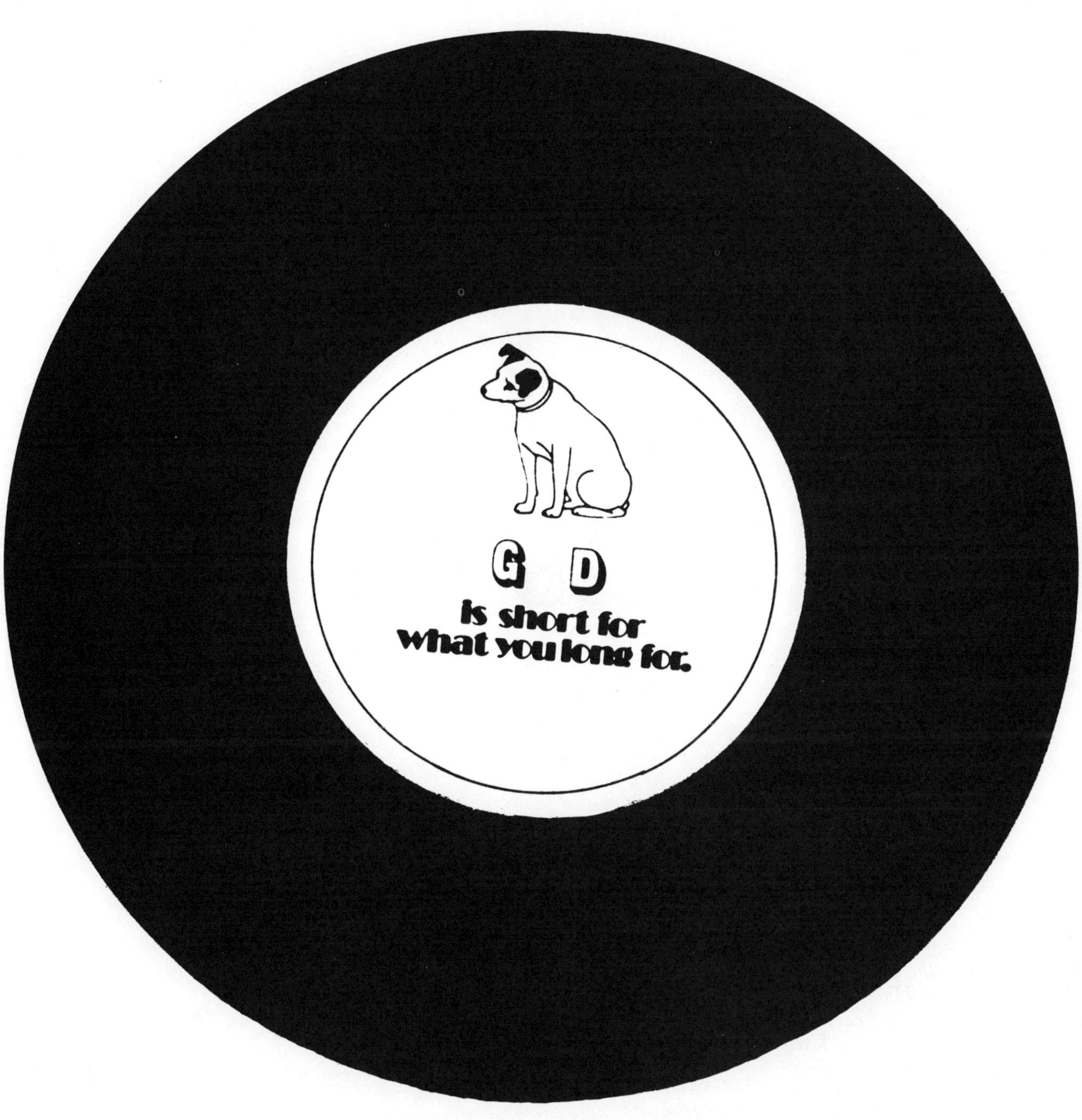

~~Graphic Design~~
Group Dynamics

The above dot is the actual calculated size of a black hole of the same mass as the earth. In his book The Key to the Universe, Nigel Calder explains that if you were 6000 kilometres away from it, the gravitational pull would feel the same as at the earth's surface, but at 60 centimetres (two feet) from it you would experience a force 100 million million times stronger. Now you see it.

Close your right eye and fixate the above dot with your left. Hold the book at arm's length. When the book is about 60 centimetres (two feet) from your face the dot on the left hand page should disappear as it falls on the blind spot of the retina of the eye. The blind spot is the point where the optic nerve leaves the retina for the brain. The optic nerve is the medium of communication between the eye and the brain. Now you don't.

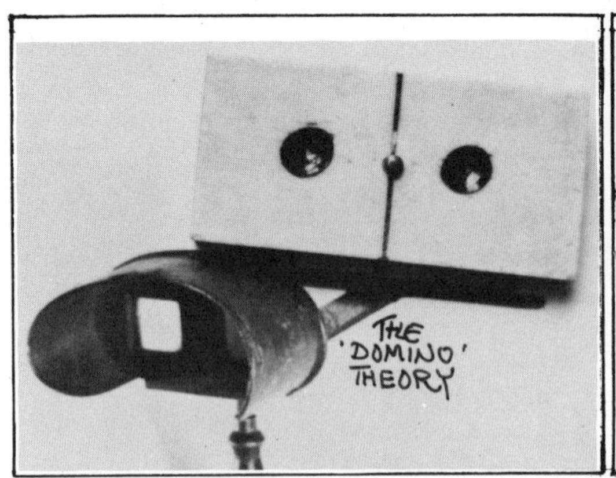

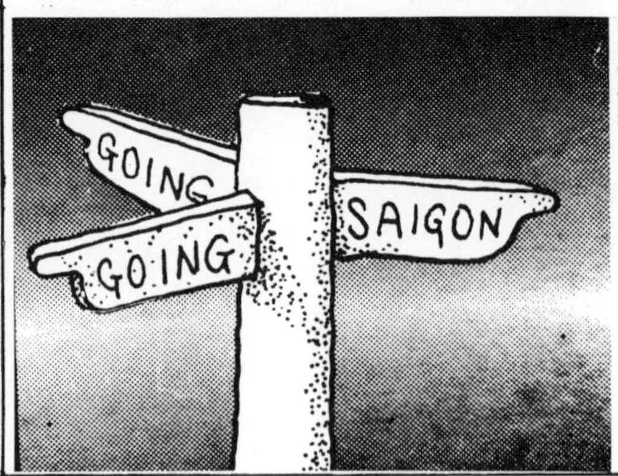

cogn. ~ISM(2, 4), **trivial'ITY**, ~NESS, nn., ~IZE(3) v.t., ~LY^2 adv. [f. L *trivialis* commonplace f. TRI(*vium* f. *via* road) place where three ways meet, see -AL]

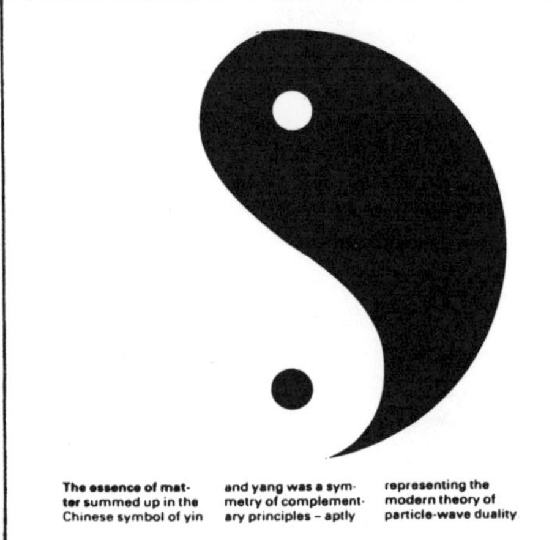

What is new is only this: the possibility that the truths which lie ahead of us are not merely extraneous to man, or incomprehensible to all but a handful of men—these negations have long been with us—but that there may be between man's survival and certain truths, between man's hopes of justice and decency and certain categories of truth, a fundamental incompatibility. It is now conceivable that the truth lies in wait for man, as it did for Oedipus, the solver of riddles, where the three ways meet. It is conceivable that the rage for insight, the hunter's cry, which infected the Western mind almost 3,000 years ago, is leading us into ambush.

Out, damned spot! out, I say! One;
two: why then, 'tis time to do't.

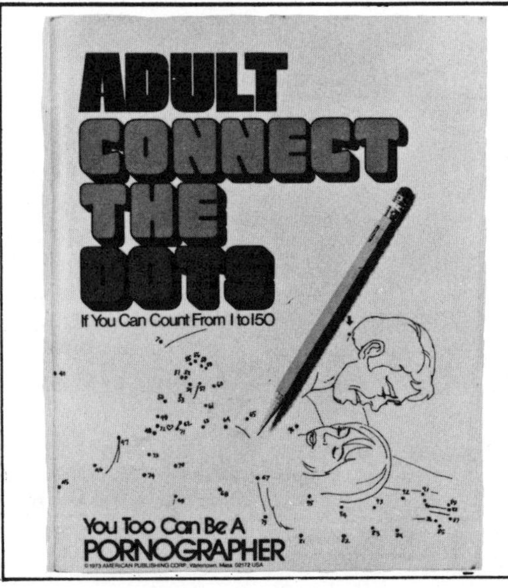

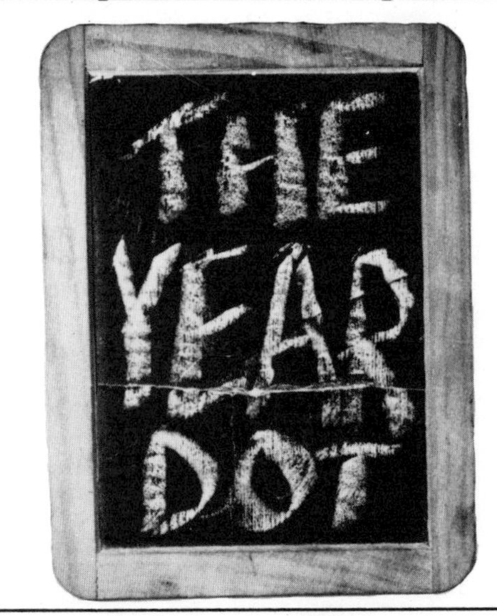

Hard core Apostrophe Theory

Assuming that the universe expands and that Einstein's field equations agree with that interpretation, the question still arises inexorably: Why? The easiest, and almost inevitable, explanation is that the expansion is the result of an explosion at the beginning. In 1927, the Belgian mathematician Abbé Georges Édouard Lemaître suggested that all matter came originally from a tremendously dense 'cosmic egg', which exploded and gave birth to the universe as we know it. Fragments of the original sphere of matter formed galaxies, which are still rushing outwards in all directions as a result of that unimaginably powerful multi-million-year-old explosion.

The Russian-American physicist George Gamow has elaborated

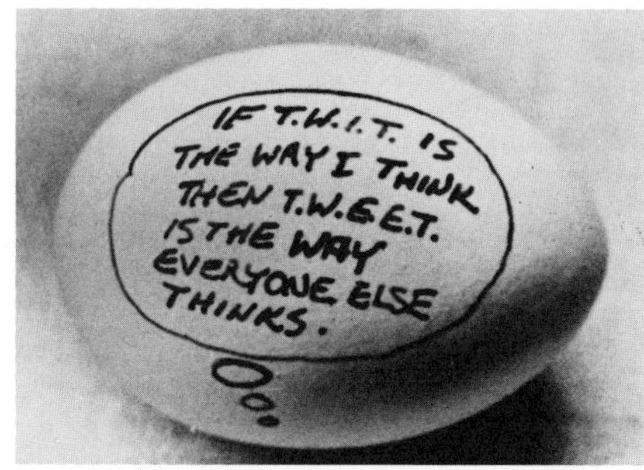

Two birds

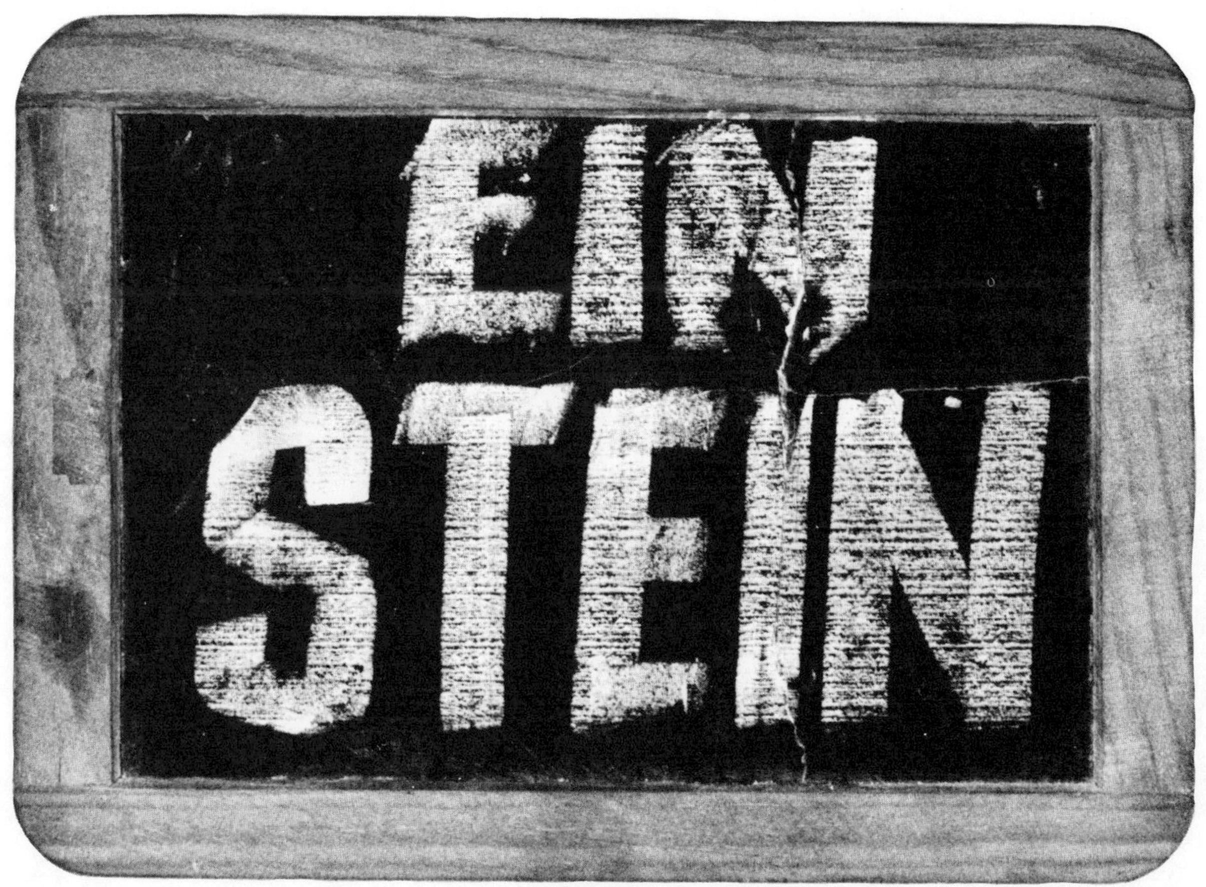

One stone

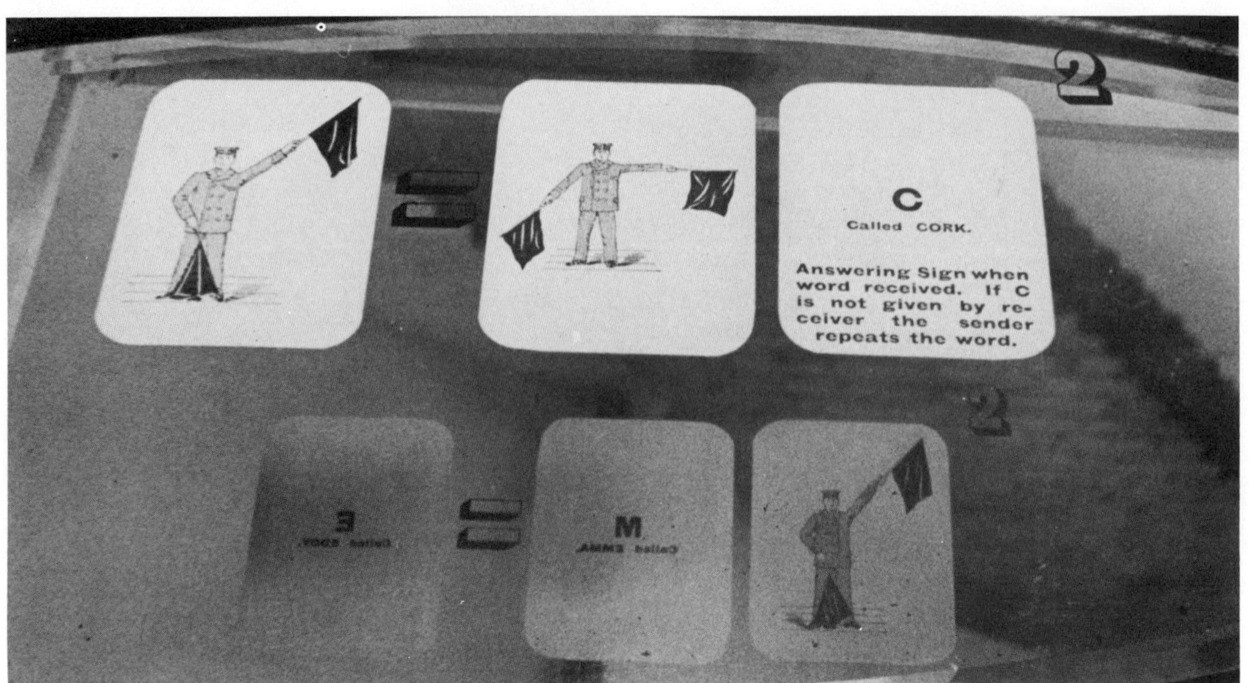
2
C
Called CORK.
Answering Sign when word received. If C is not given by receiver the sender repeats the word.
2
M
Called EMMA.

Middle c

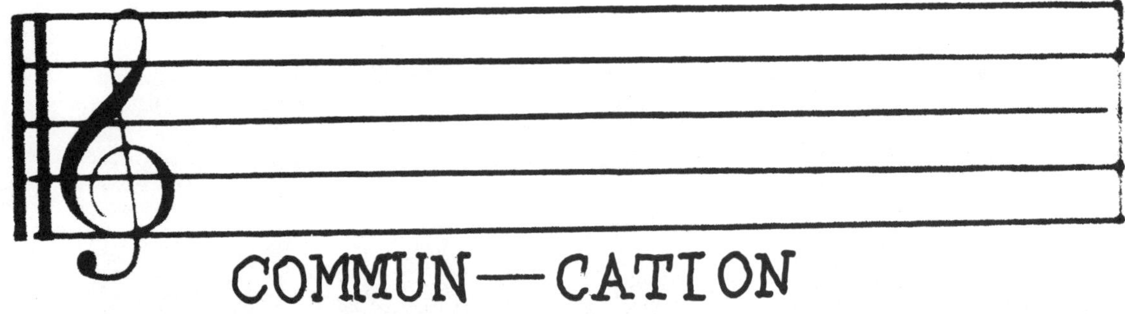
COMMUN—CATION

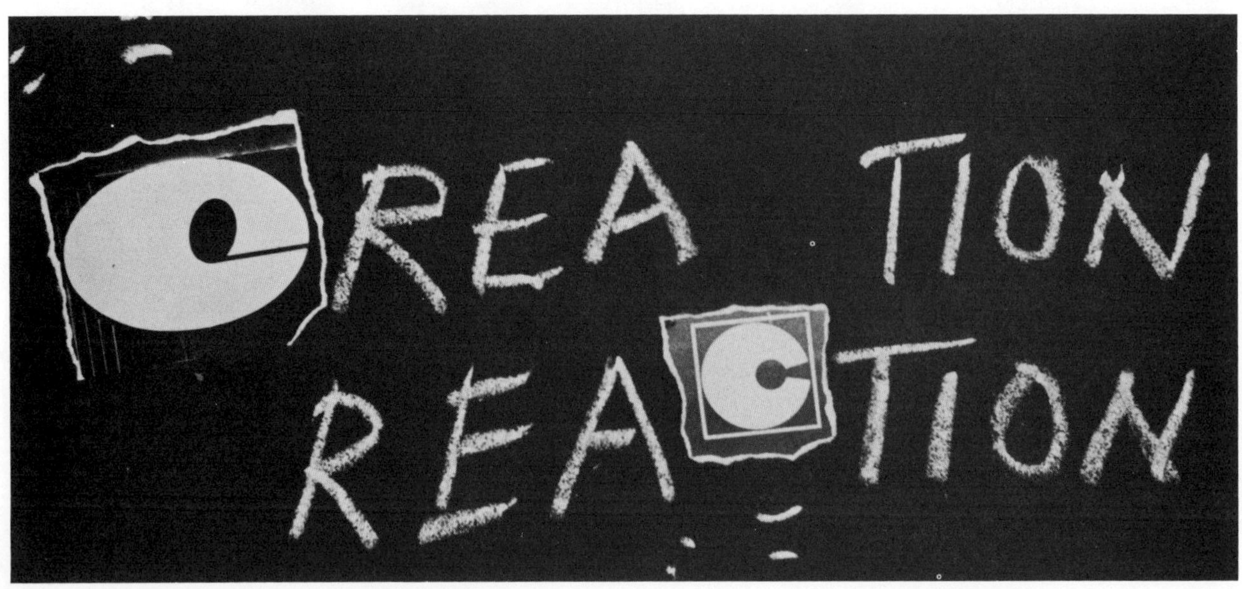
CREA TION
REACTION

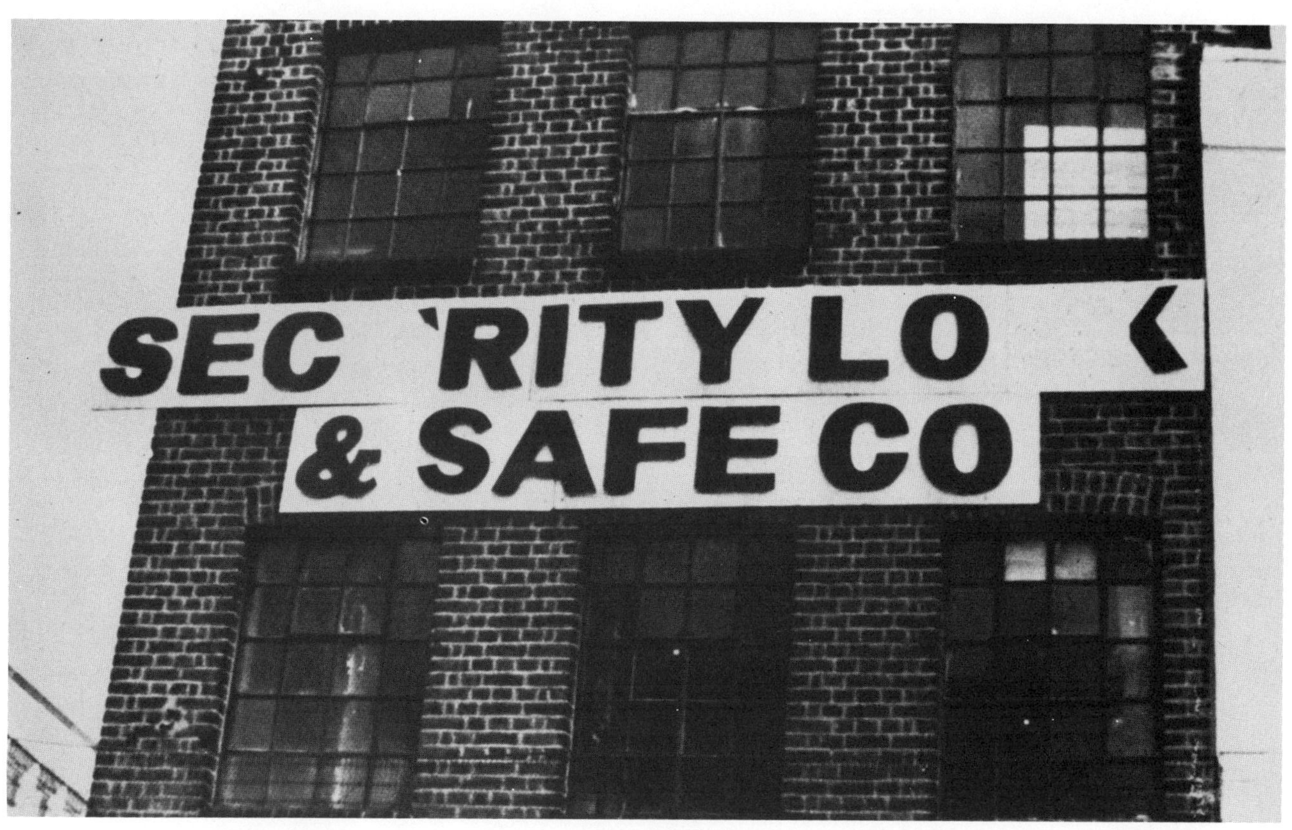

Now UC it

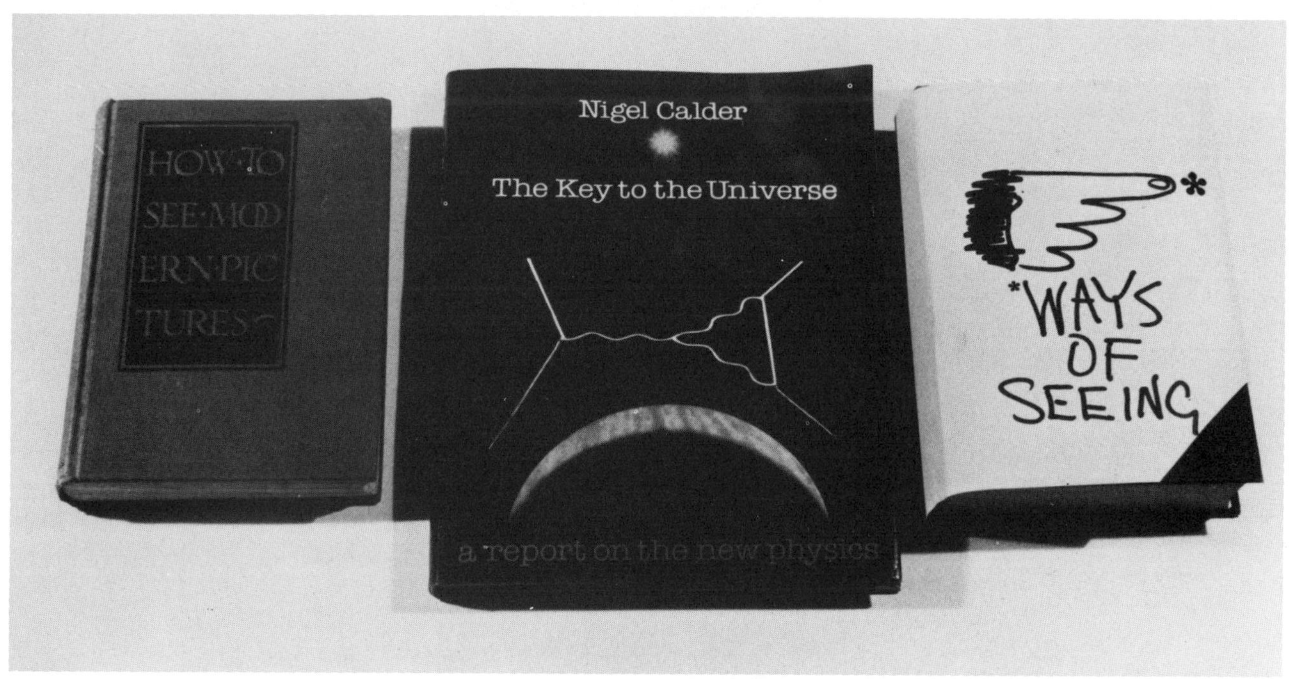

Now you don't

a Pelican 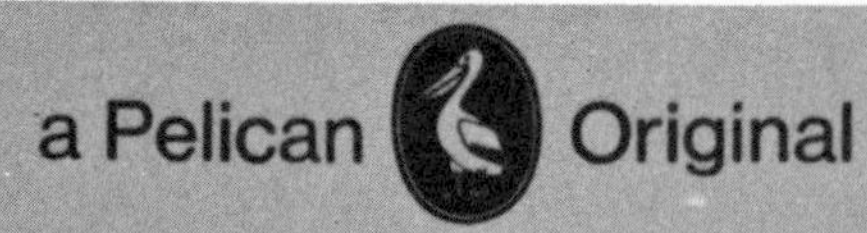 Original

WAYS OF SEEING

Based on the BBC television series with

JOHN BERGER

Seeing comes before words. The child looks and recognizes before it can speak.

But there is also another sense in which seeing comes before words. It is seeing which establishes our place in the surrounding world; we explain that world with words, but words can never undo the fact that we are surrounded by it. The relation between what we see and what we know is never settled.

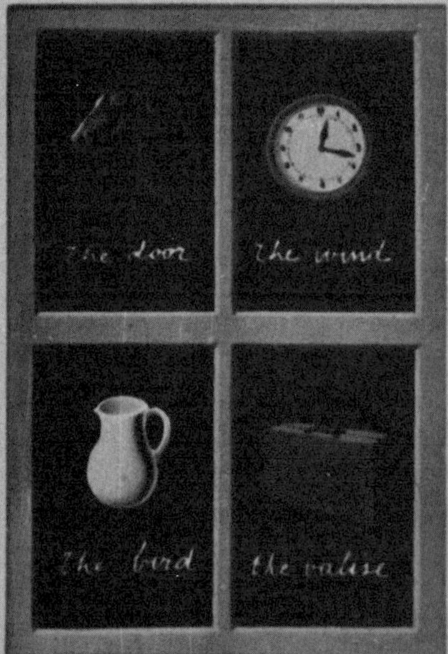

The Surrealist painter Magritte commented on this always-present gap between words and seeing in a painting called The Key of Dreams.

The way we see things is affected by what we

The Knightmare

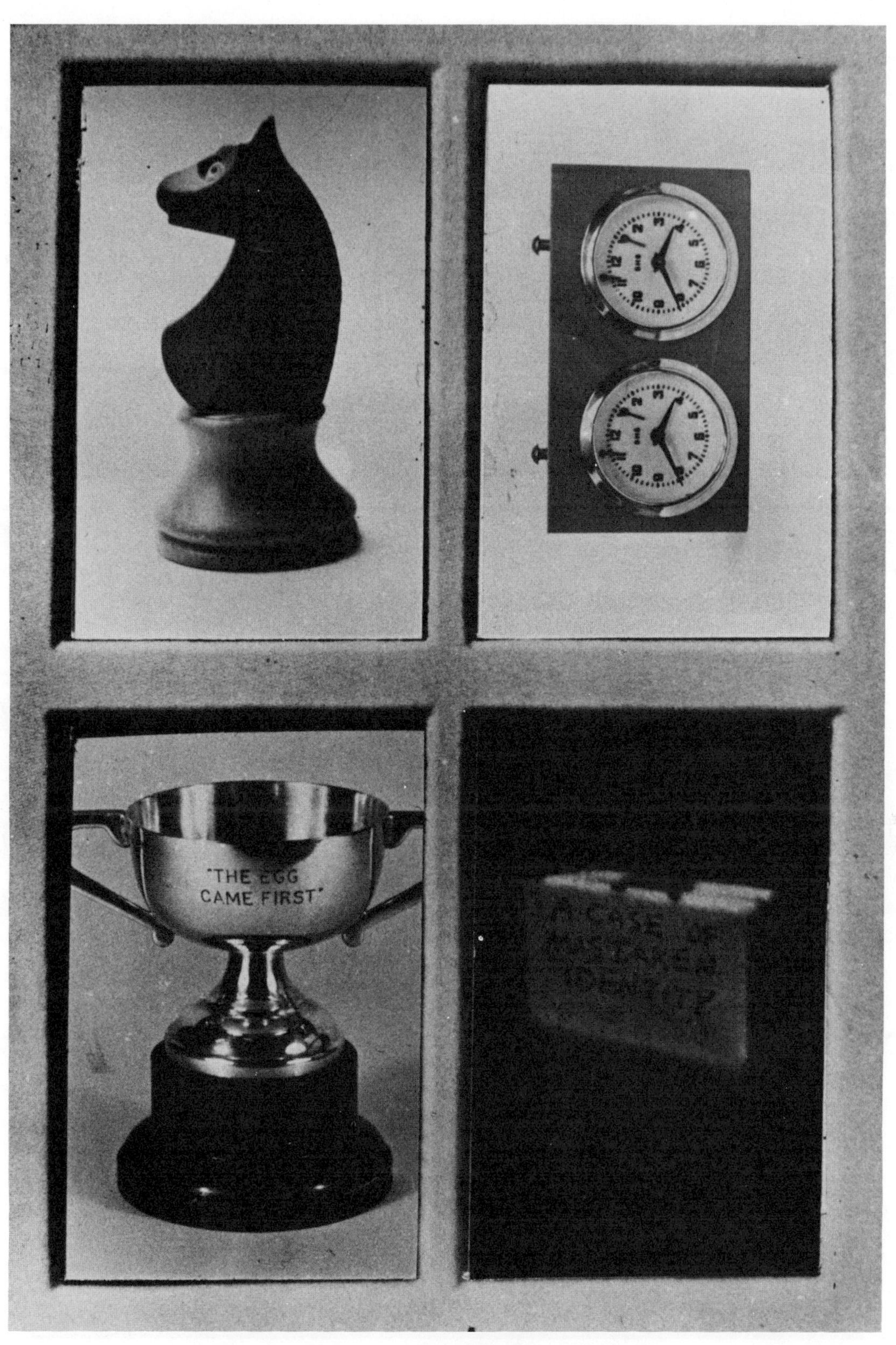

'trophy theory

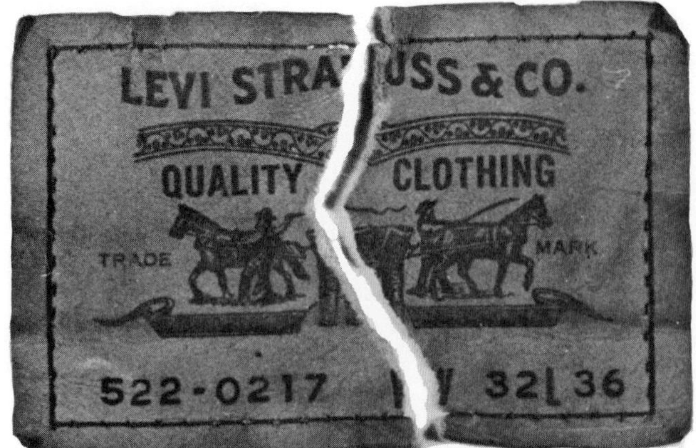

Apart

symbol.

This was originally a token, in the form of an object broken in twain, so that the identity could be proved by having the two parts match (as in James Branch Cabell's *The Cream of the Jest*). Thus the symbol became a sign. This story hides within the word, from Gr. *symbolos*, from *symballein*, from *sym,* together + *ballein,* to put, to throw.

Joking

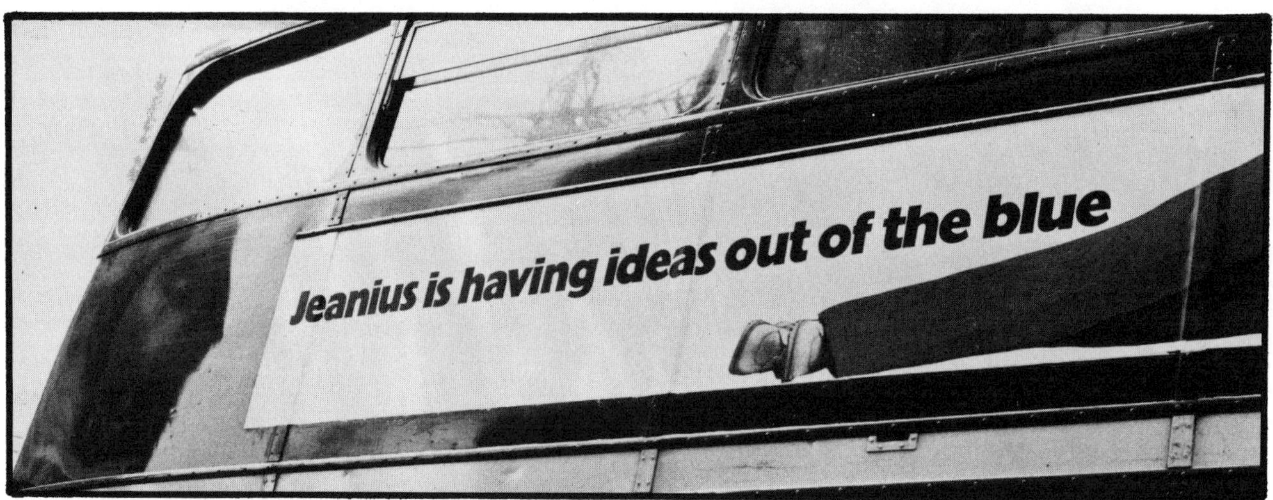

The d'nim/body relationship

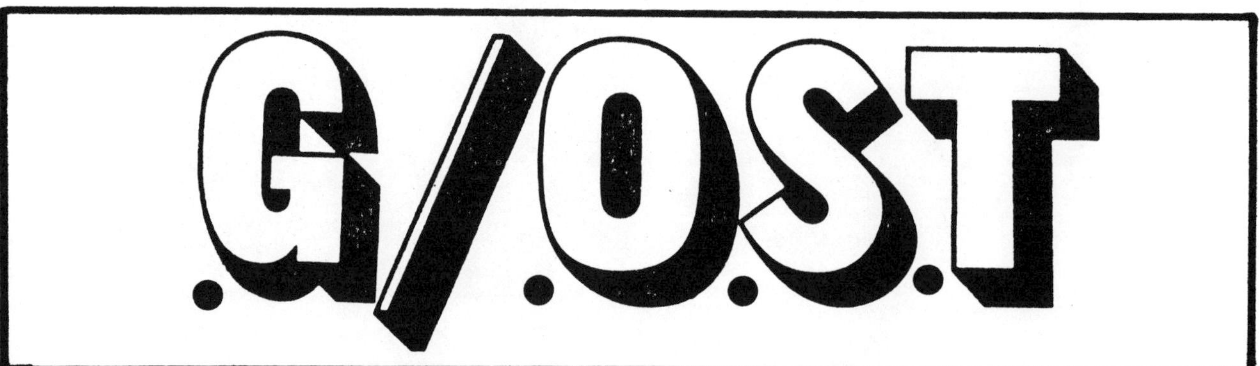

The Stroke Of Genius

"I love my love with an H," Alice couldn't help beginning, " because he is Happy. I hate him with an H, because he is Hideous. I fed him with—with—with Ham sandwiches and Hay. His name is Haigha, and he lives——"

At this point we encounter one of the most frustrating peculiarities of information theory. Although we can determine, by calculating *H*, how many binary digits per event are required with optimal encoding, the actual devising of this optimal code is an altogether different and more difficult problem, for

traversing the intervening space, and enabling particles not in direct contact to feel each other's presence. Galileo once remarked that the book of nature was written in a language of triangles, circles and squares. Were he alive in the twentieth century he might well have added the broken H.

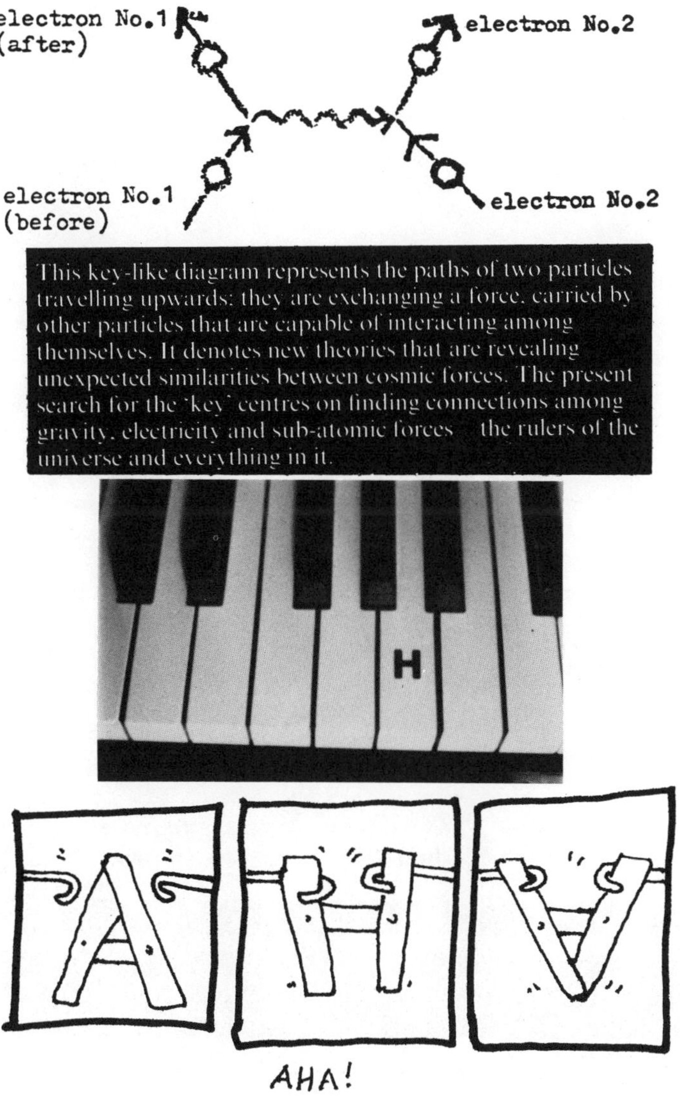

A Higher Authority

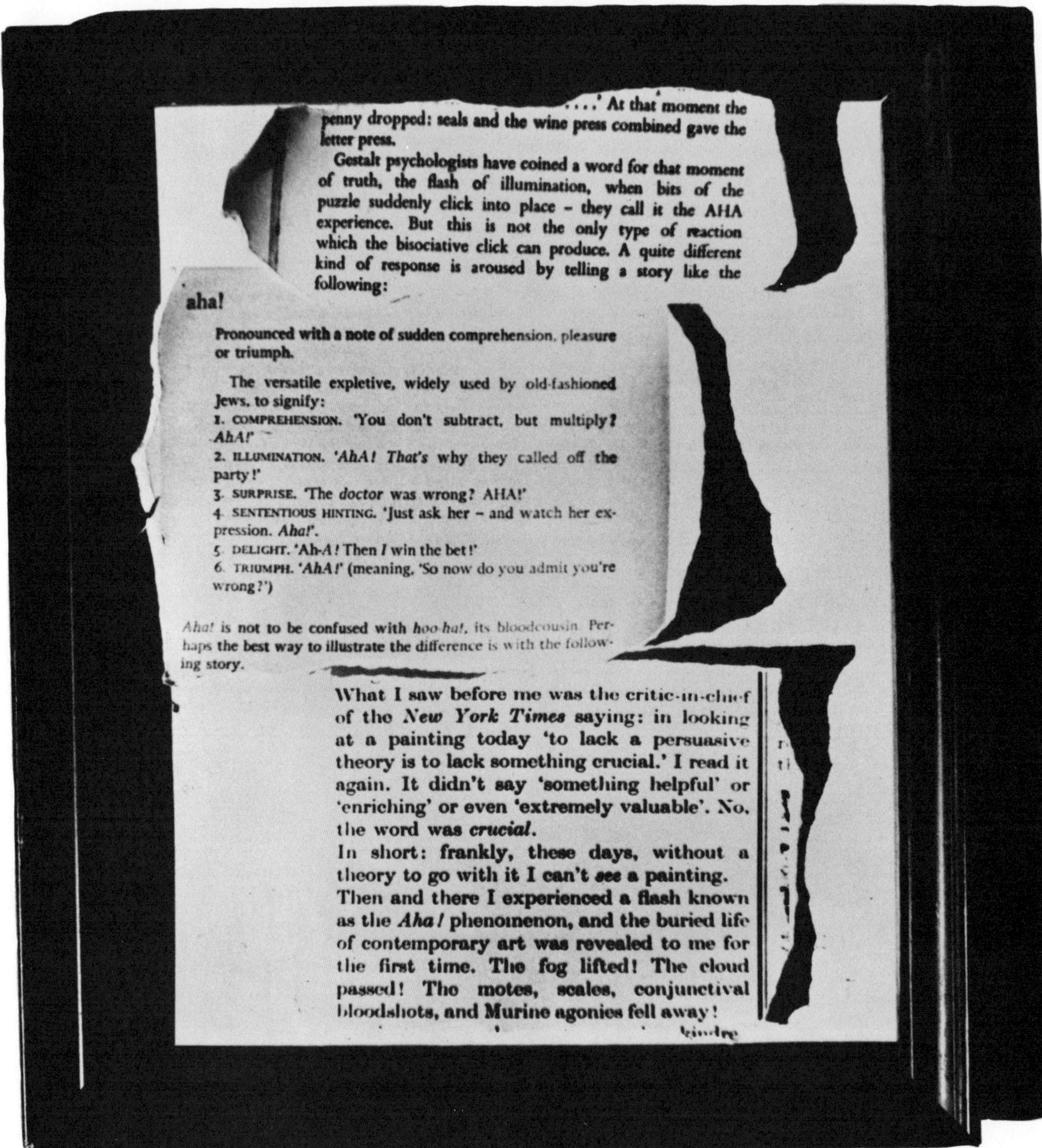

. . . .' At that moment the penny dropped: seals and the wine press combined gave the letter press.

Gestalt psychologists have coined a word for that moment of truth, the flash of illumination, when bits of the puzzle suddenly click into place – they call it the AHA experience. But this is not the only type of reaction which the bisociative click can produce. A quite different kind of response is aroused by telling a story like the following:

aha!

Pronounced with a note of sudden comprehension, pleasure or triumph.

The versatile expletive, widely used by old-fashioned Jews, to signify:

1. COMPREHENSION. 'You don't subtract, but multiply? *AhA!*'
2. ILLUMINATION. '*AhA! That's* why they called off the party!'
3. SURPRISE. 'The *doctor* was wrong? AHA!'
4. SENTENTIOUS HINTING. 'Just ask her – and watch her expression. *Aha!*'.
5. DELIGHT. 'Ah-*A!* Then *I* win the bet!'
6. TRIUMPH. '*AhA!*' (meaning, 'So now do you admit you're wrong?')

Aha! is not to be confused with *hoo-ha!*, its bloodcousin. Perhaps the best way to illustrate the difference is with the following story.

What I saw before me was the critic-in-chief of the *New York Times* saying: in looking at a painting today 'to lack a persuasive theory is to lack something crucial.' I read it again. It didn't say 'something helpful' or 'enriching' or even 'extremely valuable'. No, the word was *crucial*.

In short: frankly, these days, without a theory to go with it I can't *see* a painting.

Then and there I experienced a flash known as the *Aha!* phenomenon, and the buried life of contemporary art was revealed to me for the first time. The fog lifted! The cloud passed! The motes, scales, conjunctival bloodshots, and Murine agonies fell away!

The cru'ial theory

The name retina is from an early word meaning 'net' or 'cobweb tunic,' from the appearance of its blood vessels.

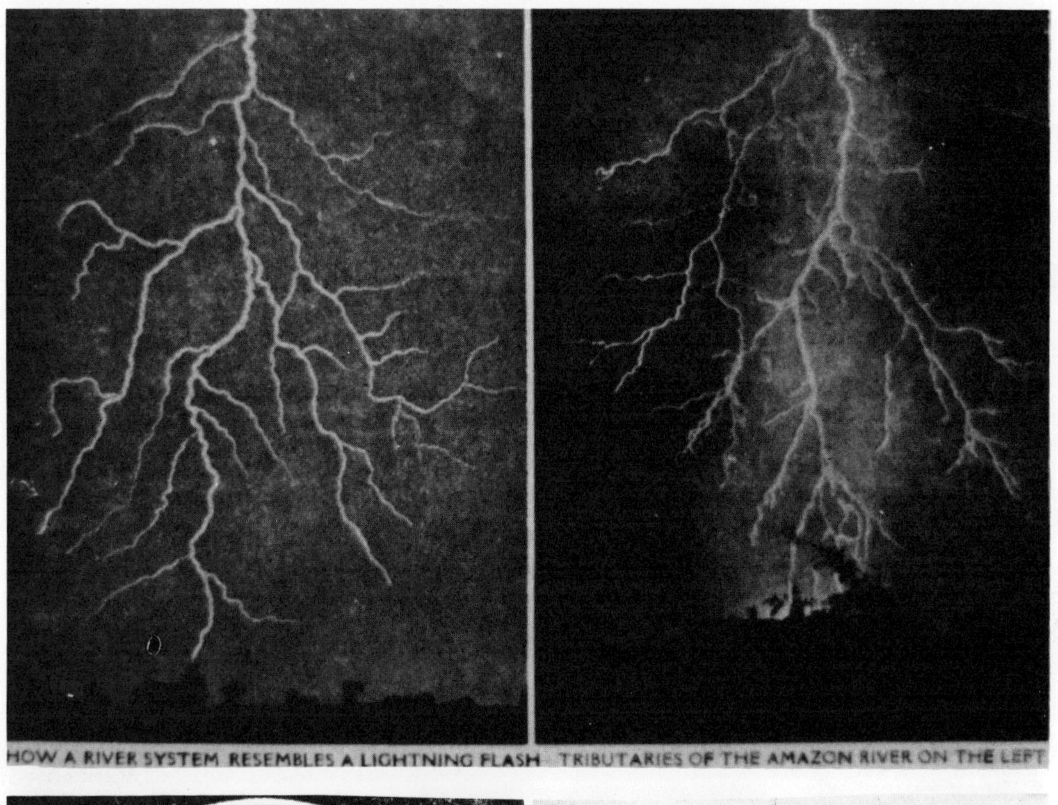

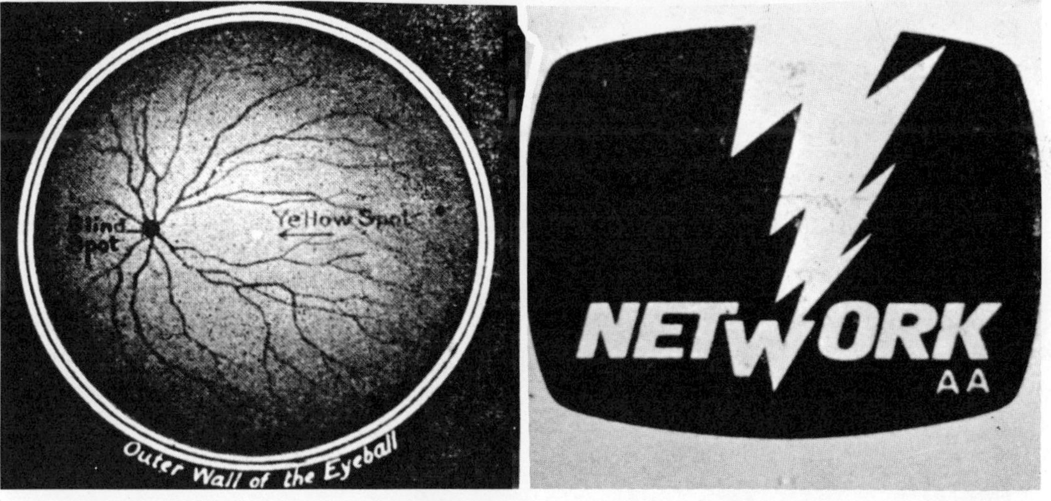

It was the astronomer Kepler who, in 1604, first realised the true function of the retina – that it is the screen on which an image from the lens is formed. This hypothesis was tested experimentally by Scheiner, in 1625. He cut away the outer coating (the *sclera* and the *choriod*) from the back of an ox's eye, leaving the retina revealed as a semi-transparent film. Scheiner saw a small upside-down image on the retina of the ox's eye.

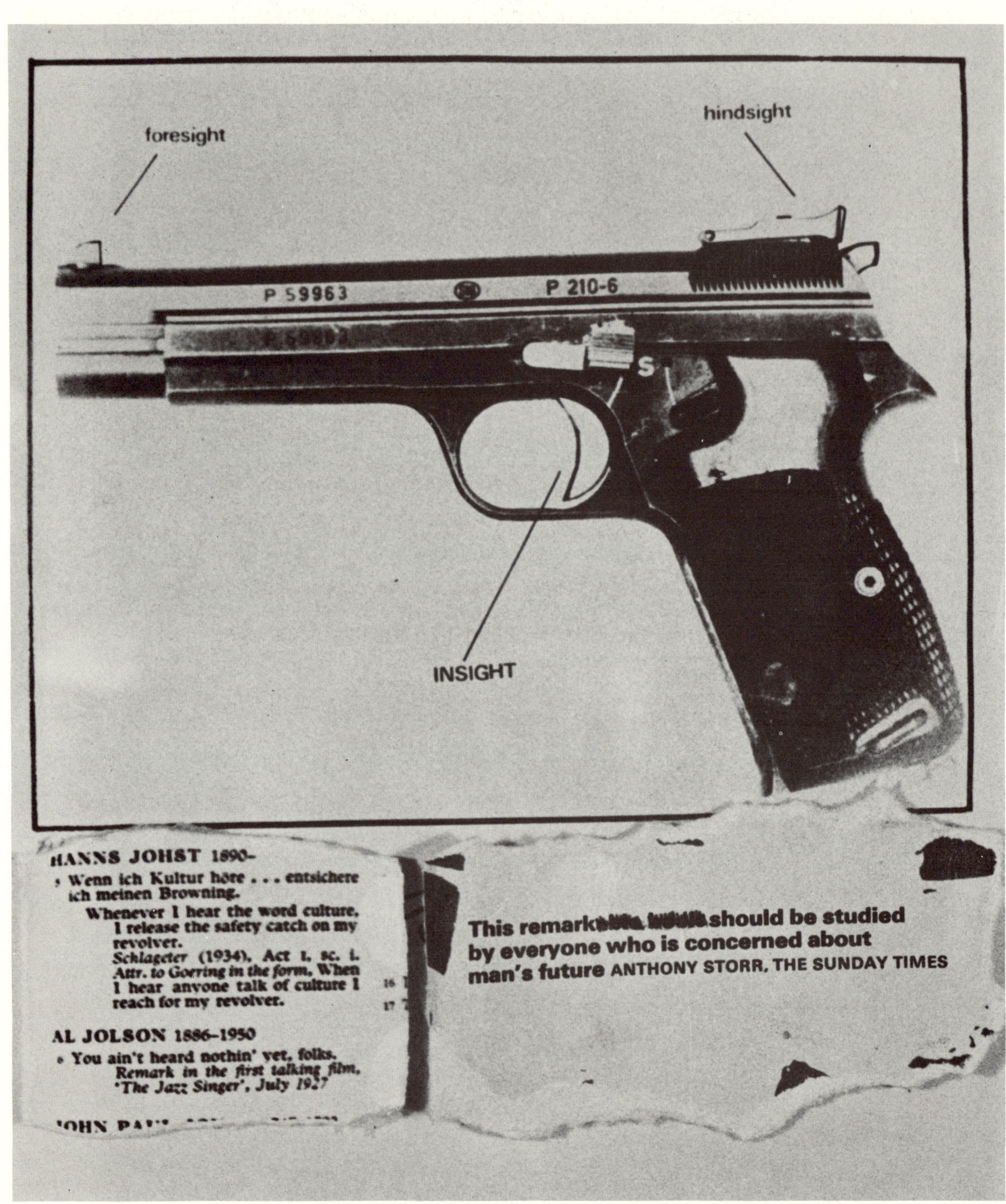

The silent picture

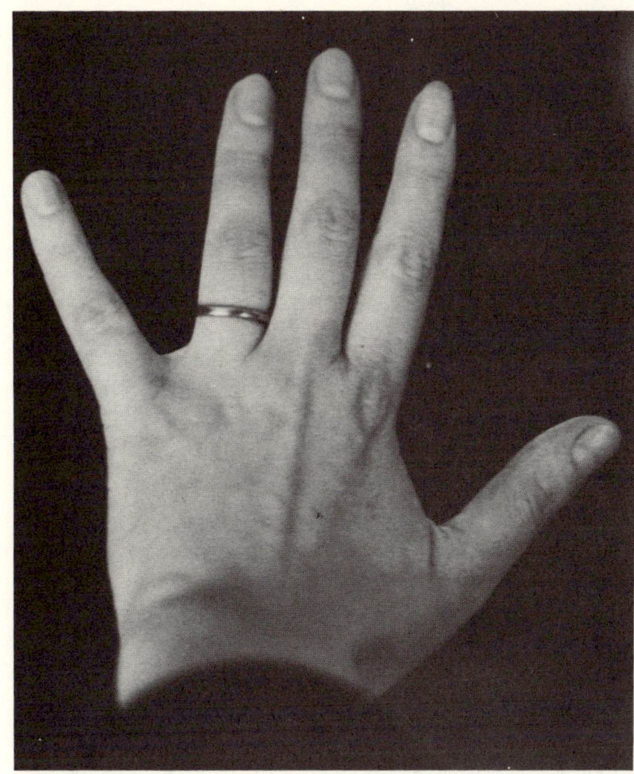

The trigger finger

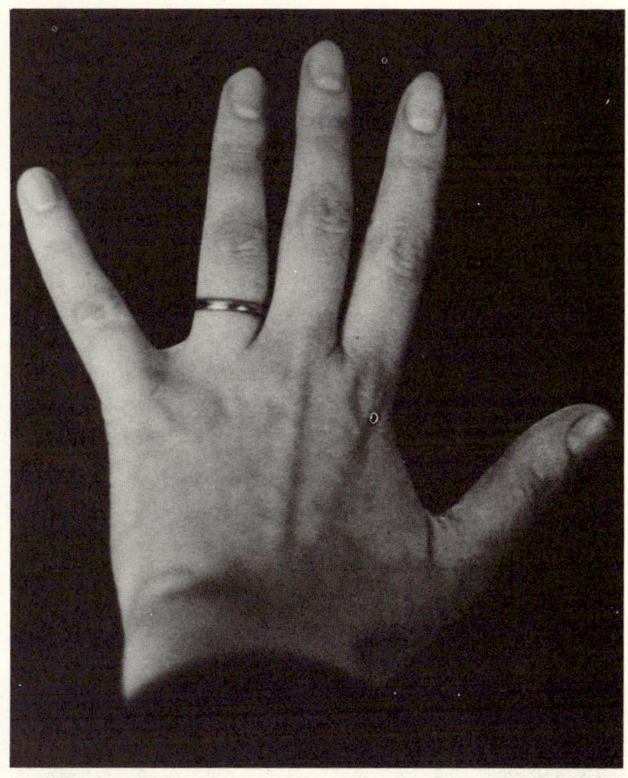

The one man band

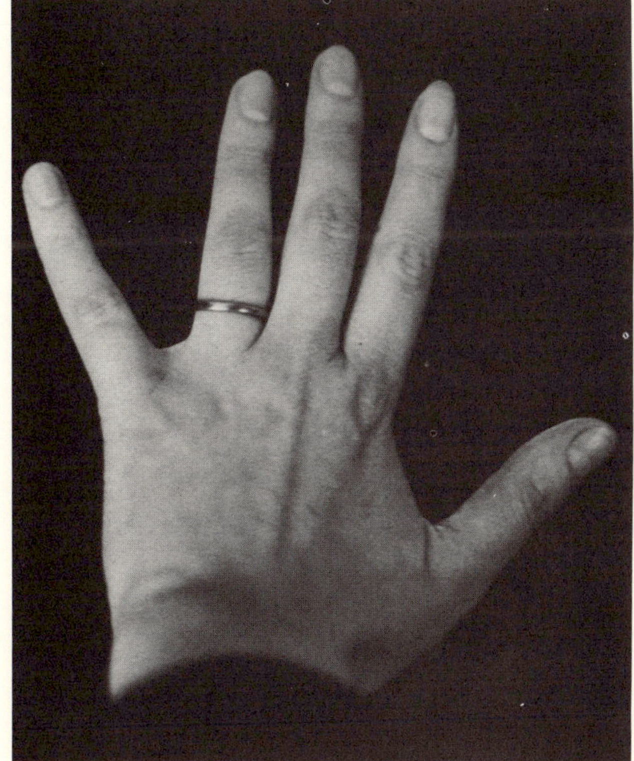

The elephant of surprise

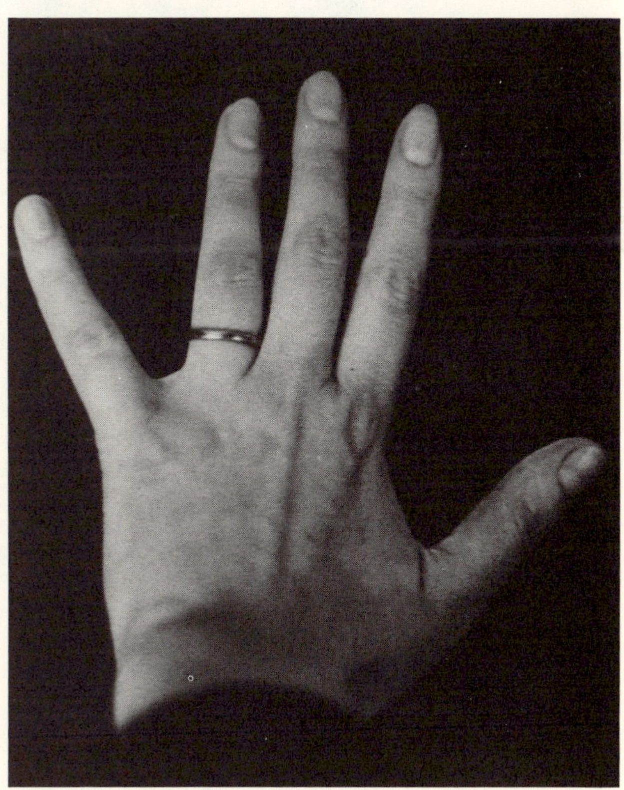

Au is for Authority

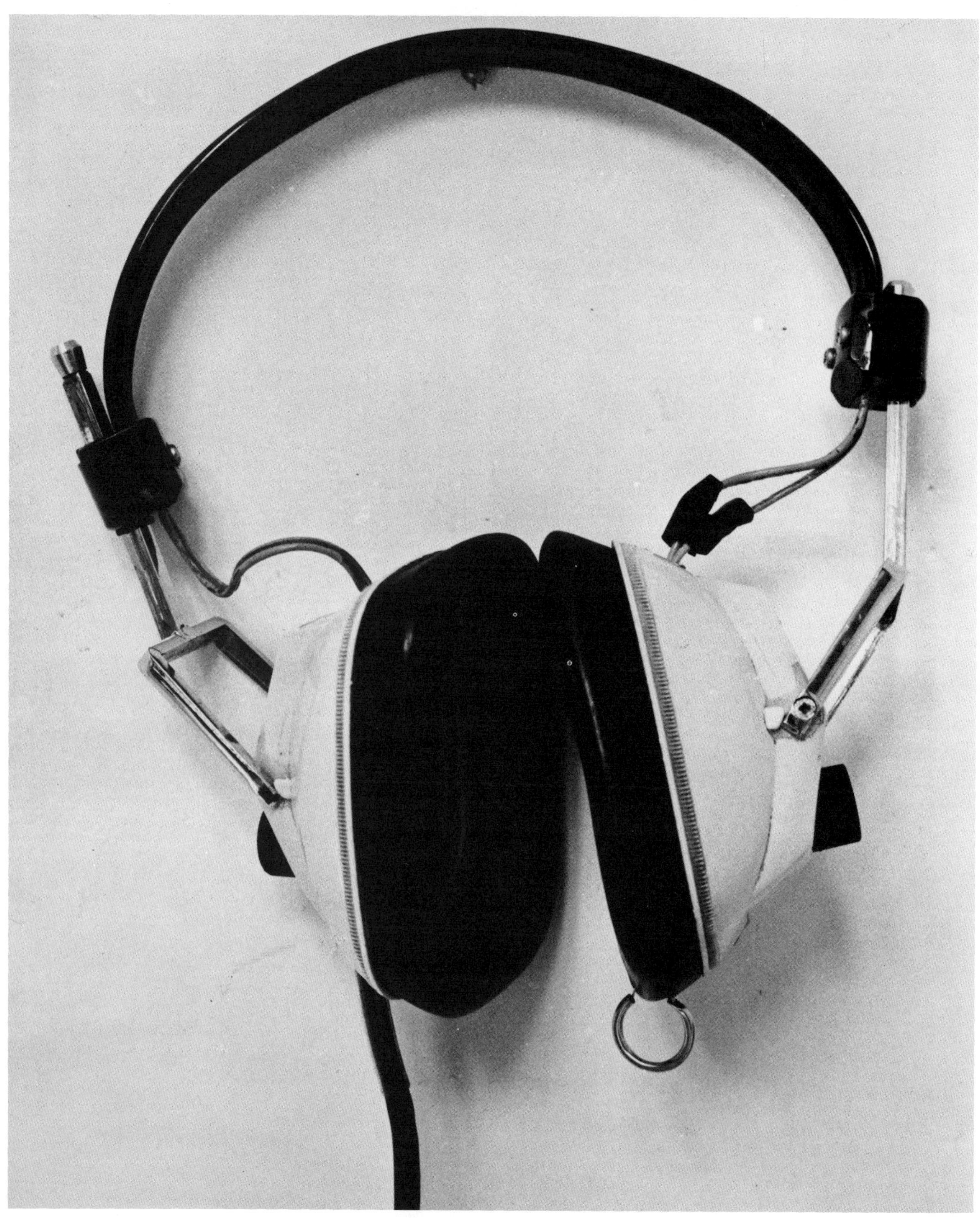

Symbol to nose ratio

The hills are alive with the sound of Hoover

A still from the soundtrack

Stop me if you've heard it

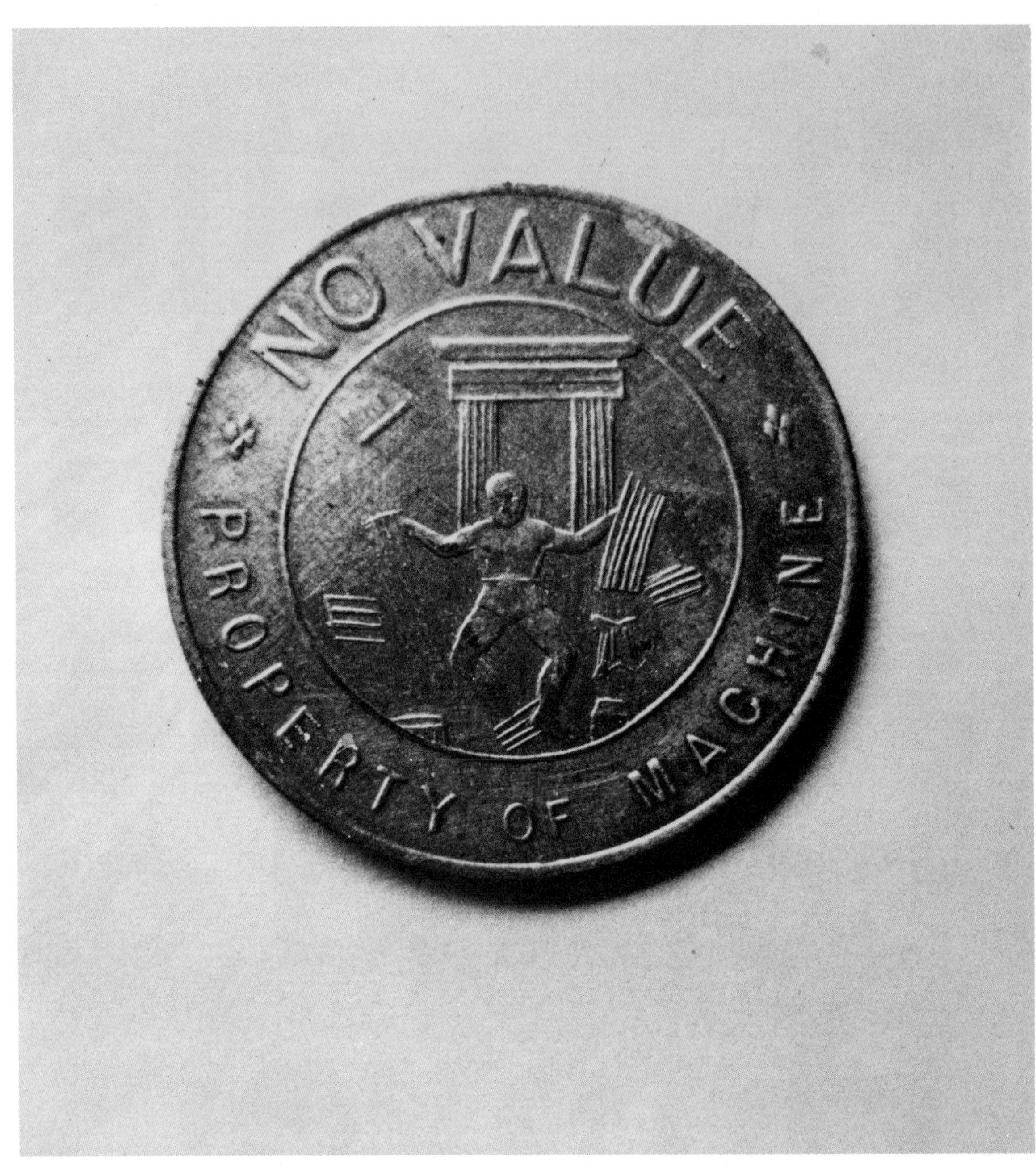

Automatopoeia

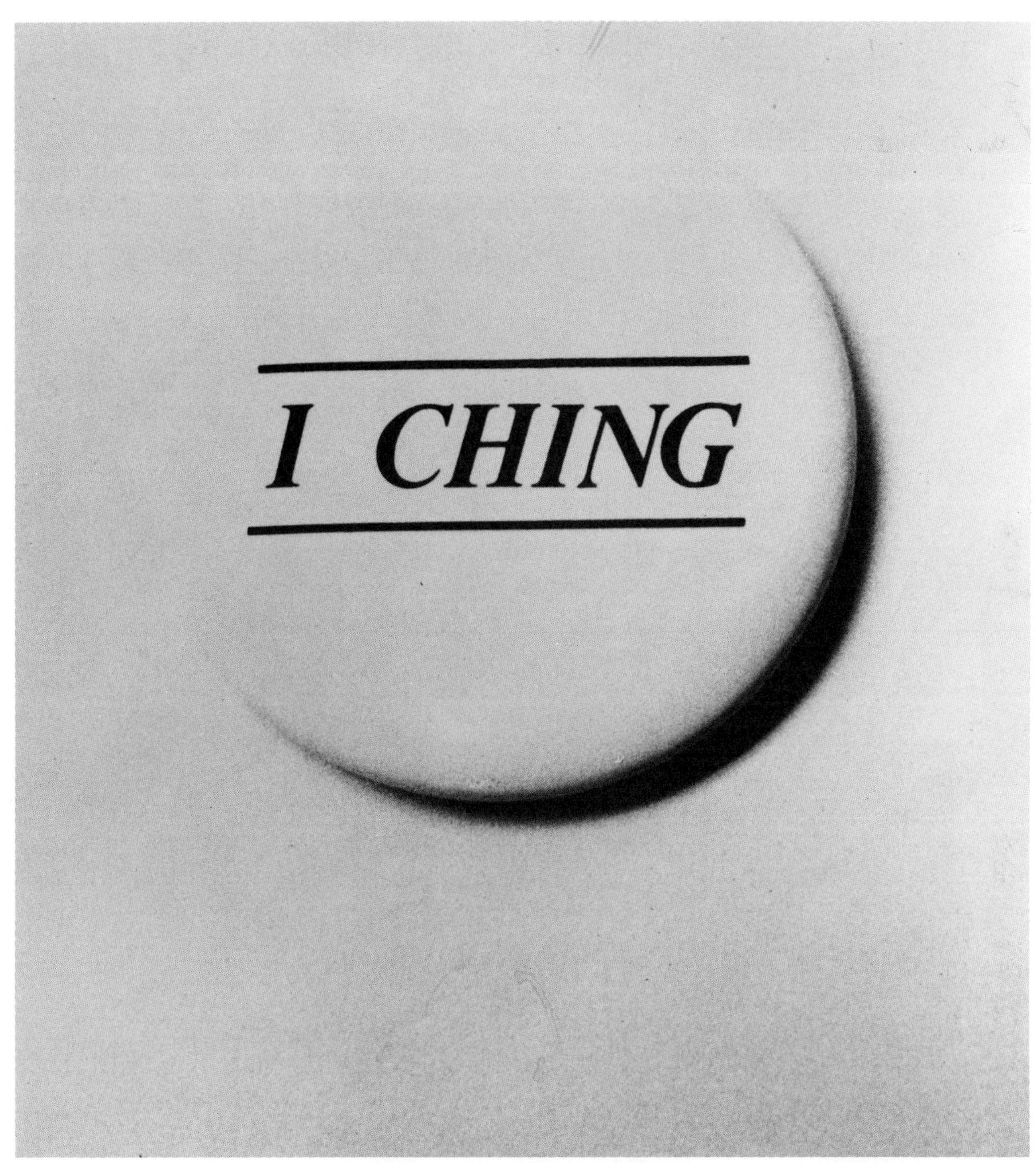

The sound of a penny dropping

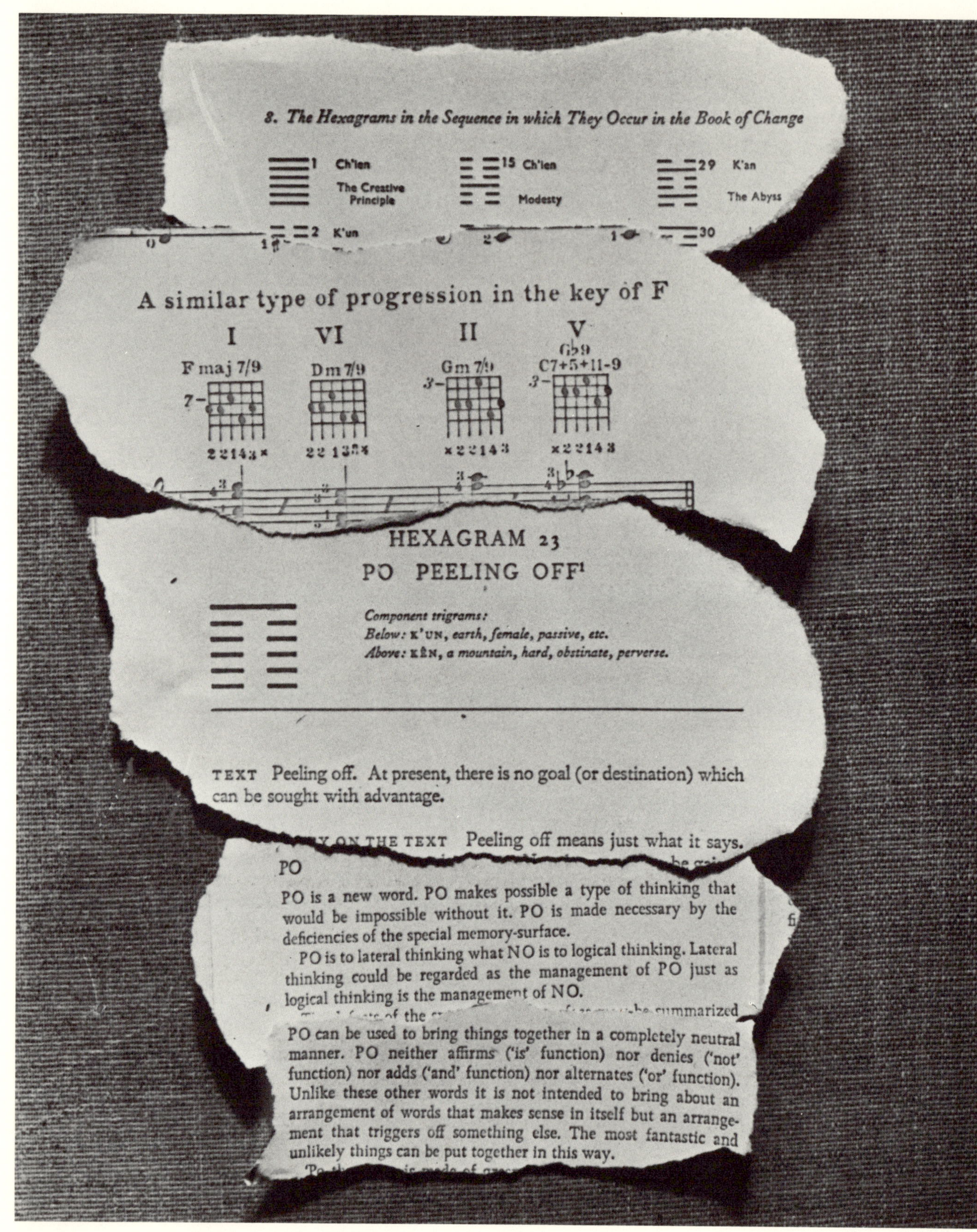

How strange the change from Asia to minor

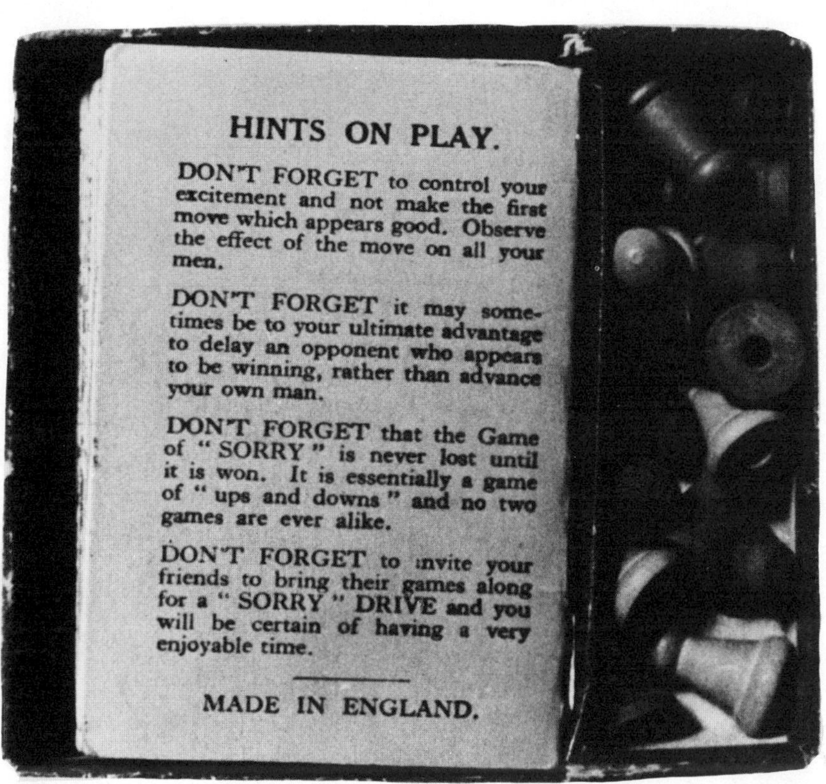
HINTS ON PLAY.
DON'T FORGET to control your excitement and not make the first move which appears good. Observe the effect of the move on all your men.
DON'T FORGET it may sometimes be to your ultimate advantage to delay an opponent who appears to be winning, rather than advance your own man.
DON'T FORGET that the Game of " SORRY " is never lost until it is won. It is essentially a game of " ups and downs " and no two games are ever alike.
DON'T FORGET to invite your friends to bring their games along for a " SORRY " DRIVE and you will be certain of having a very enjoyable time.
MADE IN ENGLAND.

'pology

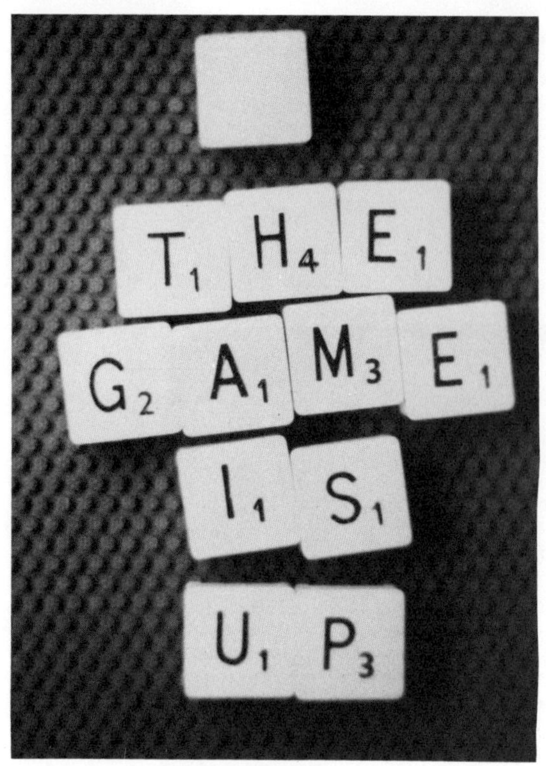

The name of the game

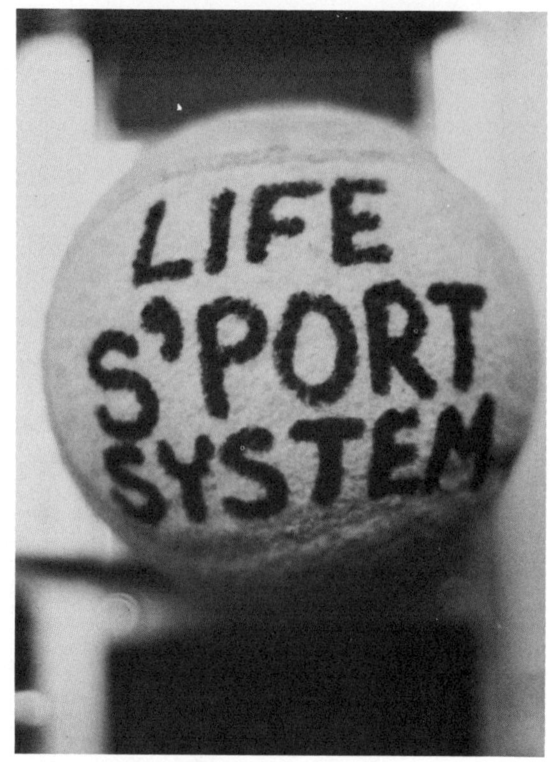

The address of the game

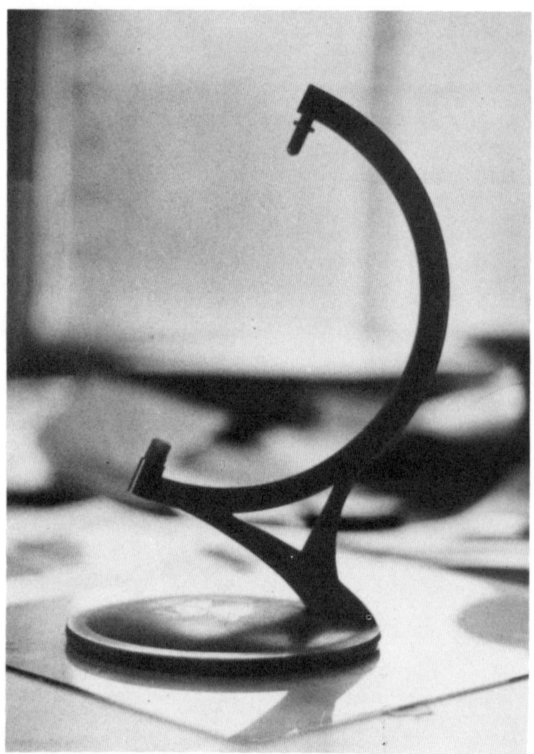

My italics

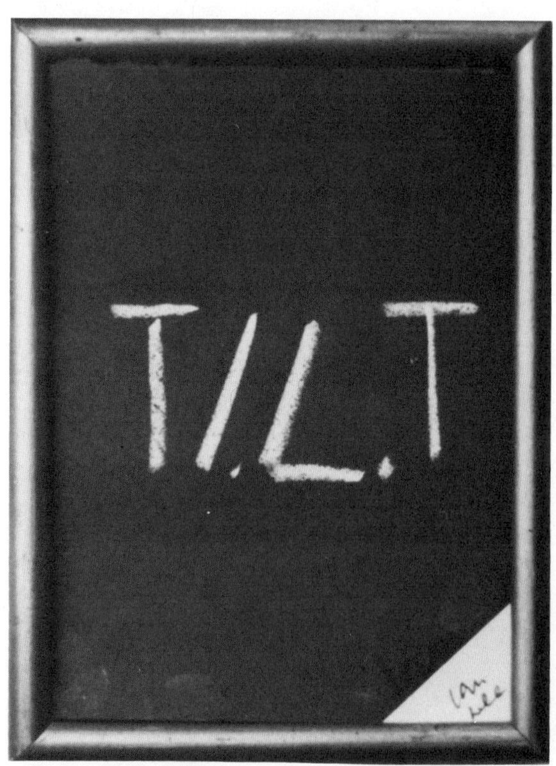

Internal ~~Logic~~ language

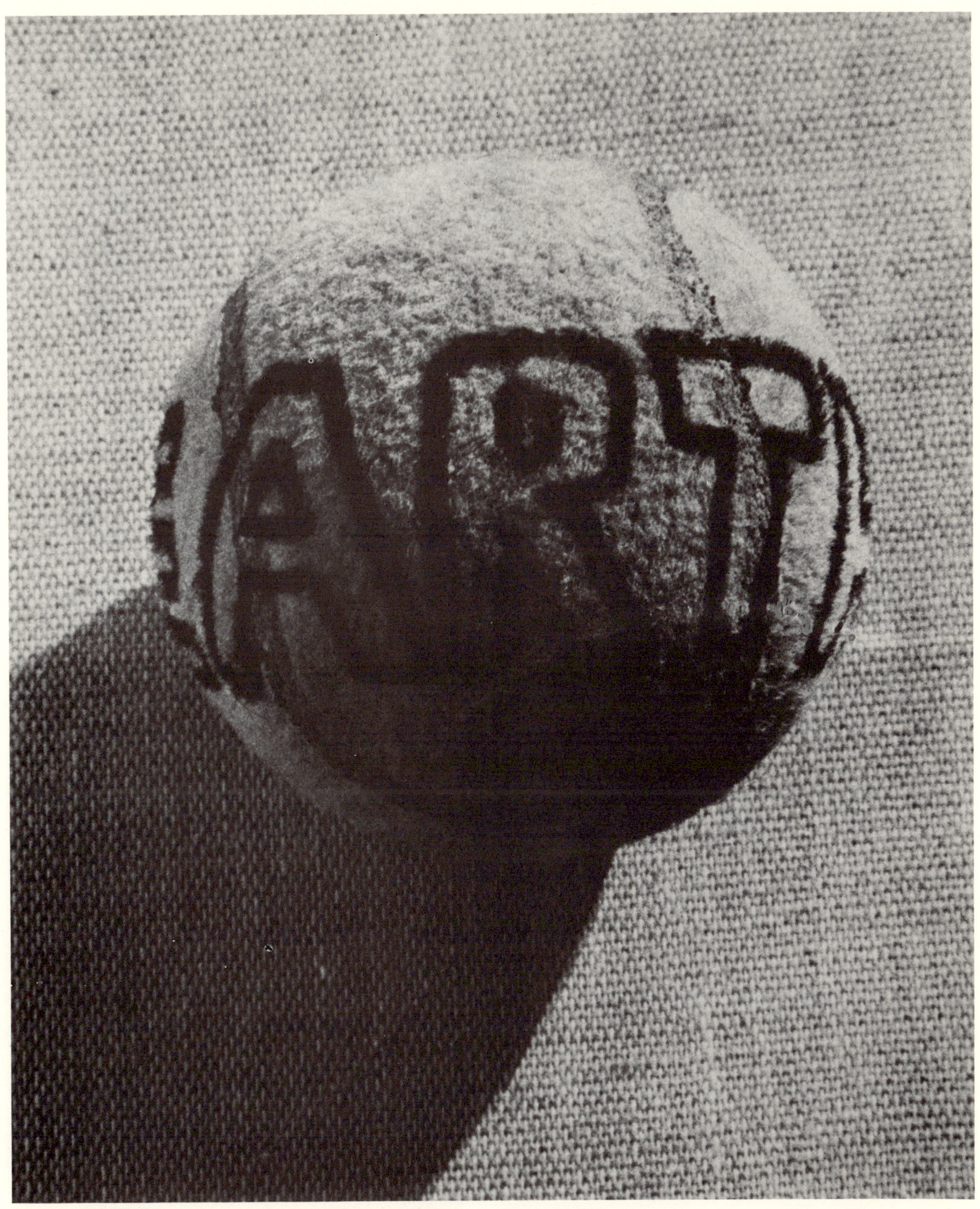

The man is the moon

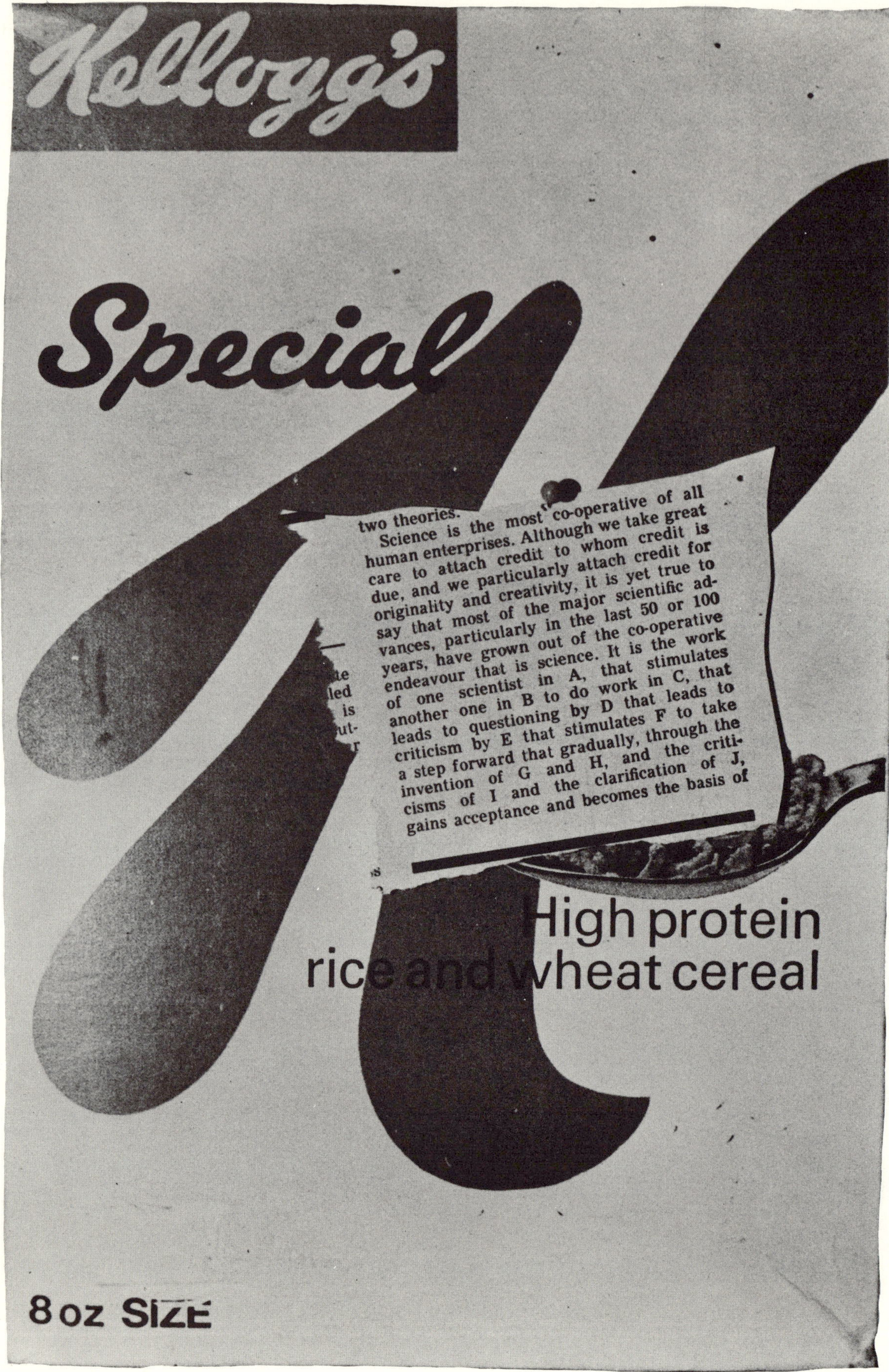
Kellogg's
Special K
two theories.
Science is the most co-operative of all human enterprises. Although we take great care to attach credit to whom credit is due, and we particularly attach credit for originality and creativity, it is yet true to say that most of the major scientific advances, particularly in the last 50 or 100 years, have grown out of the co-operative endeavour that is science. It is the work of one scientist in A, that stimulates another one in B to do work in C, that leads to questioning by D that leads to criticism by E that stimulates F to take a step forward that gradually, through the invention of G and H, and the criticisms of I and the clarification of J, gains acceptance and becomes the basis of
High protein
rice and wheat cereal
8 oz SIZE

Fig 1

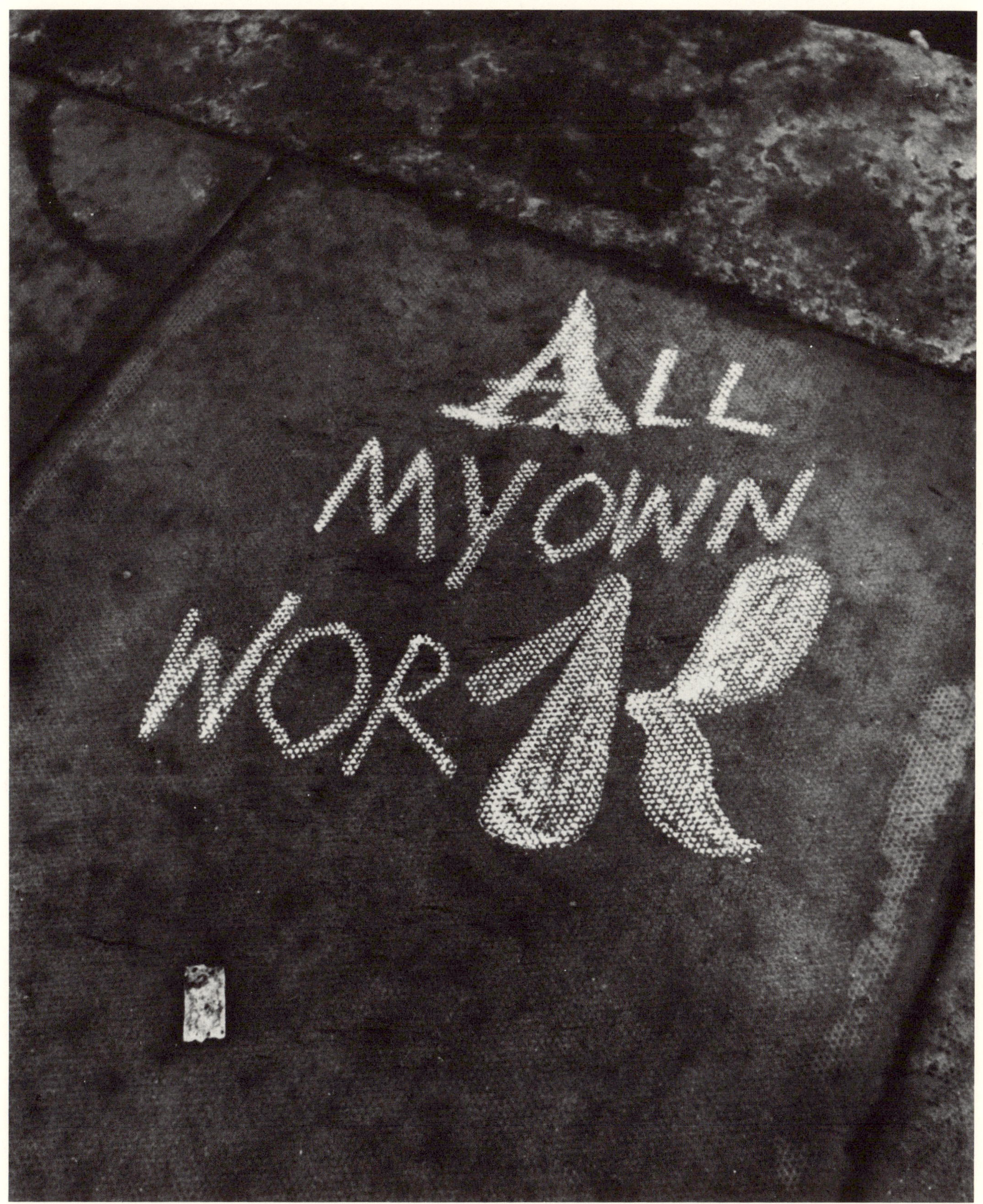

Fig 2

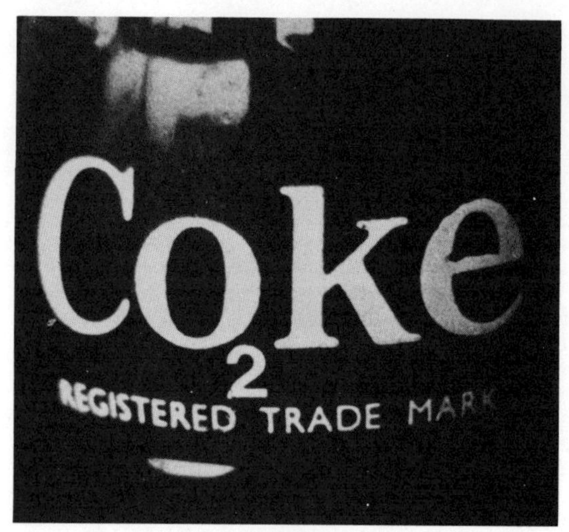

Fig 2

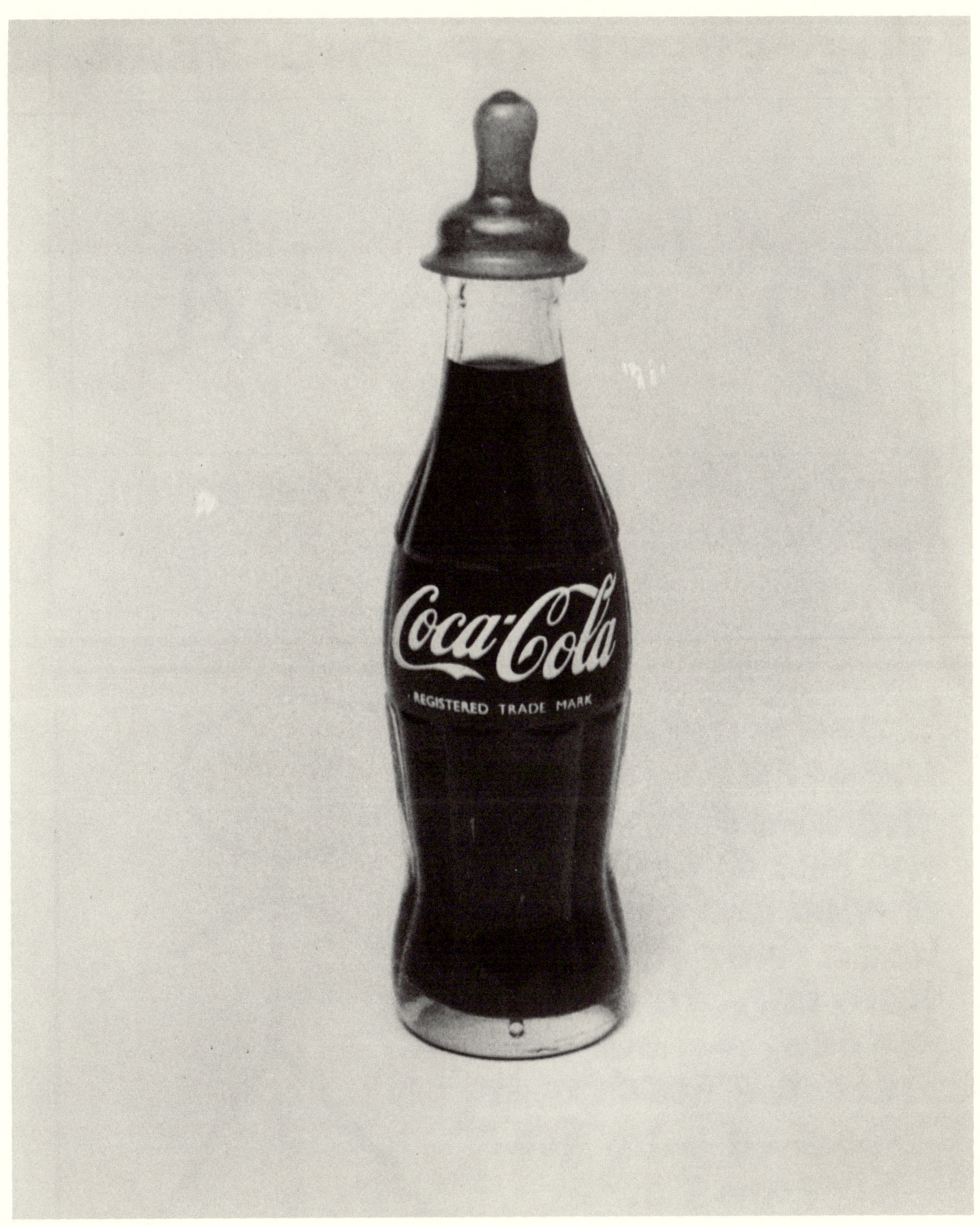

Fig 1

THE EVENT OF THE YEAR.

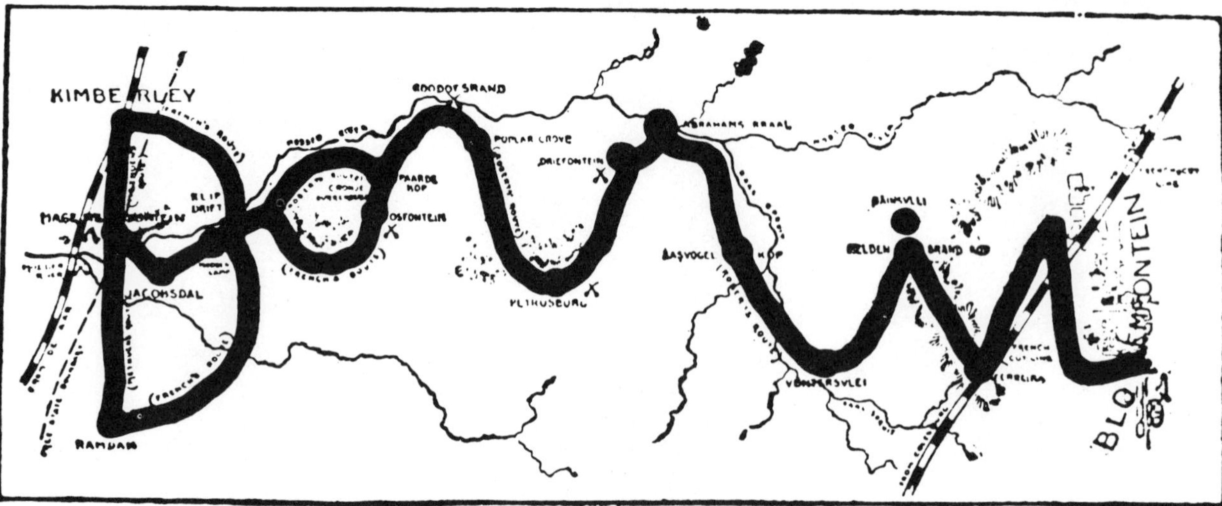

How Lord Roberts wrote BOVRIL.

Careful examination of this Map will show that the route followed by Lord Roberts in his historical march to Kimberley and Bloemfontein has made an indelible imprint of the word Bovril on the face of the Orange Free State.

This extraordinary coincidence is one more proof of the universality of Bovril, which has already figured so conspicuously throughout the South African Campaign.

Whether for the Soldier on the Battlefield, the Patient in the Sick-room, the Cook in the Kitchen, or for those as yet in full health and strength at home, Bovril is Liquid Life.

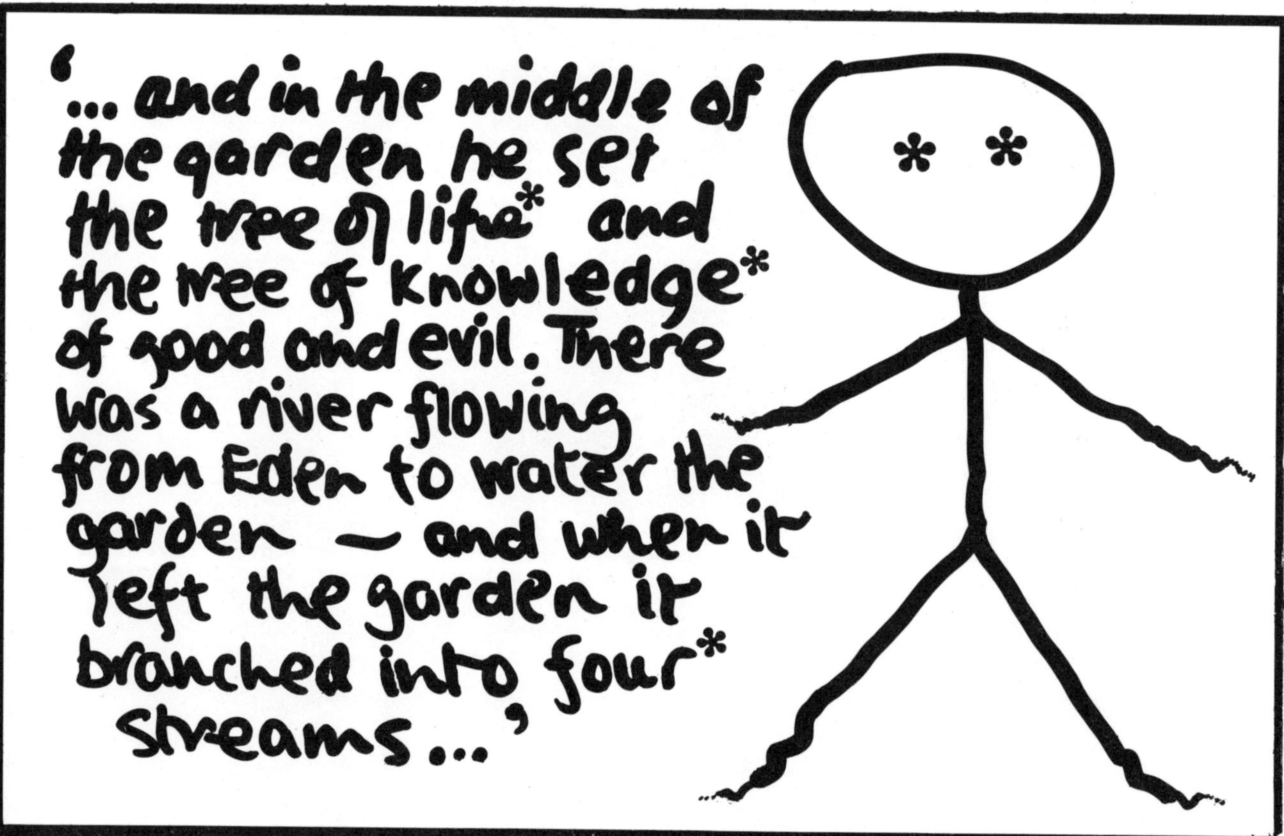

Critical Path Analysis

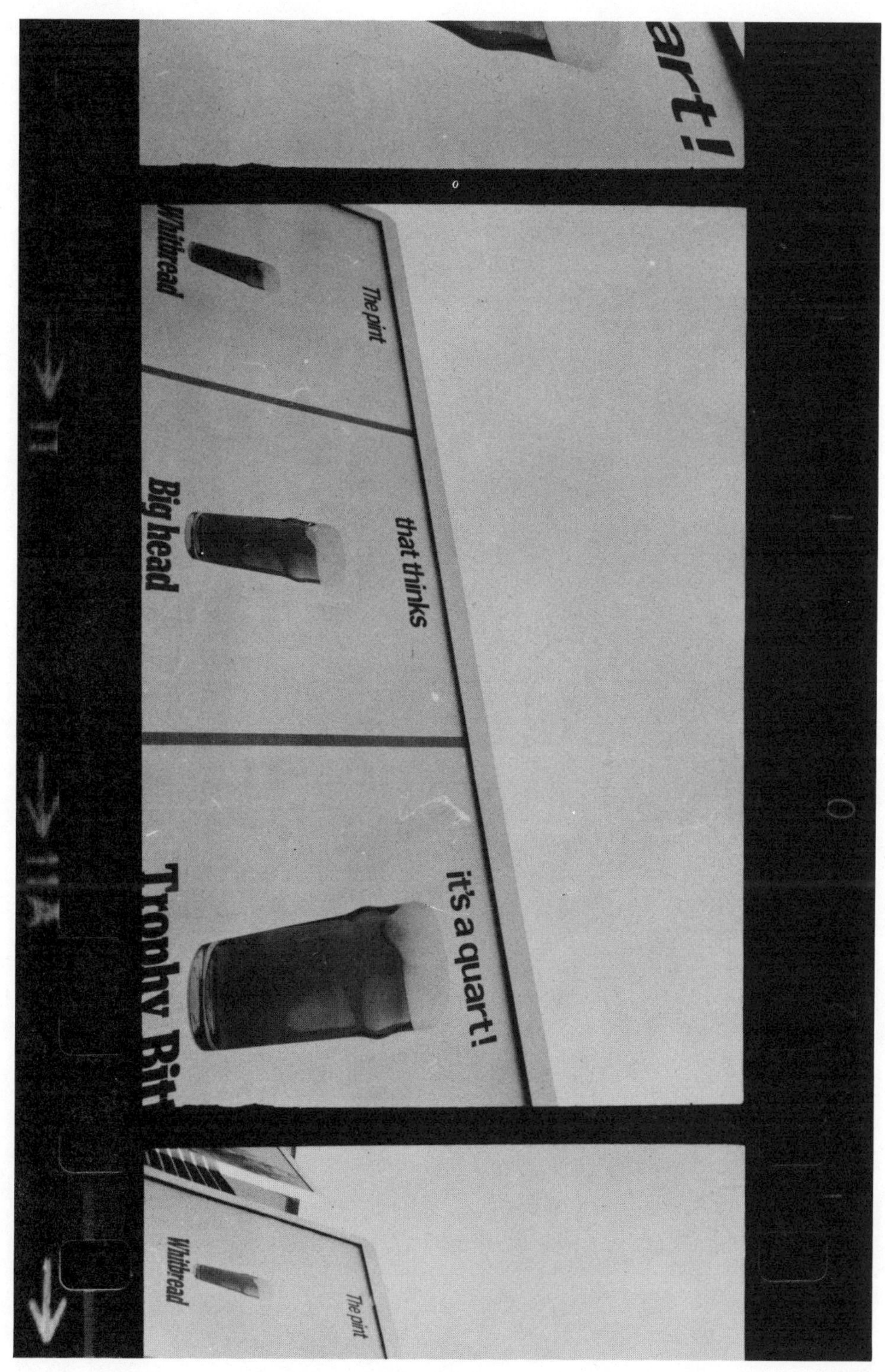

The shortest distance between two pints

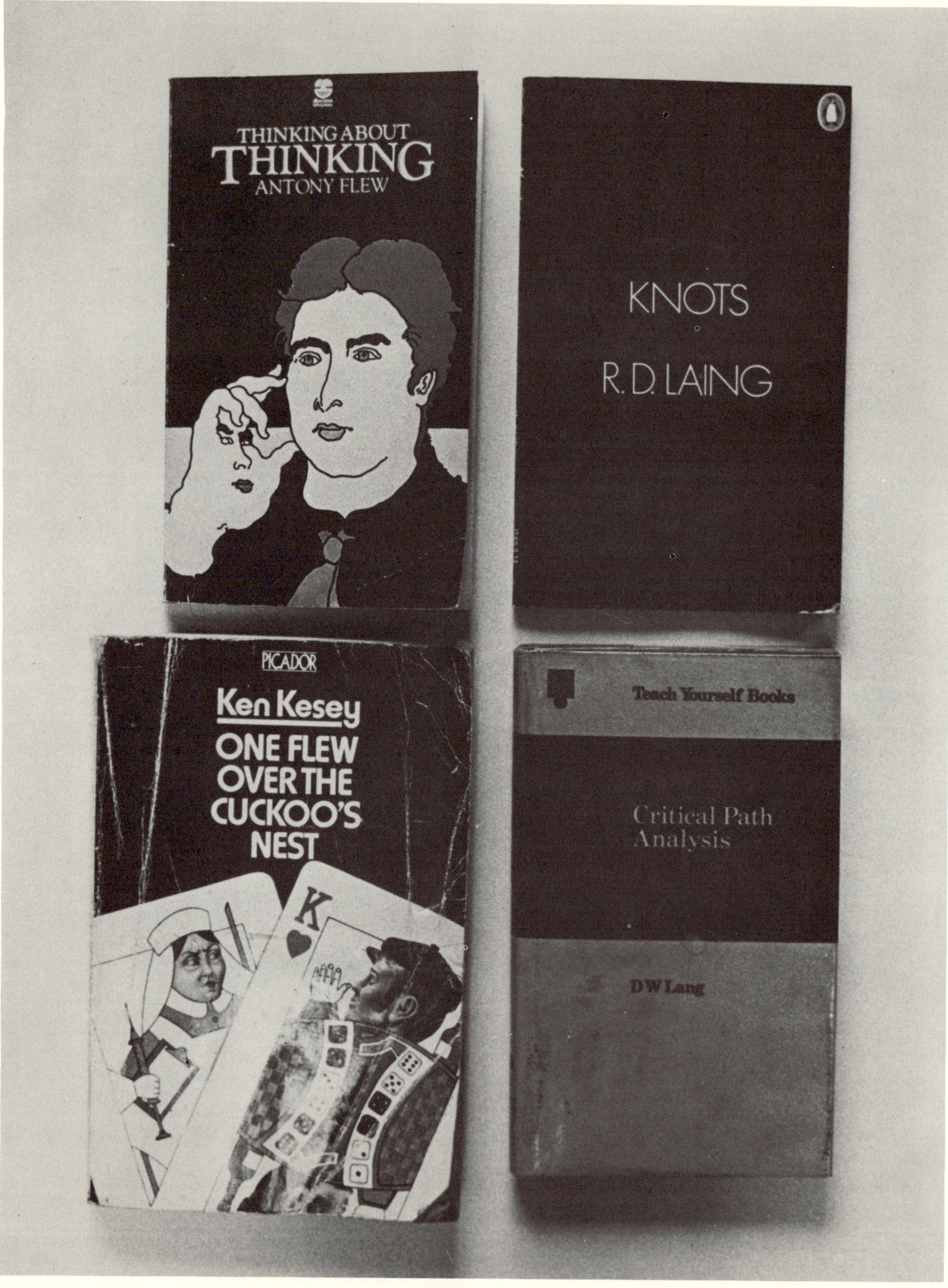
THINKING ABOUT
THINKING
ANTONY FLEW
KNOTS
R.D. LAING
PICADOR
Ken Kesey
ONE FLEW
OVER THE
CUCKOO'S
NEST
K
Teach Yourself Books
Critical Path
Analysis
D W Lang

Critical Path Analysis is the organized application of system reasoning for planning, scheduling, and controlling practical situations where many separate jobs, which make up the whole task, can happen simultaneously, almost simultaneously or in sequence such that it is difficult intuitively to establish the relationship between the separate jobs.

Fig 114 Photograph of a girl's face. Record of the eye movements during free examination of the photograph with both eyes for one minute.

C.P.A.

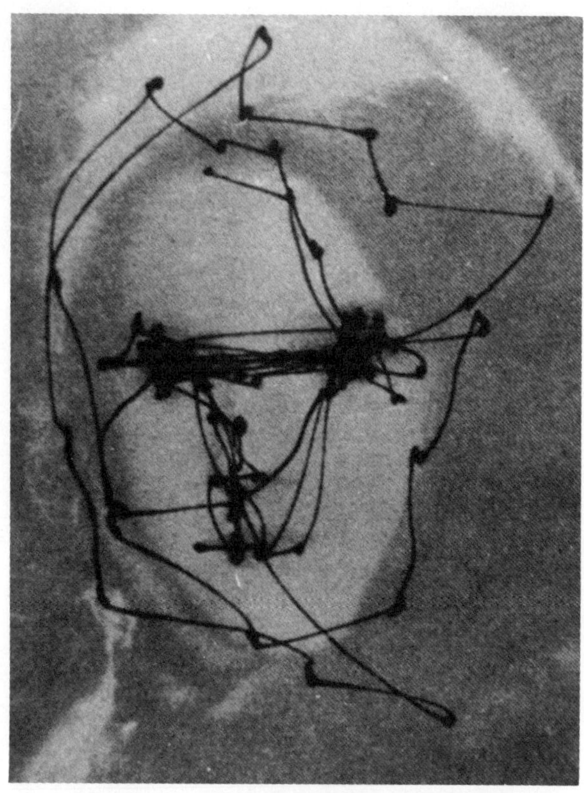

C.P.A.

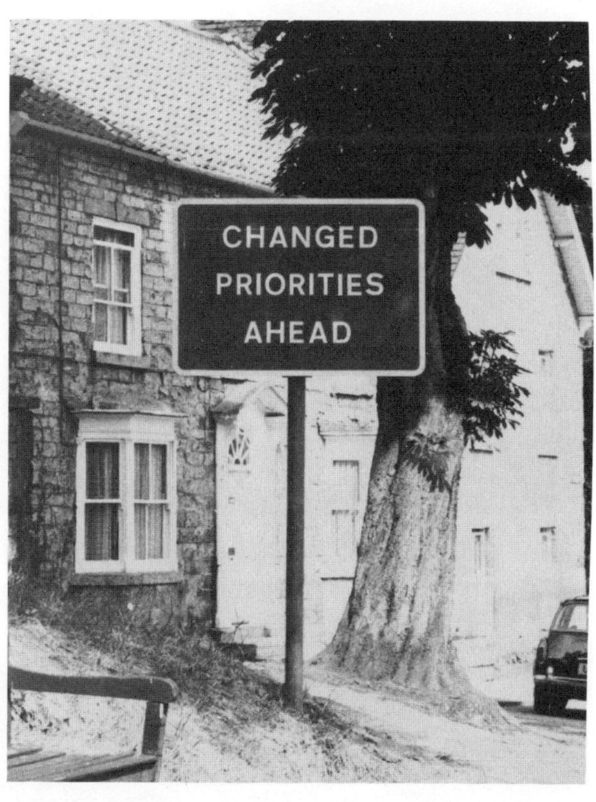

C.P.A.

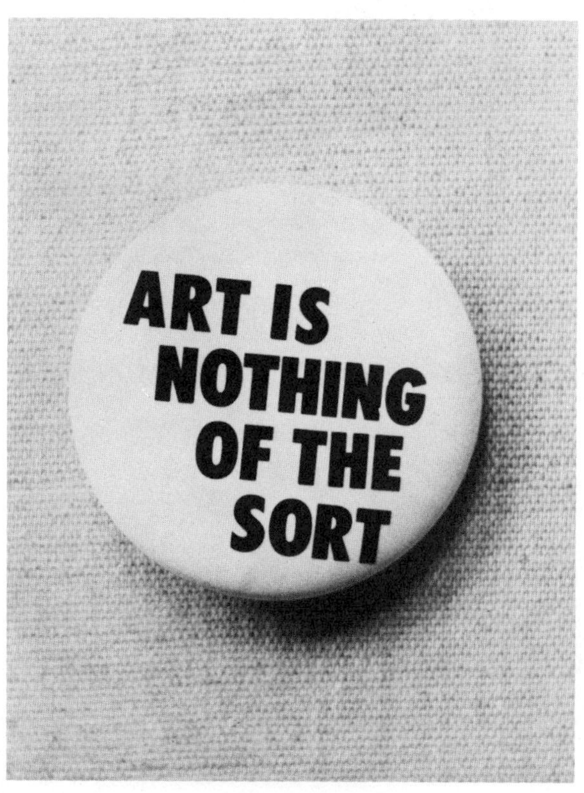

N.O.T.S.

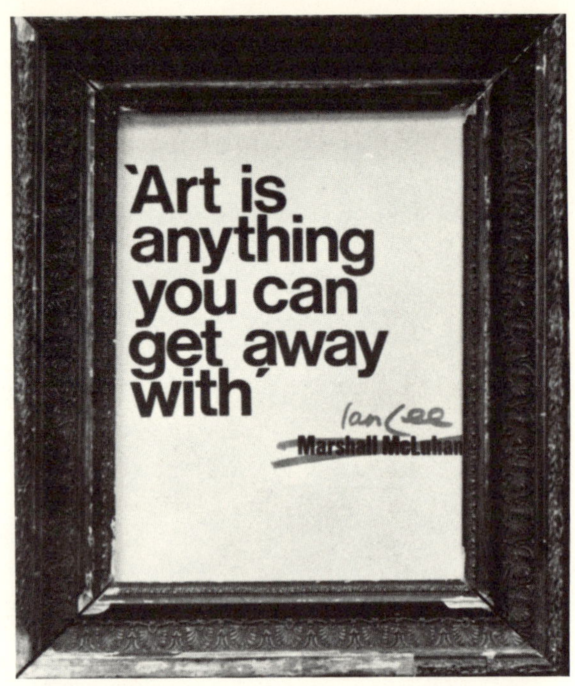

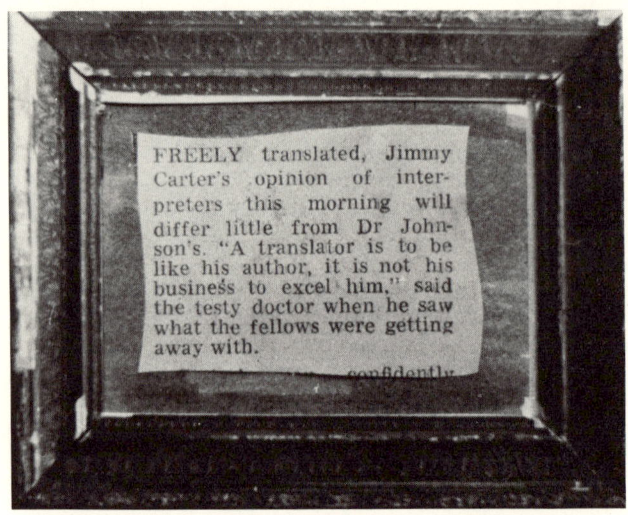
FREELY translated, Jimmy Carter's opinion of interpreters this morning will differ little from Dr Johnson's. "A translator is to be like his author, it is not his business to excel him," said the testy doctor when he saw what the fellows were getting away with.

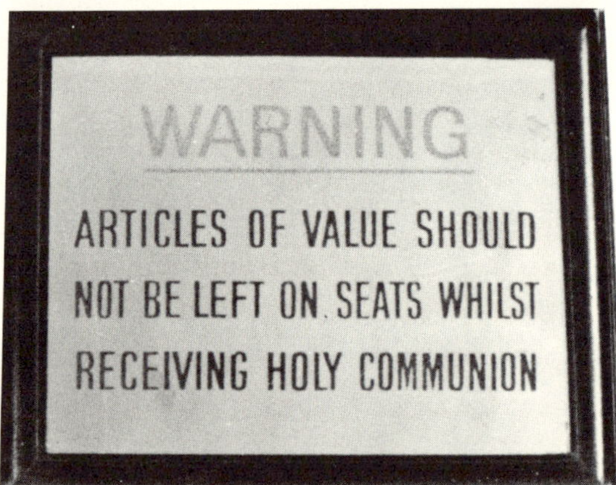

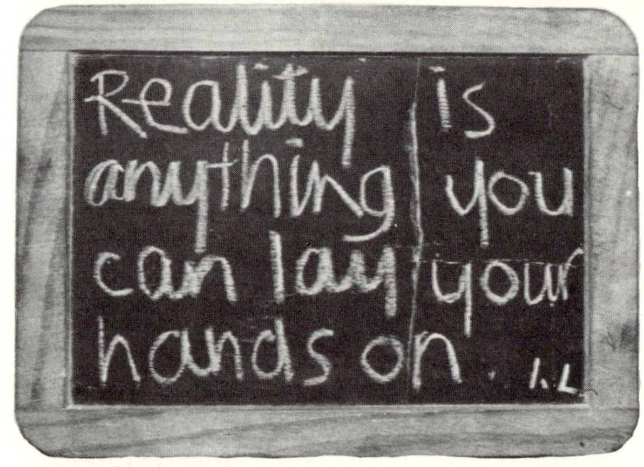

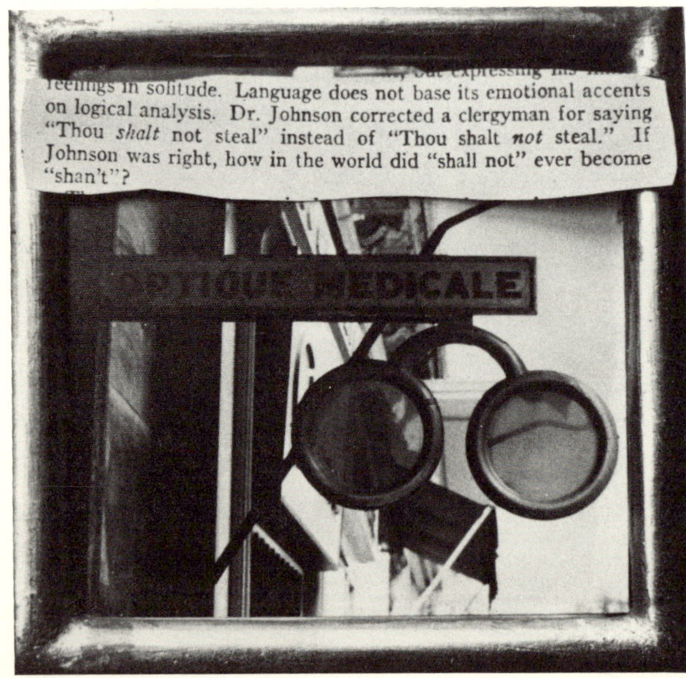
feelings in solitude. Language does not base its emotional accents on logical analysis. Dr. Johnson corrected a clergyman for saying "Thou *shalt* not steal" instead of "Thou shalt *not* steal." If Johnson was right, how in the world did "shall not" ever become "shan't"?

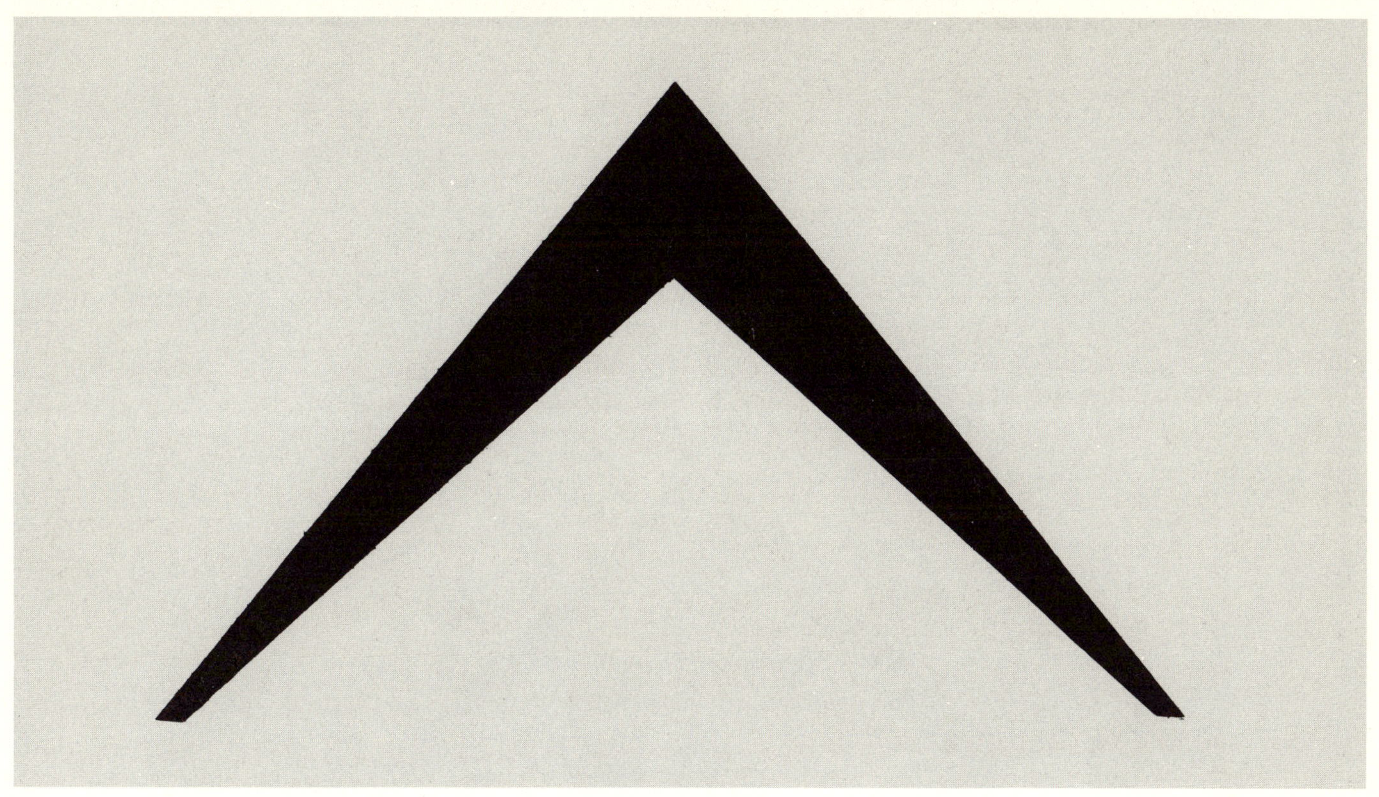

Rôle Theory

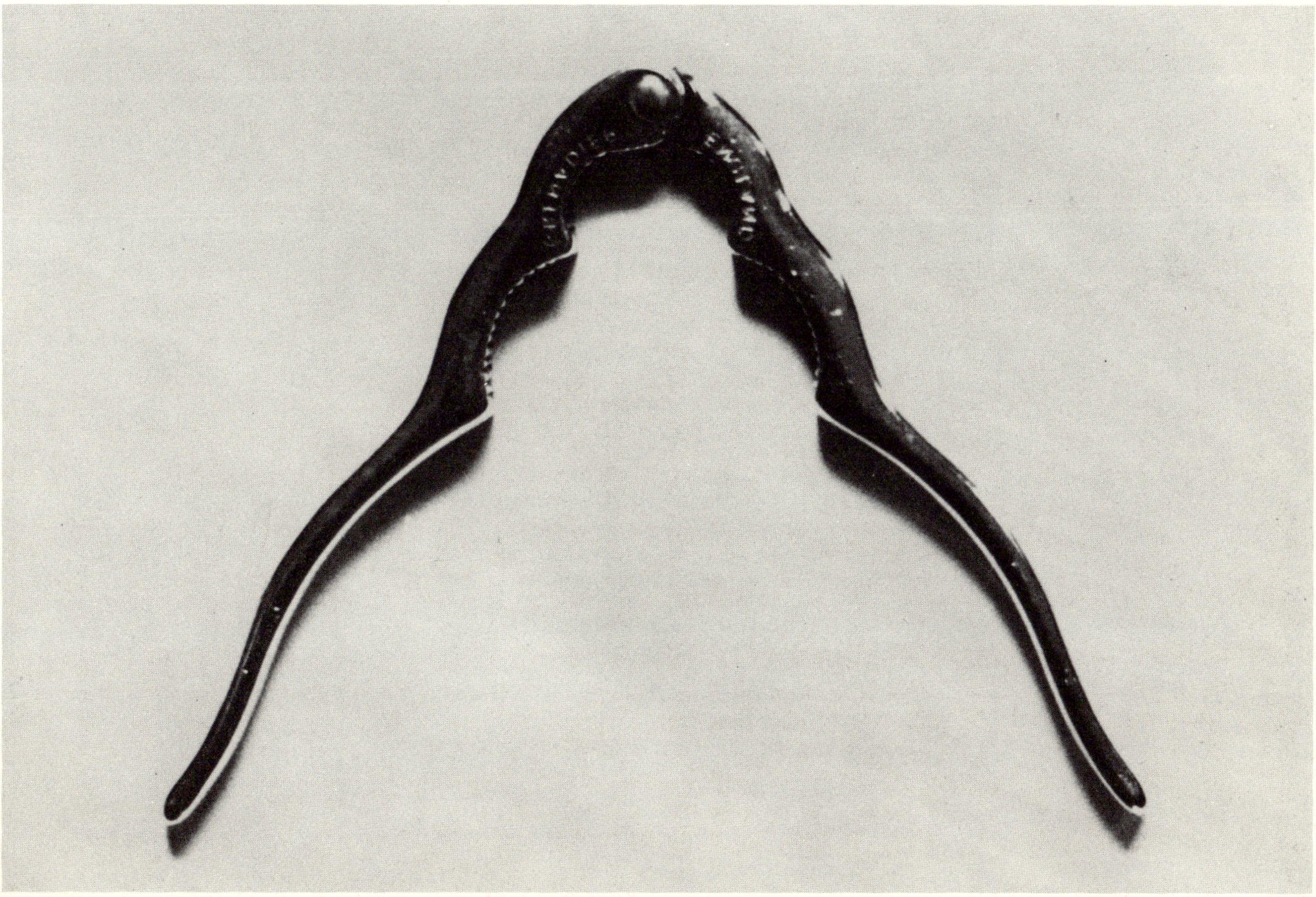

Apostrophe Theory...

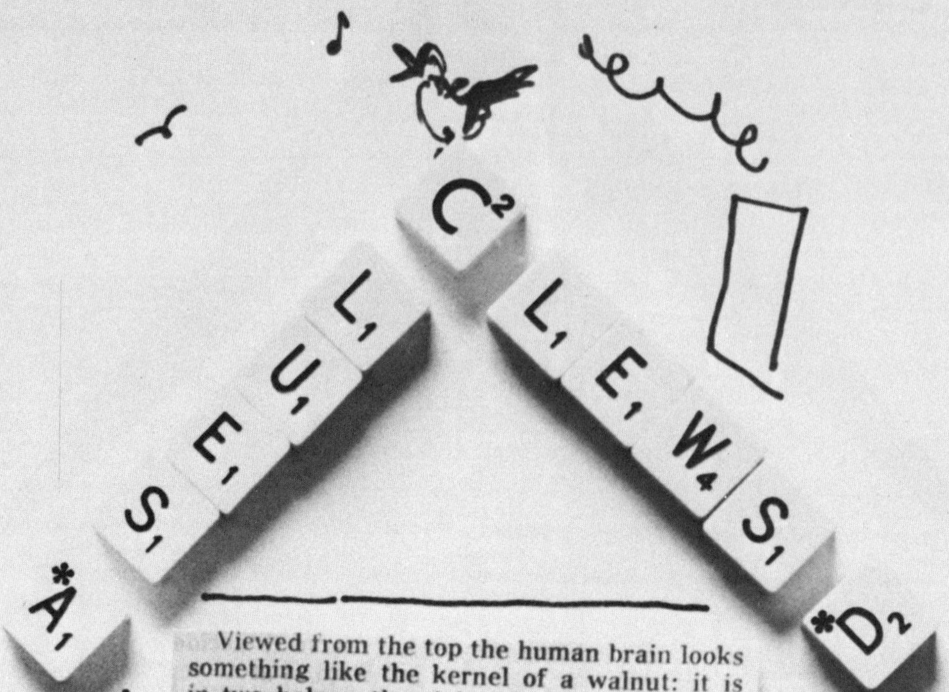

*A S E U L C L E W S *D

Viewed from the top the human brain looks something like the kernel of a walnut: it is in two halves, the right hemisphere and the left hemisphere. Because of a curious developmental quirk,

sequential information processing occurs in the left hemisphere and simultaneous processing in the right.

*A digital computer is usually a sequential machine. That is, successive portions of work are dealt with one-at-a-time, by the same sections of the computer. A store is necessary for keeping intermediate results until required, but the size of machine does not necessarily have to increase with the size of the job required.

*An analogue computer is a simultaneous machine. All sections of the computer are operational at the same time. Storage is not available, and larger jobs may require larger analogue computers.

In a digital computer, individually distinct values are processed.

In an analogue computer the values are continuously varying.
(See below for further explanation).

... in a nutshell ...

There are other signs which have gradually come to their present form from a shortened way of writing them. In an account we see that so many articles are charged @ a certain sum each. The @ is really a shortened way of writing *ad*, the Latin word for to or at. Account itself is

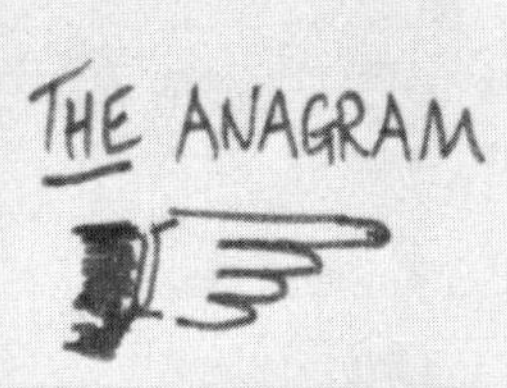

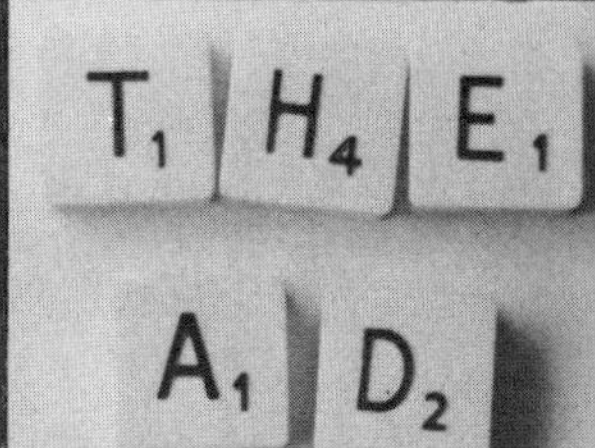

INPUT ⟶ AD ⟶ OUTPUT

AD is some acquisition device capable of receiving input data and of producing some output. A typical AD would be a computer which receives and produces information. We may regard the human mind as an AD. The input into the human mind will be the data received through sense-experience – sounds, colours, etc. The output will be a wide range of intellectual activities – for example, the ability to operate with some concept, like that of causality. The question is:

Who was that A1 D2 I saw you with last knight?

Reflection and Refraction of Light 143

The ratio of the speed of light in a vacuum to the speed in a given material is called the **index of refraction** of the material. This quantity, represented by the symbol *n*, determines the extent of the bending of

D2 'n' A1

Discovering for yourself

3. Find seven quickest routes for a Queen to move, from a1 to d5.

[Solutions to this quiz are on page 136.]

11. The Knight ♘ N

The Knight, unlike other pieces, does not move in a straight line. It moves in the shape of a letter L. These are the L-shaped patterns the Knight follows in making one move.

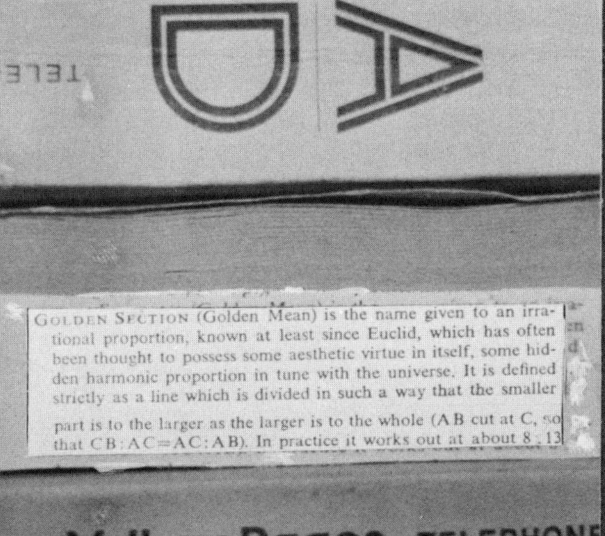

GOLDEN SECTION (Golden Mean) is the name given to an irrational proportion, known at least since Euclid, which has often been thought to possess some aesthetic virtue in itself, some hidden harmonic proportion in tune with the universe. It is defined strictly as a line which is divided in such a way that the smaller part is to the larger as the larger is to the whole (AB cut at C, so that CB:AC=AC:AB). In practice it works out at about 8 : 13

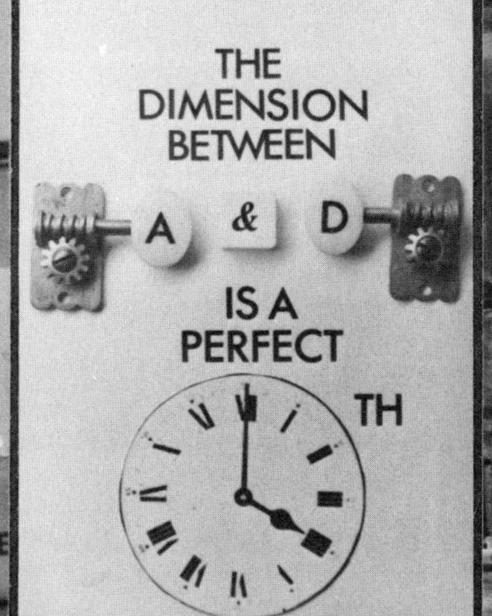

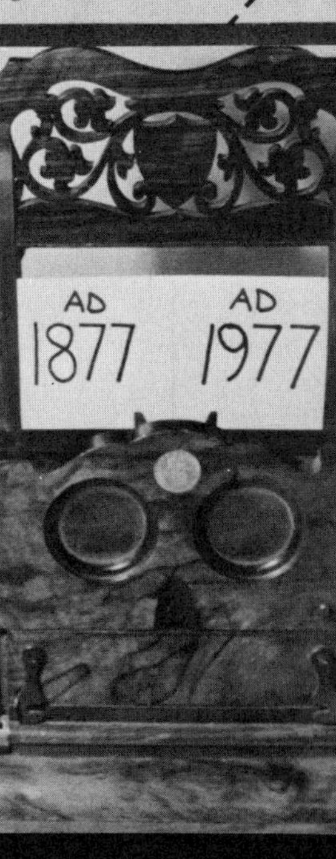

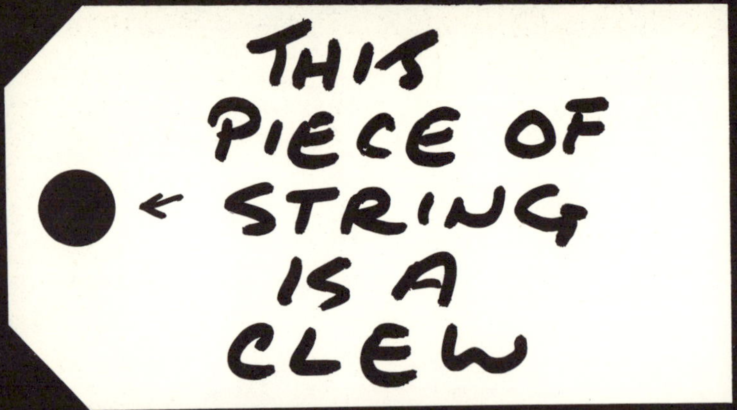

THIS PIECE OF ← STRING IS A CLEW

The question "How long is it *really*?" (or "How long is it in th eye of God") is meaningless, since there are no conceivable op erations by which an answer may be found. The full significanc of this position was accurately perceived by the physicist Philip Frank when he stated that Einstein's relativity was "a reform i semantics, not in metaphysics."

semaphore 1294

loosely, deliberate distortion or twisting of meaning, as in some types of advertising, propaganda, etc. 5. *see* GENERAL SEMANTICS

sem·a·phore (sem′ə fôr′) *n.* [Fr. *sémaphore* < Gr. *sēma*, a sign (see SEMANTIC) + *-phoros:* see -PHOROUS] 1. any apparatus for signaling, as by an arrangement of lights, flags, and mechanical arms on rail-

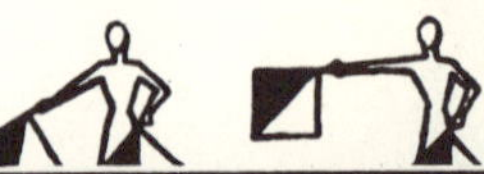

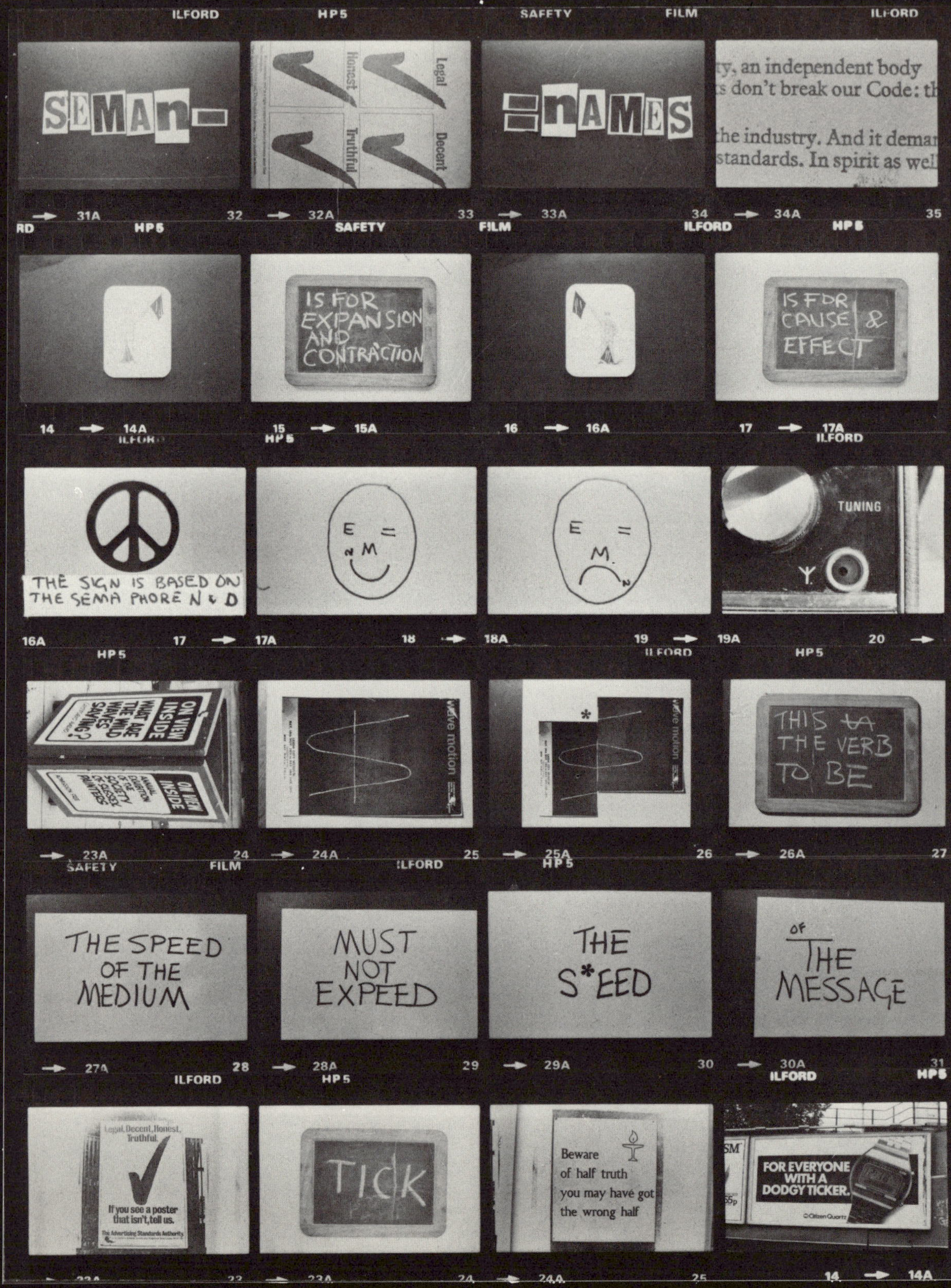

SEMAn-

Honest Legal Truthful Decent

NAMES

ty, an independent body
s don't break our Code: th
he industry. And it demar
standards. In spirit as well

IS FOR EXPANSION AND CONTRACTION

IS FOR CAUSE & EFFECT

THE SIGN IS BASED ON THE SEMA PHORE N & D

TUNING

ON VIEW INSIDE WHAT ARE THE WILD WAVES SAYING?

wave motion

THIS IS THE VERB TO BE

THE SPEED OF THE MEDIUM

MUST NOT EXPEED

THE S*EED

OF THE MESSAGE

Legal, Decent, Honest, Truthful. If you see a poster that isn't, tell us. The Advertising Standards Authority.

TICK

Beware of half truth you may have got the wrong half

FOR EVERYONE WITH A DODGY TICKER.

We are unaware of the ticking of the clock, but aware that it has stopped. While reading we are unaware of the shape of the letters because the skill of transforming them into words is fully automatized, and awareness is focused on the meaning behind the shapes – a phenomenon known as the 'transparency' of language.

But some of the light passes from the first medium into the second. For many substances the amount of light which penetrates is very small; but for others, which have been called 'transparent,' a considerable fraction of the light enters. The behaviour of the light in passing from one medium to another must now be studied, and it is well to remember throughout that the proportion of light reflected or transmitted depends to a great extent upon the angle of incidence of the light, as well as upon the nature of the media concerned. The case of light passing from air to some other substance, such as water or glass, will first be considered. The ray is always bent towards the normal on entering a more dense medium. This bending is called **refraction.**

Do you understand what I mean?

Refraction finds its most useful application in **lenses**, which are an essential part of many optical devices, such as microscopes, projectors, spectacles, telescopes, cameras, range finders, etc. The purpose of a lens is to change the curvature of light waves—that is, to bend the rays— usually in order to form an image.

The ability of a lens to bring light to a focus is is where the heart lies. But also, where the hearth, the early center of home life. Hence, the center or common point of anything. (L. *focus*, hearth). The L. is from Gr. *phos*, from *phaos*, light, from *phainein*, to show,

YOU QUANTUM

metaphors, may serve to focus into one meaning many different meanings. This point is of some importance, since so much interpretation comes from supposing that if a word works one way it cannot simultaneously work in another way and have simultaneously another meaning.'

metaphormosis

Note that L. *lens*, *lent—*, a seed, is used now in Eng. of the *lens* of glass (from the shape);

*

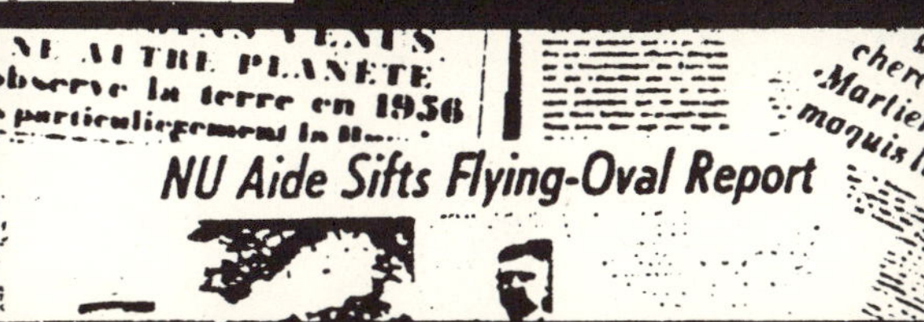
...AUTRE PLANETE
observe la terre en 1956
NU Aide Sifts Flying-Oval Report
cherch
Martien

YOU QUANTUM... : ME CHANICS

Light passing through air that is not all at the same temperature is refracted. This accounts for the twinkling of the stars

2·7 A lens can be thought of as a pair of converging prisms, forming an image from a bundle of rays. The image is far brighter than from a pinhole, but it is generally distorted in some degree, and the depth of focus is limited.

I REMEMBER THE STAR OF DAVID WHEN HE WAS JUST A TWINKLE IN HIS MOTHER'S EYE!

*

As someone wrote the other day, remarking in passing that the entire galaxy was once compressed into a primeval seed a tenth of a millimetre long, the necessary calculations are in quantum mechanics, a language that few can speak or are ever likely to.

symbol.
This was originally a token, in the form of an object broken in twain, so that identity could be proved by having the two parts match (as in

blurrb

the Cabalistic symbol of two overlapping triangles. These two triangles should be seen as inscribed in a circle: they represent the poles, the tropics, and the ecliptic, besides having the addeo meaning of the male and female elements coming together to generate the cosmos.

the seemingly innocuous *obiter dicta*, the words in passing, that give the game away.

What I saw before me was the critic-in-chief of the *New York Times* saying: in looking at a painting today 'to lack a persuasive theory is to lack something crucial.' I read it again. It didn't say 'something helpful' or 'enriching' or even 'extremely valuable'. No, the word was *crucial*.

In short: frankly, these days, without a theory to go with it I can't *see* a painting.

Then and there I experienced a flash known as the *Aha!* phenomenon,

The symbol '*e*' stands for the quantum energy, 'ν' (the Greek letter 'nu') for the frequency, and '*h*' for 'Planck's constant', which gives the proportional relation between quantum energy and frequency.

nu?

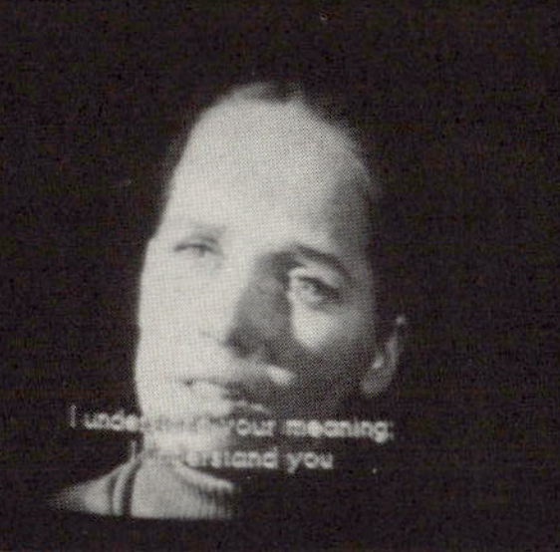

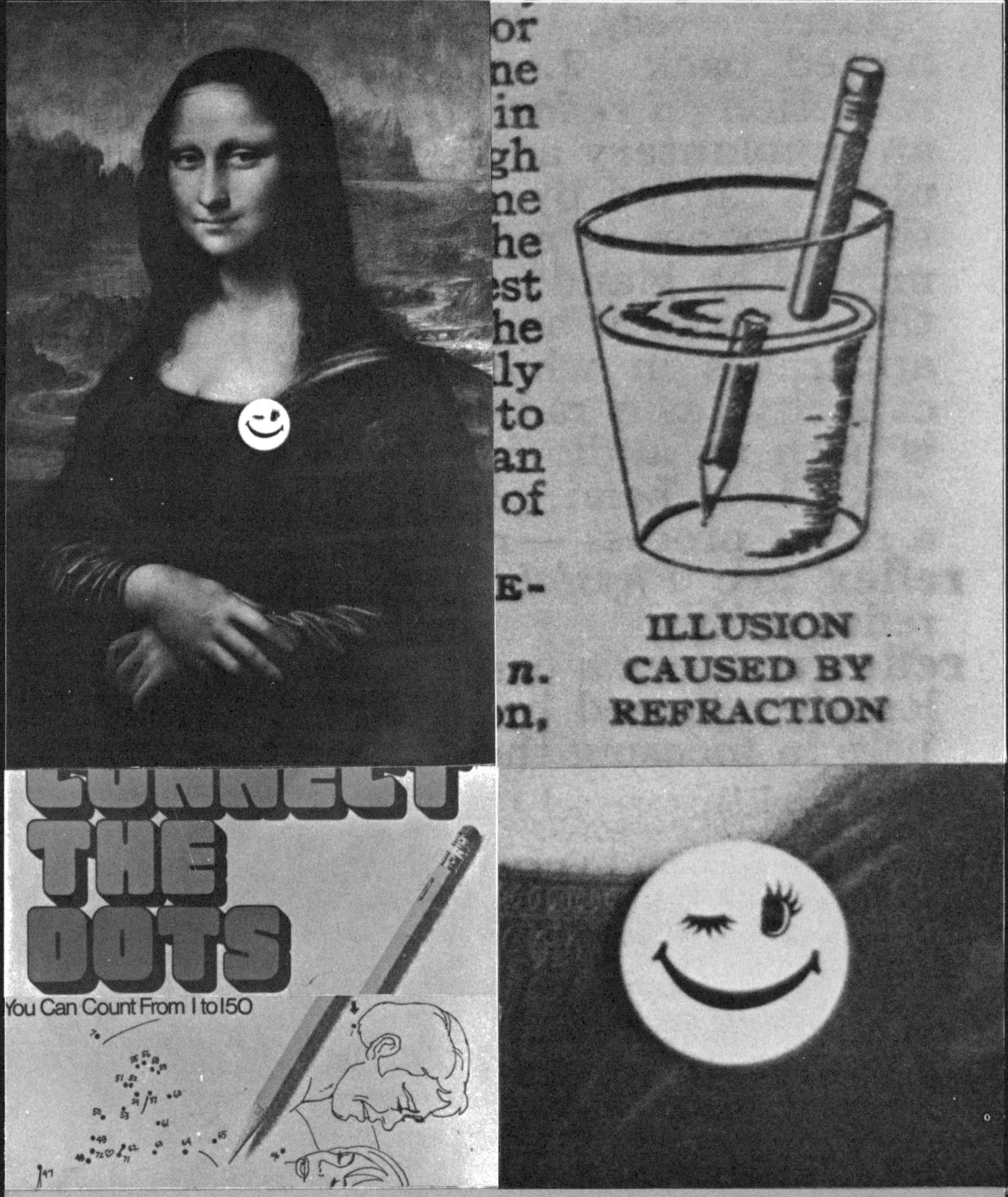

obvious in the fantastic dream landscape in the background. The horizon on the left side seems to lie much lower than the one on the right. Consequently, when we focus the left side of the picture, the woman looks somehow taller or more erect than if we focus the right side. And her face, too, seems to change with this change of position, because, even here, the two sides do not quite match. But with all these sophisticated

indistinct, by letting them merge into a soft shadow. That is why we are never quite certain in what mood Mona Lisa is really looking at us. Her expression always seems just to elude us. It is not only vagueness, of course, which produces this effect. There is much more behind it. Leonardo has done a very daring thing, which perhaps only a painter of his consummate mastership could risk. If we look carefully at the picture, we see that the two sides do not quite match. This is most

To understand what the physicists meant by a gauge theory, it may be helpful to think of a piece of decorated wallpaper and the kind of symmetry which it represents. It is quite different from, say, the simple left right symmetry of the human body. The same pattern is repeated over and over again. The task facing the designer of wallpaper is to make sure that complicated patterns will repeat reliably when the paper-hanger joins two lengths of wallpaper side by side.

Consider for a moment the following joke situation:

Question: In what way are understanding a joke and solving a problem the same?

Answer: (after some delay). Well . . . I really can't see how the two are very similar at all . . .

Despite the fact that most of us would probably answer in the same way, the distinguished Gestalt psychologist Kurt Koffka (1935) began his analysis of problem solving with precisely this question.

6 What name is given to the change in direction of a ray of light as it goes through a non-uniform material, or as it passes from one material into another?

Is interpretation a medium or a message?

Critical Path Analysis

22. A dot is made on a piece of paper, and a prism is laid on the paper over the dot. An eye in certain positions now seems to see two dots. Draw a diagram to explain this.

Make a sketch, approximately to scale, showing the paths of the rays through the system. What is the nature of the final image?

By the way.. this is a clew

The one not in the secret is then called back, and is allowed to ask each player in turn the same three questions. And they in their replies should mix up the various meanings of the chosen word. Like this:

John: How do you like it?
Joan: Up in the air.
John: When do you like it?
Joan (thinking of the tool)*:* When I'm putting up a bookshelf.
John: Where do you like it?
Joan (thinking of the opposite of patterned): On the wallpaper.

Properly designed paper has consistency across an expanse of wall. The 'designer' of a universe would have a similar problem of ensuring consistency. For example, if the laws of nature were different from one galaxy to the next, you might ask: where is the 'join' in space where the laws change, and would not very peculiar things happen there? The prime discoveries of astronomy could be summed up by saying the universe was like wallpaper.

The Hatter opened his eyes very wide on hearing this; but all he *said* was, "Why is a raven like a writing-desk?"

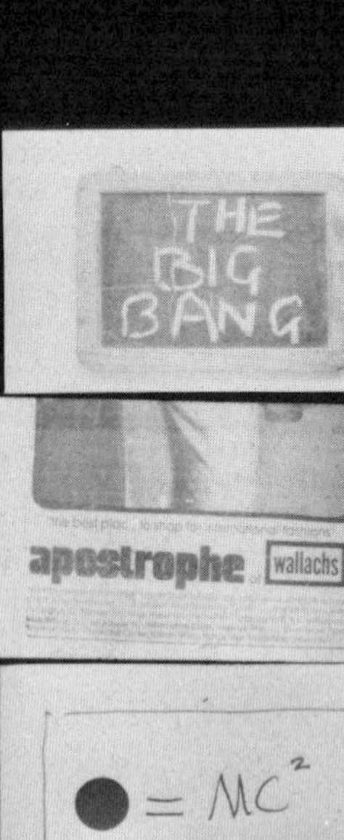

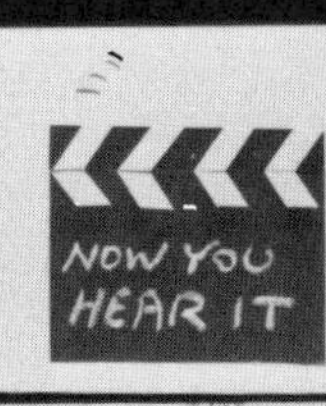

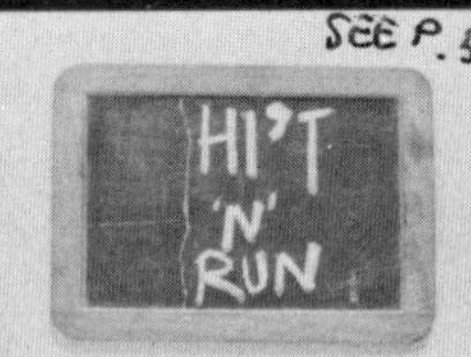

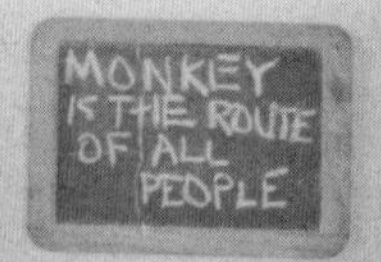

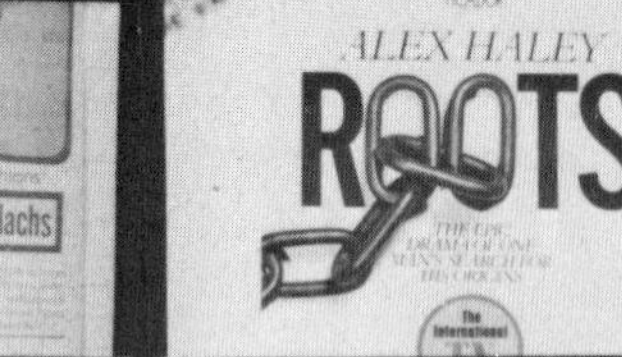

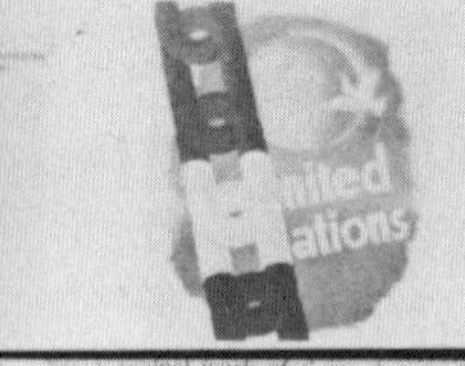

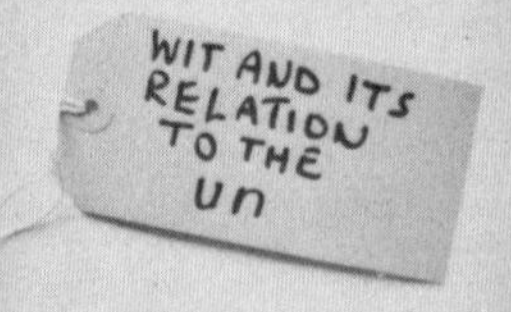

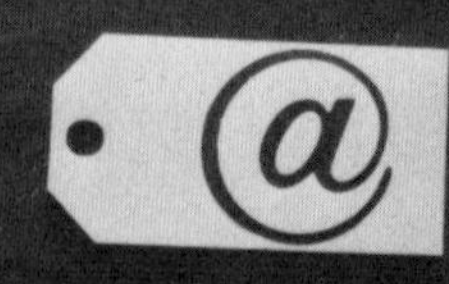

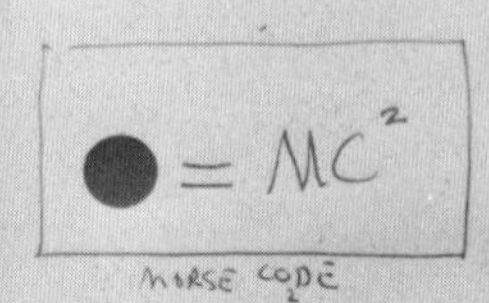

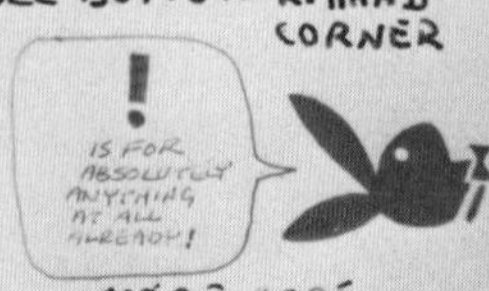

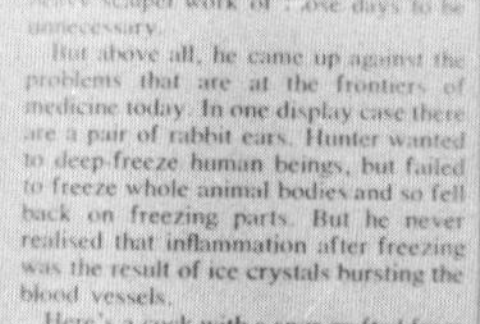
heavy scalpel work of those days to be unnecessary.

But above all, he came up against the problems that are at the frontiers of medicine today. In one display case there are a pair of rabbit ears. Hunter wanted to deep-freeze human beings, but failed to freeze whole animal bodies and so fell back on freezing parts. But he never realised that inflammation after freezing was the result of ice crystals bursting the blood vessels.

Here's a cock with a spur grafted from

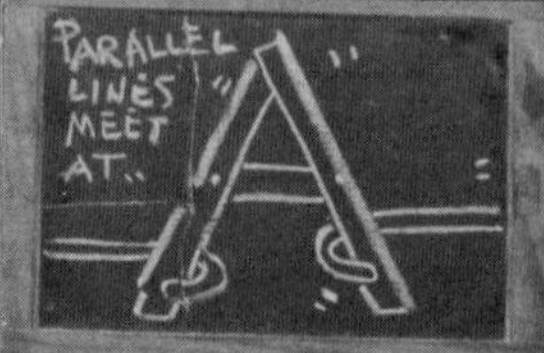

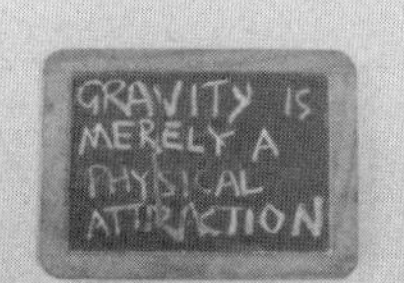

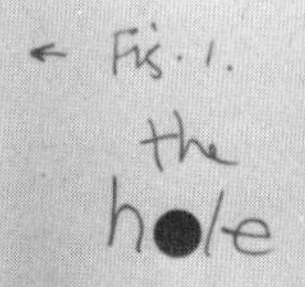

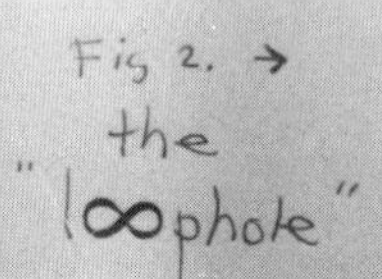

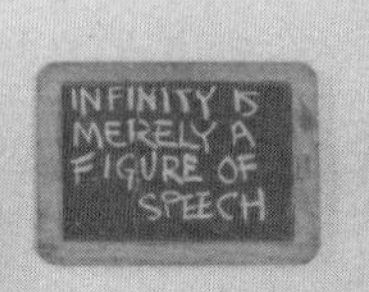

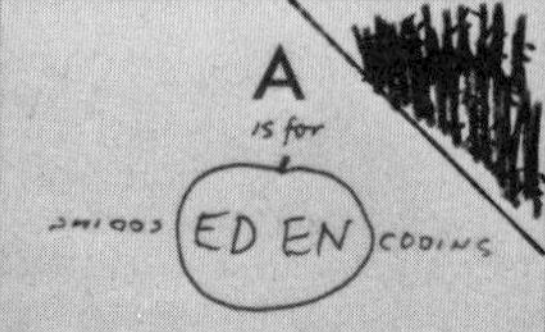

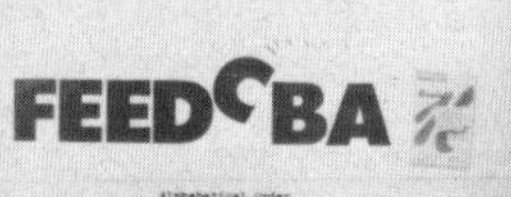

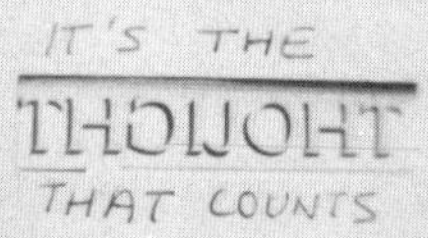

cogito
ogre
sum
PUN

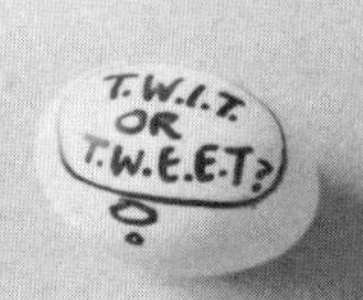

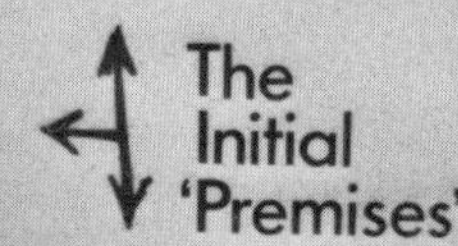

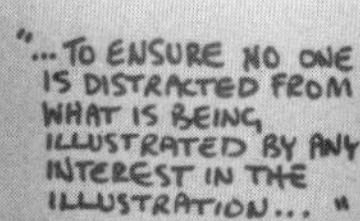

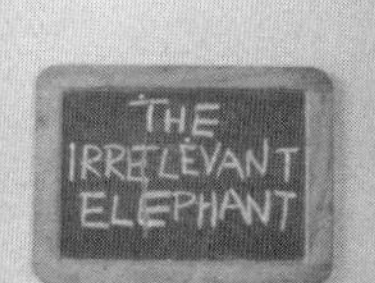

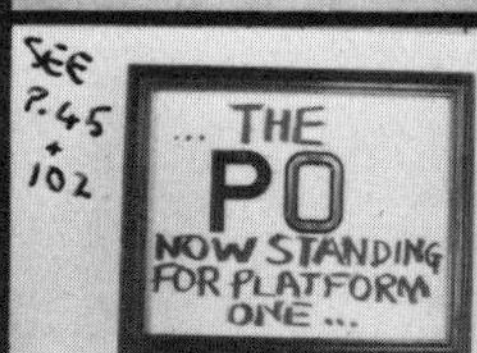

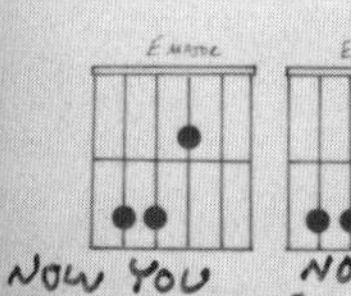

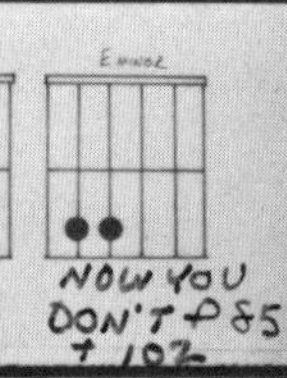

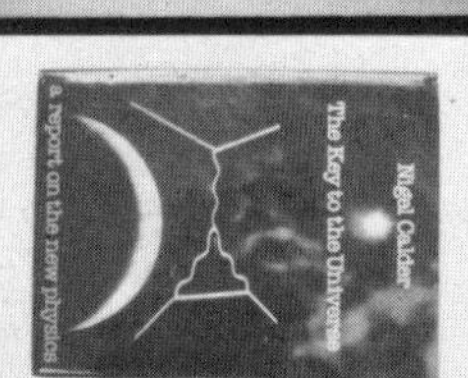

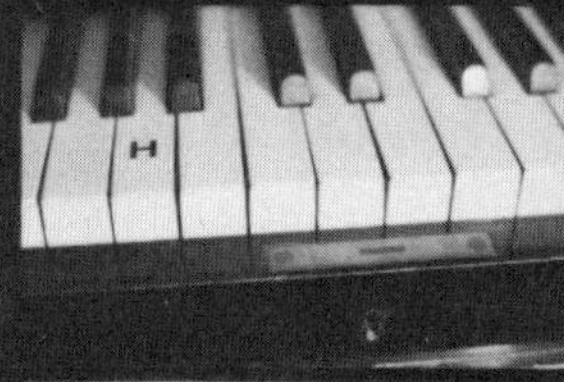

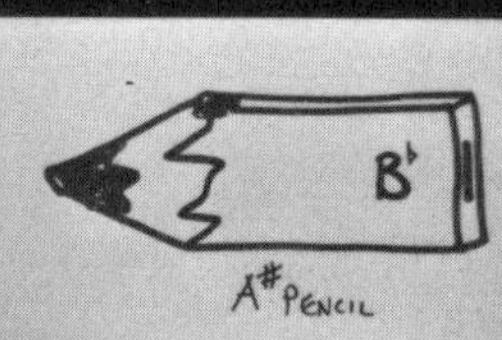

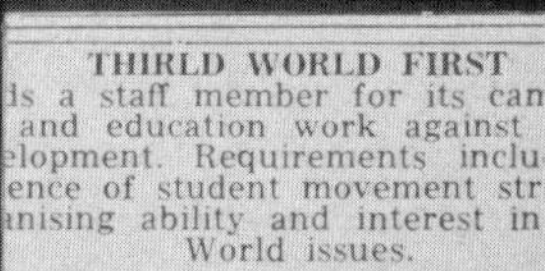
THIRLD WORLD FIRST
ds a staff member for its can
and education work against
elopment. Requirements inclu
ence of student movement str
nising ability and interest in
World issues.
d large SAE for application
to:
3W1 (T).

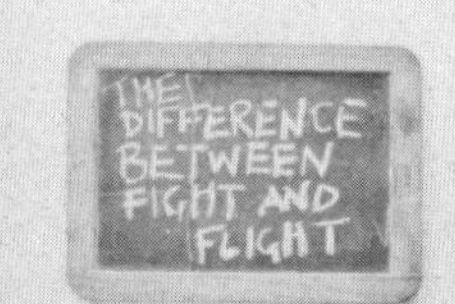

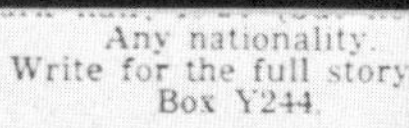
Any nationality.
Write for the full story to:
Box Y244.

KNIGHT
in rather dented armour (attractive, 6' 2" 29) seeks MAIDEN with tin opener or some knowledge of panel-beating.
Photo, phone exchanged ALA.
Box Y311.

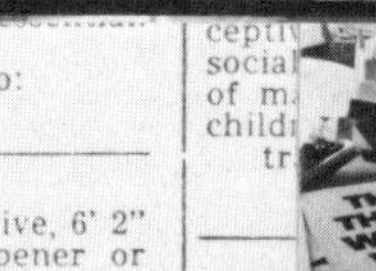

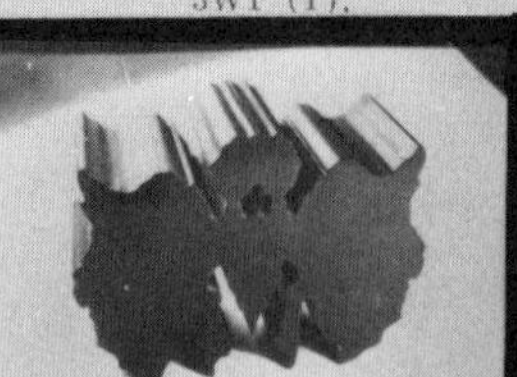

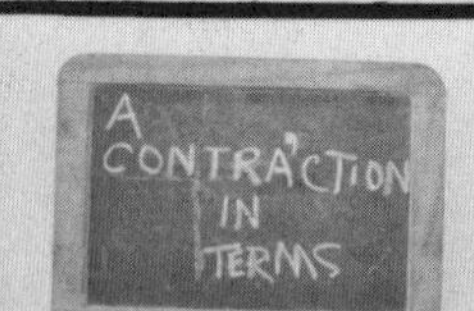

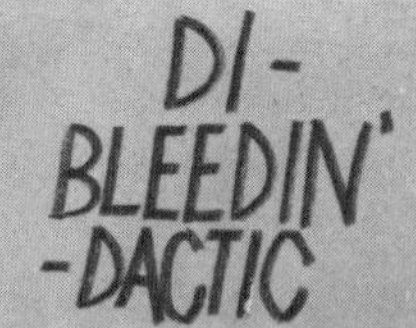

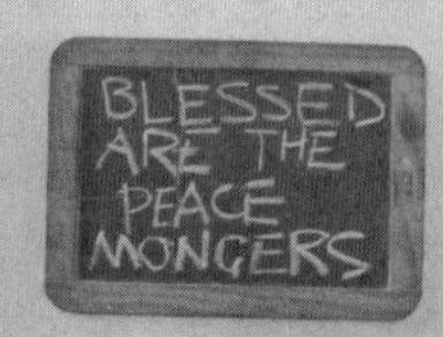

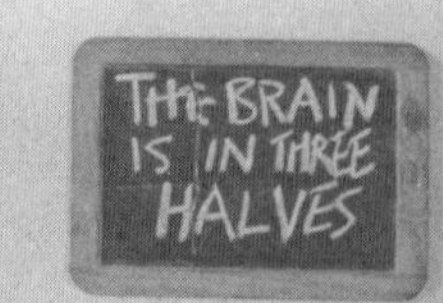

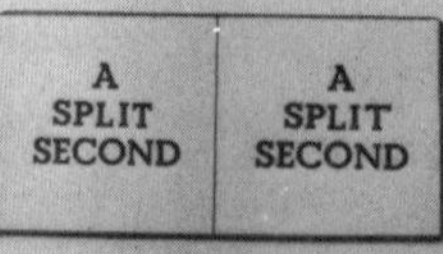

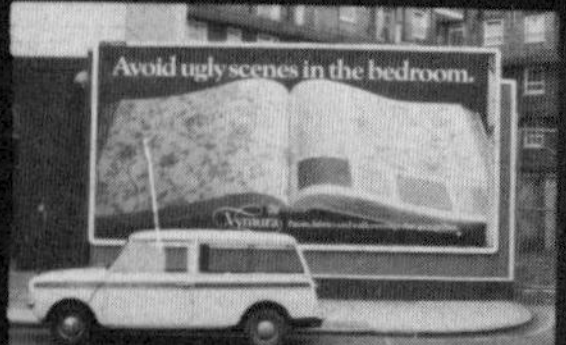

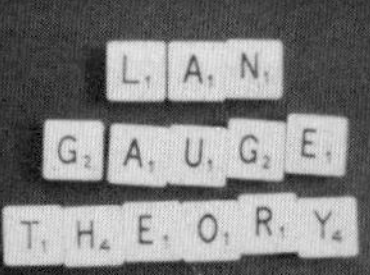

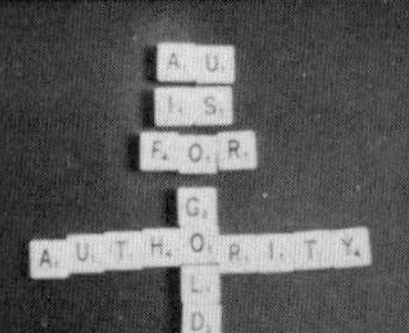

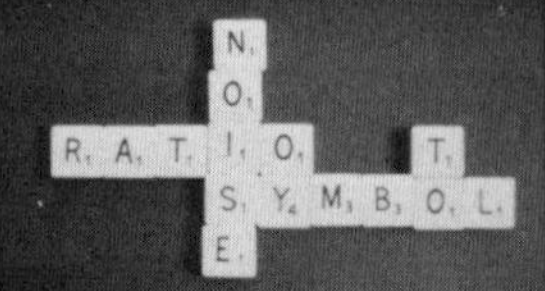

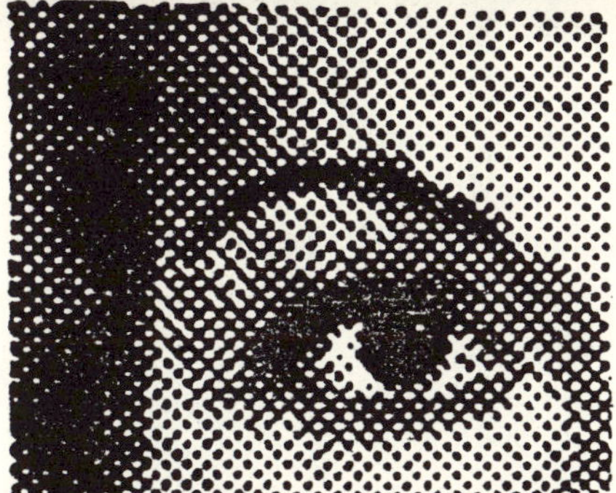

Fig. 185. Dot structure of enlarged portion of a screened picture

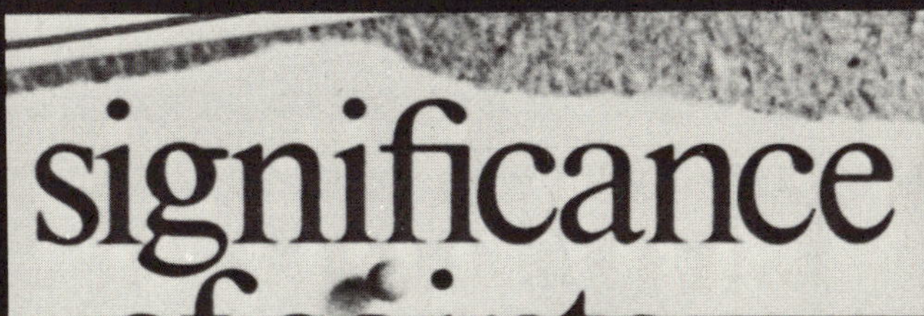

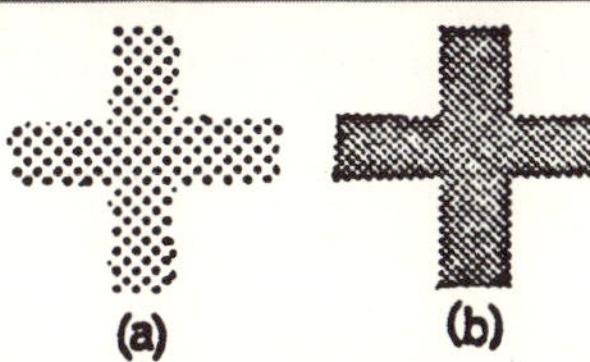

(a) (b)

Fig. 186. Cross composed of few dots (a) blends into a solid figure when many more dots are added (b)

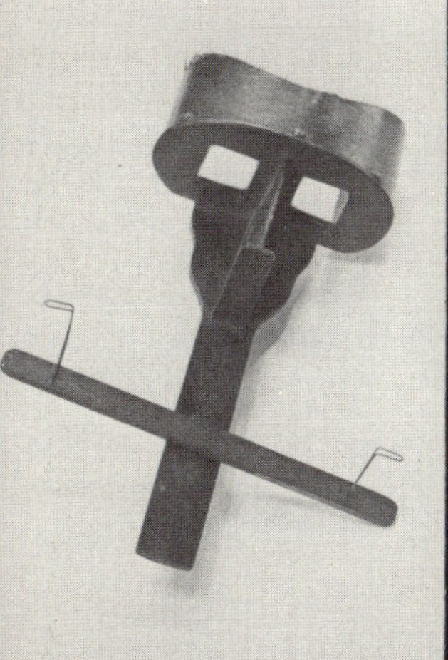

proved that our impression of solidity is derived from each eye receiving a different view of the same object. He illustrated this by drawing two pictures from different points of view and placing them at either end of a bar, in the centre of which were two mirrors placed at an angle, and upon their surfaces the picture was viewed. By means of this instrument he produced artificially the impression of solidity in pictures upon flat surfaces and called it a "Stereoscope" (from the Greek *stereos*, meaning "solid.") Five years later, Sir David Brewster introduced another form, in which the pictures were seen through two prisms; and this again, in 1849, was improved by Duboscq, of Paris, who substituted convex lenses for the prisms, and thus clear definition was obtained. Wheatstone's reflecting stereoscope,

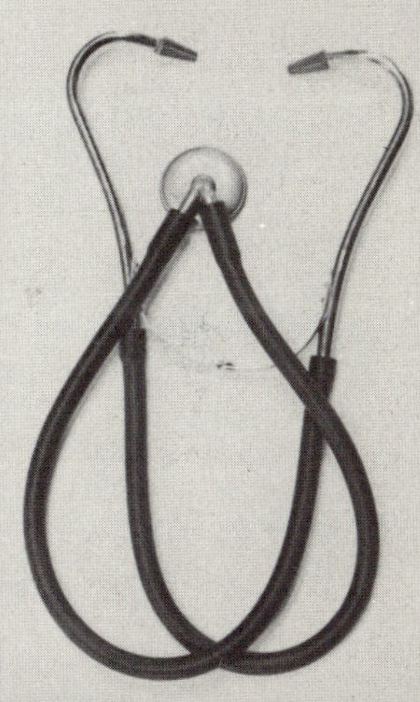

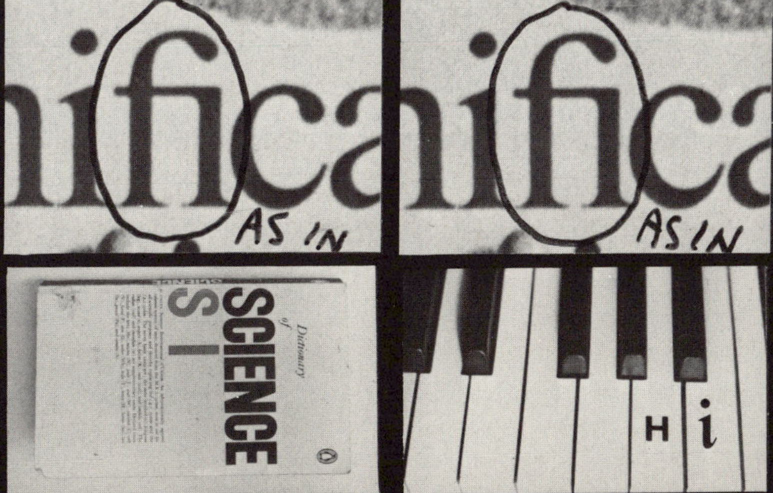

DOTTING THE I's AND CROSSING THE T's

SP'CE TIME,

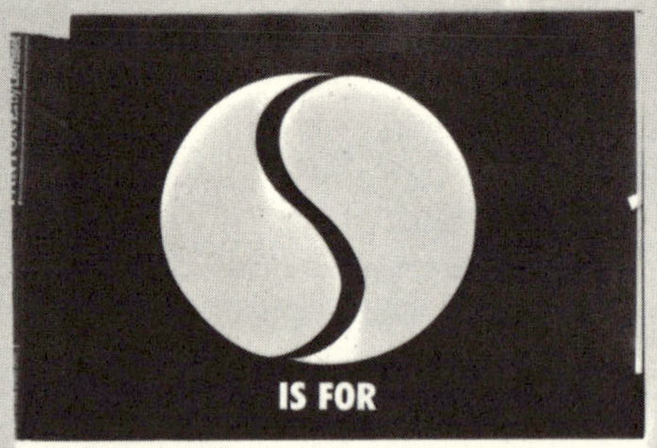

THE / OF
GENIUS

THE MEDIUM
THE MESSAGE

"... one per cent / and
ninety-nine per cent S ..."

@ Edison

THE
FUNCTION
OF
PUNCT'ION

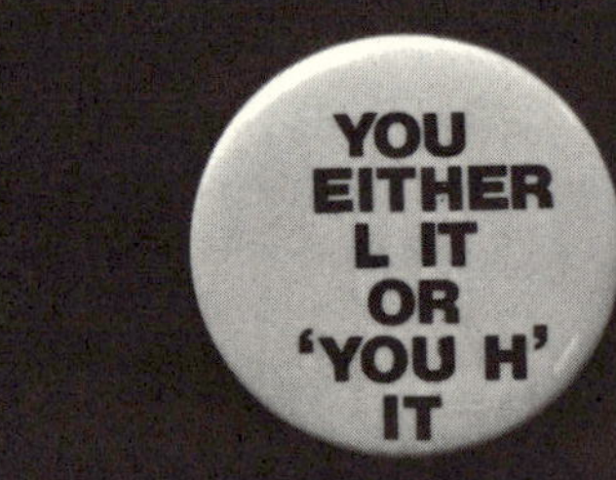

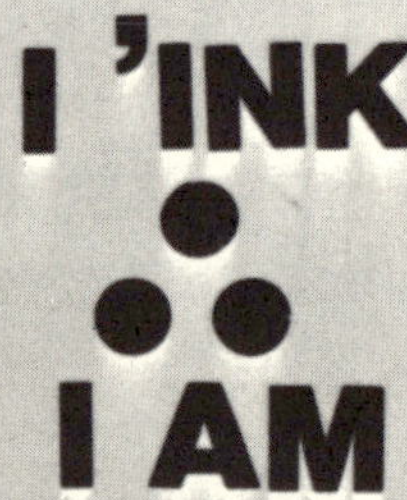

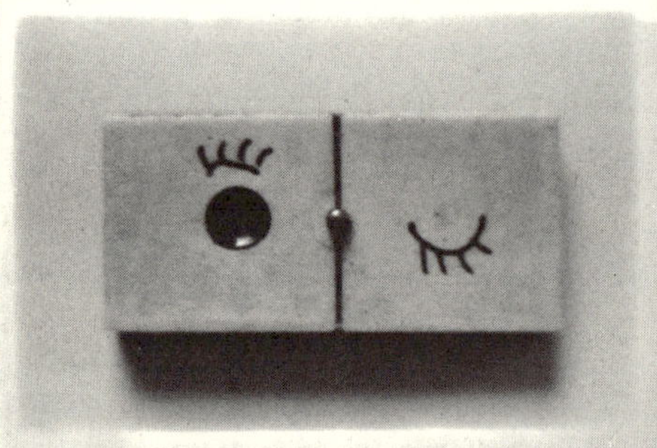

'AHA

The Apostrophes

THERAPY BEGINS
AT H

The Theories

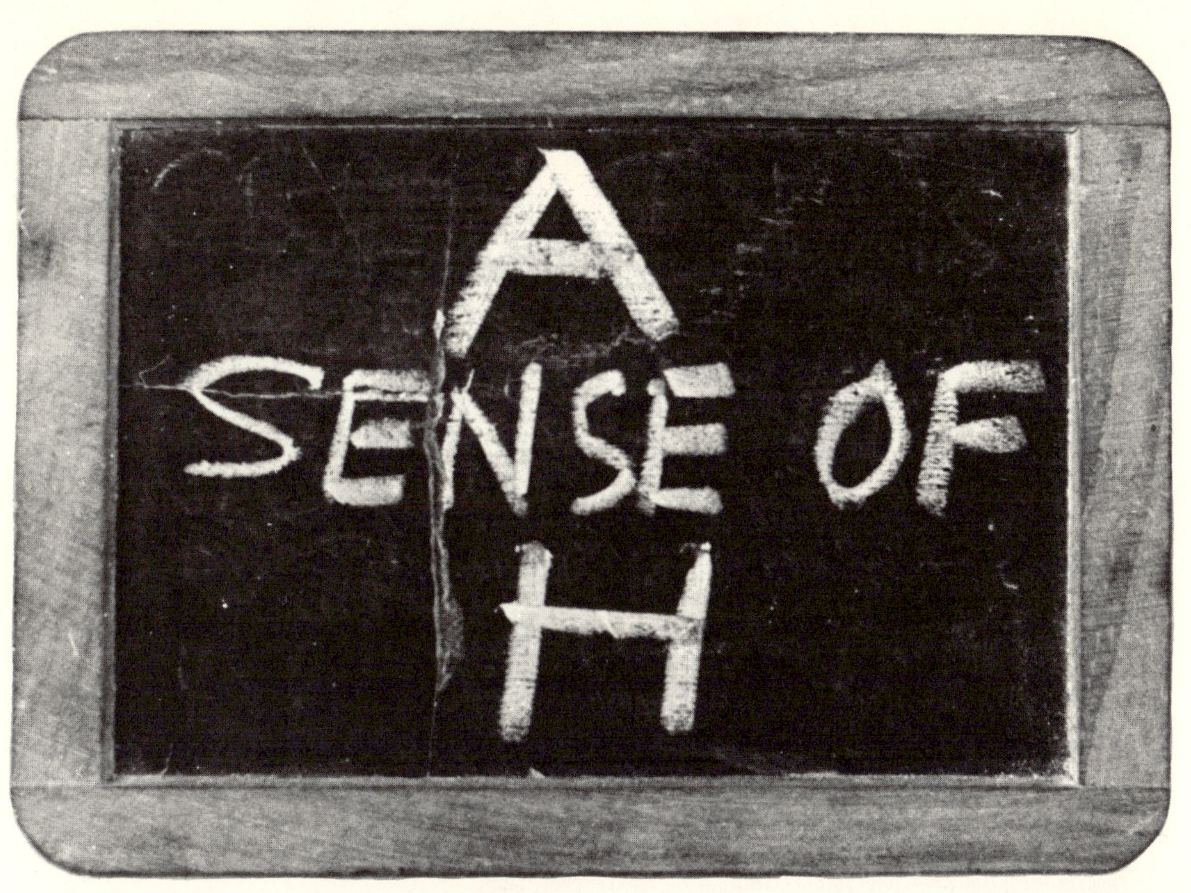

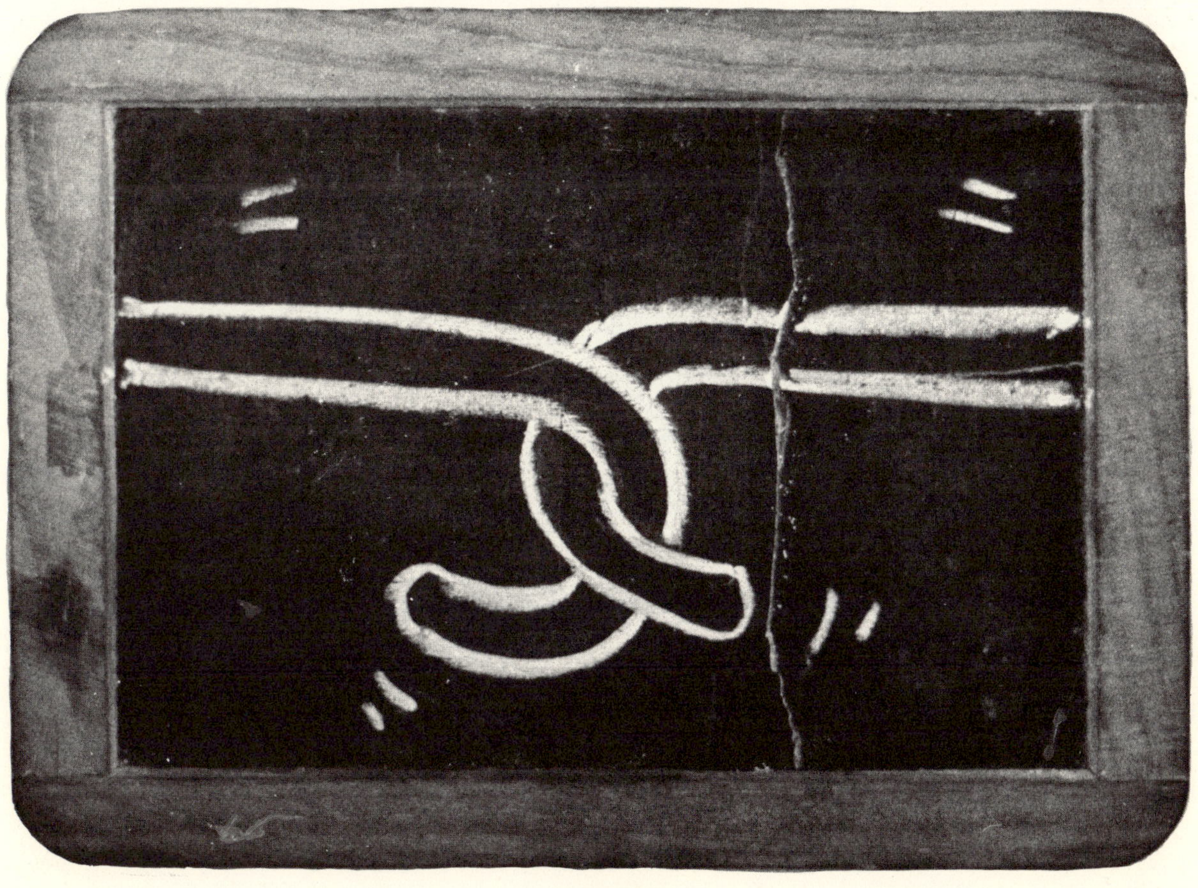

See page 93

Acknowledgments

Page

7 Richard Burton in *The Observer,* 11 July 1976, talking about his friend, the late Stanley Baker.
Other words and ideas from Joseph T. Shipley, *Dictionary of Word Origins,* Philosophical Library, New York 1945.

12 The 'elephant' of surprise from J.R. Evans, *The Junior Week-End Book,* Victor Gollancz, London 1952. (Clews to the maid's 'lack' of intelligence can be found 'dotted' around the rest of the book.)

15 Lewis Carroll, *Alice's Adventures in Wonderland,* G. Bell edition, London 1933.
Graffiti from the wall of the Swiss Cottage Library, north London.

19 *Walker's Rhyming Dictionary,* Routledge & Kegan Paul, London 1969.

21 Object relations 'of the third kind' from a psychoanalytic paper by Dr H. Ezriel of the Tavistock Institute, London.

27 The 'Zenital' Trading Company, Kentish Town, London, is now a grocery store.

36 Charles Darwin, *The Origin of Species.*

40 Letter to Charles Darwin, Francis Galton, *Inquiries into Human Faculty,* Dent, London 1907.

41 From the colour supplement of a British Sunday newspaper.

42 On retinal rivalry, R.L. Gregory, *Eye and Brain,* World University Library, London 1966.
Brain hemispheres and the Stroop Effect, *New Scientist* magazine.
On metaphor, Eric Partridge, *Usage and Abusage,* Penguin Books, 1974.
On mental illness, Thomas Szasz, *The Second Sin,* Routledge & Kegan Paul, London 1974.

44 On Milton, Eric Partridge, *Usage and Abusage.*
Graffiti beside the statue of Freud, Swiss Cottage, London.
Cover of *The Concept of Meaninglessness,* Edward Erwin, Johns Hopkins University Press, Baltimore 1970, reproduced by permission of the Press.
Watergate Fish Bar, Brecon, Wales.
On linking images, Edward de Bono, *The Mechanism of Mind,* Pelican Books, 1971.
On the word Nu, Leo Rosten, *The Joys of Yiddish,* Penguin Books, 1971.

45 Resonance; sleeve notes from an executive toy.

46 Gauge Theory, *New Scientist* magazine.
Hello mum and streaker photographed during televised cricket match.

47 Gauge Theory, Nigel Calder, *The Key to the Universe,* BBC Publications, London 1977.
How, when and where, *The Junior Week-End Book.*

48 Original photograph (c) Roger Perry 1976.
Virtue is square, Edward Erwin, *The Concept of Meaninglessness.*

49 Victor Frankl, *The Doctor and the Soul,* Pelican Books, 1973.

53 Canon Fleming, *The Art of Reading and Speaking,* Edward Arnold, London 1914.

54 Cover reproduced by courtesy of Penguin Books.

59 Cover reproduced by courtesy of Penguin Books.

60 Misprint in Freud's christian name, *The International University Reading Course* (undated but presumably before 1939).

63 Stimulus-Response theory, Arthur Koestler, *The Ghost in the Machine,* Pan Books, London 1967.

65 History's exclamation point, Marshall McLuhan, *The Medium is the Massage,* Penguin Books, 1967.

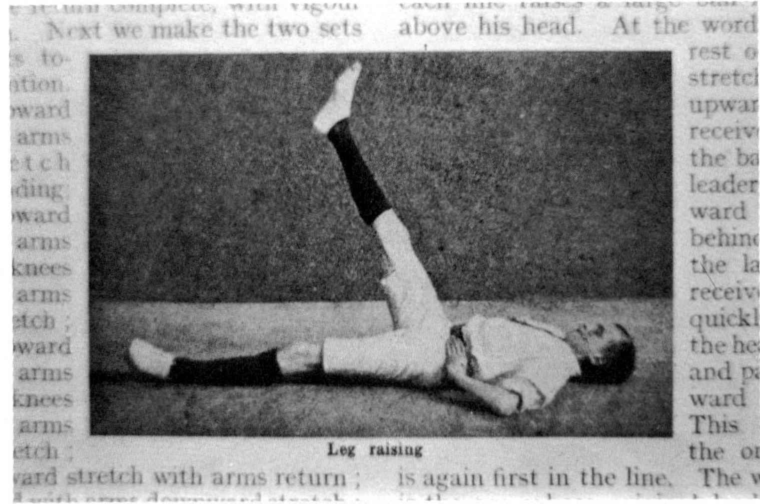

Consciousness pulling

66 Cover reproduced by courtesy of Penguin Books.
68 Howard R. Pollio, *The Psychology of Symbolic Activity*, Addison Wesley, Reading, Mass. 1974.
69 Glass of tea, Nathan Ausubel, *A Treasury of Jewish Folklore*, Crown, New York 1955.
Sour cream, Leo Rosten, *The Joys of Yiddish*.
Suspension bridge, Sigmund Freud, *Wit and its Relation to the Unconscious*, Routledge & Kegan Paul, London (n.d.).
75 Dust cover and spine, Marshall McLuhan, *Understanding Media*, R.K.P. (Routledge & Kegan Paul), London 1968.
79 Interest in the illustration, Anthony Flew, *Thinking About Thinking*, Fontana, London 1975.
86 Oedipus, George Steiner, 'Has Truth a Future?', *The Listener*, Jan. 1978.
Adult Connect the Dots, The American Publishing Corporation, Watertown, Mass. 1973.
87 Isaac Asimov, *Guide to the Physical Sciences*, Pelican Books, London 1975.
88 The Key of C. C for Chappell Music Co. and the Chubb Lock Co.
89 *The Key to the Universe*, by permission of BBC Publications. Cover designed and photographed by Michael Freeman.
The Security Lock and Safe Co. This building has now been demolished.
90 Cover reproduced by courtesy of Pelican Books.
93 The H diagram, Nigel Calder, *The Key to the Universe*.
94 AHA (top) Arthur Koestler, *The Ghost in the Machine*.
AHA (centre) Leo Rosten, *The Joys of Yiddish*.
AHA (bottom) Tom Wolfe, 'The Painted Word', *Harpers and Queen*, Feb. 1976.
95 The retina, R.L. Gregory, *Eye and Brain*.
97 Au is the chemical symbol for gold (Latin *Aurum*).
102 John Blofeld, *The Book of Change (I Ching)*, George Allen and Unwin, London 1970.
Ivor Mairants, *Guitar Chord Encyclopaedia*, Francis Day and Hunter, London 1957.
Po, Edward de Bono, *The Mechanism of Mind*.
110 Bovril, Diana and Geoffrey Hindley, *Advertising in Victorian England*, Wayland, London 1972.
112 Covers by permission of Fontana Books, Penguin Books and Picador Books.
Teach Yourself Critical Path Analysis by Douglas W. Lang, cover reproduced by permission of the publishers, Hodder & Stoughton.
113 Alfred L. Yarbus, *Eye Movements and Vision*, Institute for problems of Information Transmission, Moscow, Plenum Press 1967.
120 E.H. Gombrich, *The Story of Art*, Phaidon, London 1964.
121 Gauge Theory, Nigel Calder, *The Key to the Universe*.

All photography, design and artwork by the author except where otherwise indicated.

My thanks to A. for her initial inspiration and to Paul Forrester for the use of his darkroom.

Apostrophe Theory is dedicated to my mother and father.

is:	**isn't:**
natural, effective, systematic, refreshing, simple, effortless, spontaneous, easily learned scientifically verifiable, practiced twenty minutes morning and evening to develop the full potential of the individual.	a lifestyle, self-hypnosis, concentration, contemplation, mind control, a philosophy, a yoga exercise, an intellectual practice, a religion, a diet, a special way of dressing, or difficult to learn.

Apostrophe Theory